AA9 0024768 36

373.14|HAM
D/H₁₁

I0658697

De La Sulle Resource,
Dublin.

WITHDRAWN FROM STOCK
MARINO INSTITUTE OF EDUCATION

MARINO INSTITUTE OF EDUCATION

by the same author

The Teacher and Counselling

THE TEACHER
AND PASTORAL CARE

DOUGLAS HAMBLIN

BASIL BLACKWELL·OXFORD

© Basil Blackwell, 1978
Reprinted 1979

All Rights Reserved. No part of this publication may be
reproduced, stored in a retrieval system, or transmitted,
in any form or by any means, electronic, mechanical,
photocopying, recording or otherwise, without the prior
permission of Basil Blackwell & Mott Limited.

British Library Cataloguing in Publication Data

Hamblin, Douglas
   The teacher and pastoral care.
   1. Personal service in secondary education
   I. Title
   373.1'4   LB1620.5

   ISBN 0–631–18670–0
   ISBN 0–631–18680–8 Pbk

TO:
Kate, Maggie,
Sheila and Viv.

Phototypeset in V.I.P. Bembo by
Western Printing Services Ltd, Bristol
Printed and bound in Great Britain by
Billing & Sons Limited
Guildford, London and Worcester

CONTENTS

PREFACE

Teachers work hard in their pastoral role and yet too often do not get the rewards they deserve. This book is offered in true humility as a help to the vast majority of teachers who care deeply about their pupils and who are engaged in a search for ways of coping with the problems of the age.

Inevitably, the book only scratches the surface of fundamental issues and provides a starting point for tackling urgent problems. These limitations I deeply regret, but my faith in the creativity and integrity of my fellow teachers is such that I believe they will build with skill and zest on the foundations provided.

So many people have helped that it seems almost impossible to acknowledge them. All my present and past students have contributed in their various ways, many of them through the testing and developing, in their schools, of the ideas offered in this book. I would like to thank Sue Russell and Peter Seabourne for materials on pages 36 to 40 from the long-established induction course at their school, Phil Davies for materials from his induction course and Dewi Williams for the three exercises on pages 74 and 75 which were developed by a small group of students with whom he worked. Grateful acknowledgement is also made to Maggie Bradbury, Kate Doherty, Lynne Chapman, Chris Brown and John Wignall for their help in checking my original typescript. To all the foregoing I would say that they have given more than they know and far better than they would care to say.

Special thanks are due to two other people. Sheila Toms undertook the task of constructing the index—a task she has done with care and intelligence. Freda Swift has been more than a typist—her foresight, care and determination to achieve a standard of excellence in the production of the manuscript has made her contribution extremely valuable. It is almost impossible to thank her sufficiently—I have had to try to live up to her standards.

In conclusion, it is clear that this book belongs to all of them in a very special way, although this does not mean that they have to take responsibility for its defects. Those are mine alone.

Swansea.
May 1977.

INTRODUCTION

This book is written from the standpoint of one who has found teaching to be a deeply satisfying activity. It has called for every scrap of integrity, intelligence and imagination that I possessed, and without doubt I was often found wanting, but the sense of excitement still persists. We all know that teaching is not a one-way process and my colleagues and pupils have always contributed more than I. These remarks are made because it seems fair to indicate the attitudes which underpin the approach to pastoral care offered in this book.

Pastoral care is not something set apart from the daily work of the teacher. It is that element of the teaching process which centres around the personality of the pupil and the forces in his environment which either facilitate or impede the development of intellectual and social skills, and foster or retard emotional stability. The pastoral effort is also concerned with the modification of the learning environment, adapting it to meet the needs of individual pupils, so that every pupil has the maximum chance of success whatever his background or general ability.

Thus the primary task of the pastoral team is to develop an environment which adapts to the needs of pupils of all abilities and backgrounds. Whilst their attitudes to school have to be taken into account, it is more important that they should face realistically their need to acquire verbal and conceptual skills. If this is not done then we may be imposing upon pupils activities which seem meaningless and offer them the conditions for failure rather than success. Marland [1974] points out that the pastoral care system exists to help the school achieve its objectives, not as a welfare system dealing with crises, the causes for which lie outside the school.

Within the school staffroom one hears complaints that certain individuals or groups of pupils absorb an undue proportion of the staff's attention—and this often means the administration of punishments in a ritualistic way. Neither the agent of punishment nor the recipient believe that it does any good, yet the charade is continued until the pupils truant or reach the statutory leaving age. In both cases, a sense of relief is then felt, if not always expressed!

Problems like this can be dealt with more successfully when staff working parties systematically examine the pupil's attitudes towards school, towards authority and towards learning in general, taking into consideration the methods of teaching and discipline within the school. This approach can reveal other problems. It is right for the pastoral team to pay attention to truancy, but it must be remembered that psychological truancy, when the pupils are physically present but are emotionally and motivationally absent, is a far more severe problem.

It is ironic that even in a book arguing against the separation of the pastoral and the curricular it is still necessary to isolate the pastoral task for the purposes of exposition. By doing this, a second irony is brought out into the open—the fact that the true failure of the secondary school is in the academic field. We have not learned how to help many pupils move from concrete and rigid styles of thinking to abstract and flexible styles. We seem to be unable to help pupils with attenuated language skills to use language in a creative manner. Good relationships have often been stressed as a pre-requisite for adequate learning; yet inappropriate teaching methods and tasks can prevent the growth of positive bonds between teacher and pupil.

Glaser (1972) puts forward a compelling argument for the creation of an adaptive learning environment. When this is created within classrooms, then the sense of frustration spinging from lack of success will go, and there will be time to deal in depth with the social and personal problems of pupils. Pastoral care should be an integral part of life within the classroom.

We must all realize the possibility that self-defeating strategies are inherent in our procedures. Sometimes we find that in the fourth and fifth years we are endeavouring to modify attitudes and behaviour that we have unwittingly induced in these pupils during the first three years of the secondary school. This insight at least suggests that we can correct the situation, rather than remain its victims.

This book will deal with these processes in a practical way, whilst avoiding the temptation to produce solutions. Suggestions based on wide experience will indicate the ways in which some schools and teachers have tackled these problems. The writer holds the opinion that there are many solutions to these problems. Some of them will work in some schools and with some pupils. What is viable in one school is counter-productive in another. Perhaps this book will be most helpful if it persuades the reader to abandon the delusory search for *the right way* and look for a method which suits his own school.

REFERENCES

Glaser, R. (1972) "Individuals and learning: the new aptitudes", *Educational Researcher*, Vol. 1, No. 6.

Marland, M. (1974) *Pastoral Care*, London: Heinemann.

CHAPTER ONE: KEY POINTS

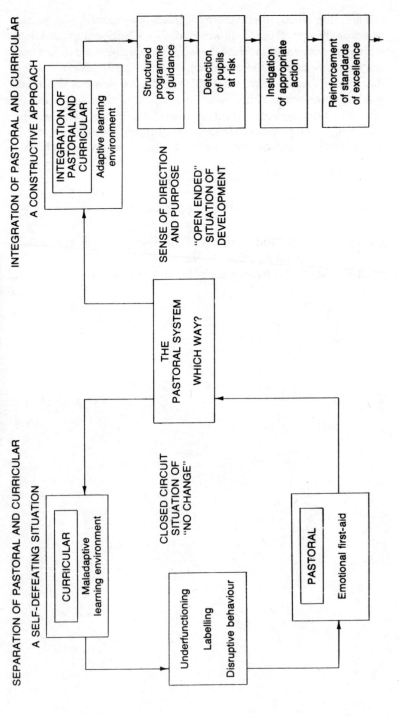

SEPARATION OF PASTORAL AND CURRICULAR

A SELF-DEFEATING SITUATION

INTEGRATION OF PASTORAL AND CURRICULAR

A CONSTRUCTIVE APPROACH

CURRICULAR
Maladaptive learning environment

Underfunctioning
Labelling
Disruptive behaviour

PASTORAL
Emotional first-aid

CLOSED CIRCUIT SITUATION OF "NO CHANGE"

THE PASTORAL SYSTEM

WHICH WAY?

INTEGRATION OF PASTORAL AND CURRICULAR
Adaptive learning environment

SENSE OF DIRECTION AND PURPOSE

"OPEN ENDED" SITUATION OF DEVELOPMENT

Structured programme of guidance

Detection of pupils at risk

Instigation of appropriate action

Reinforcement of standards of excellence

SOME BASIC PROCESSES AND ISSUES

Summary

THE CENTRAL ARGUMENT

An effective pastoral system is more than a device for providing emotional first-aid for adolescent tensions in a complex society, or a welfare activity for alleviating poor home conditions. The key ideas in this theme are given below.

INTEGRATION OF THE PASTORAL AND THE CURRICULAR

The argument calls for a carefully planned integration of the pastoral and the curricular aspects of the comprehensive school, based on the realization that the true failure of the secondary school lies in the field of learning. Inappropriate teaching methods, rather than indiscipline, can cause sterile relationships. We have not yet learned to construct an adaptive learning environment which meets the needs of widely differing groups of pupils. The pastoral system can help this, by examining the processes which either impede or facilitate learning.

DISTORTIONS OF THE PASTORAL SYSTEM

Distortions of the pastoral system commonly found in schools are discussed. These include the tendency for it to become a punitive system which actually reduces the efficiency of year or house head, causes some teachers to abdicate professional responsibility for the maintenance of order, and increases ineffective punishments. To criticize ineffective punishment, however, is not to claim that the pastoral system does not have a positive disciplinary function. It is strongly argued that the important contribution to discipline made by the pastoral system consists in the elimination of inconsistent discipline, the early detection of pupils "at risk", and the establishment of procedures which prevent minor difficulties escalating into crises.

PROCESSES AND REMEDIES

The processes involved in the allocation of positive and negative reputations are discussed, together with the concept of critical incidents, providing a framework for a structured programme of guidance. This programme equips pupils with some of the skills necessary for success in school. The concept of the school as a signal system, sending messages which shape the self-picture of the pupils within it, is introduced.

The underlying argument is that the pastoral system represents a planned attempt to make the socializing aspects of the teacher's task more productive. This socializing function requires the school to develop a compassionate, morally educated person who can recognize his own contribution to his success or failure in life.

The thinking behind this chapter

Pastoral care should be undertaken by teachers who are prepared to examine continuously their own actions. Some strategies, although ostensibly helpful, contain self-defeating elements and actually reinforce the conditions they are meant to remove. We need to learn to ask the simple questions, "What have we got to give our pupils?", "Do they want it?" and "If they do want it, is the price too high?". Some attempt is made to answer these questions in this chapter.

I am aware that my answers are only tentative. After all, truth is conditional, fragmentary and a product of limited perspectives within a particular situation. Popper (1973) says that nothing is permanently established and nothing unalterable. Yet whilst we must learn to look for tests and accept refutations, we must not abandon our current theories and practice lightly. There is no virtue in a blind adherence to change for change's sake.

The suggestions made in this book show that there are a number of routes to any goal. The most effective one for a particular school can only be found through knowledge of the school as an inter-related collection of parts, each of which influences the functioning of others, and for this an intimate knowledge of the school system is essential. The pastoral team should try to detect, and deal with, problems due to sterile relationships within the school and of in-appropriate educational methods. But we must avoid making the pastoral system a mechanism for draining off, in an unthinking way, tensions produced in the school, leaving the real causes untouched. Sixth-form pupils often wryly remark that tension reduction is the real function of the school council: hence they react with suspicion to it.

Pastoral care can be centred around the focal concerns of particular age groups, or can be concerned with the structural aspects of the school within which pupils have to resolve the developmental tasks of adolescence. It is sensible to take both into account. The pastoral care system should never become a device for labelling pupils as inadequate, but should be a means of instituting constructive inno-vations, rather than propping up the *status quo* and inhibiting change. The dual approach allows us to face the fact that pupils are not only questioning the content of important roles in school and society, but see no significance in them. A lack of commitment is found in a number of our pupils. These attitudes seem to have little personal significance for their holder, yet can prevent him from taking up a responsible role within the school and in later life.

Separation of the curricular and the pastoral

Many writers have shown that devices such as setting have tended to fragment the basic teaching group, making it harder for the teacher to maintain a consistent relationship with a pupil. Bazalgette (1974) found that in commerce and industry young people worked in small, relatively stable task groups, allowing supervizors to get to know them reasonably well, whilst the presence of older workers could provide models of competence. When he compared a com-prehensive school with work, he found that secondary school pro-

MARINO INSTITUTE OF EDUCATION

cedures apparently prevented form tutors gaining real knowledge of a pupil. The system of options and setting by ability in particular subjects, could make fifth-year pupils need to relate to twelve different teachers a week, excluding their form tutor. The unintended consequence was a lack of knowledge of the pupils. Individual programmes of this type need not lead to this, but curricular devices can create contingencies for which we need to devise effective action. The claim to be child-centred is a hollow one in these circumstances.

Such a situation is exacerbated by the tendency to appoint one deputy head who is responsible for the academic side, and another for the pastoral. Obviously this is likely to institutionalize the split between the pastoral and the curricular, and as yet, insufficient attention has been given to communication between the two systems, although we feel that the dichotomy is counter-productive and should not exist.

Marland (1974) has drawn our attention to the way in which the pastoral system which is divided from the academic life of the school is in danger of being seen as inferior. It is then perceived as a tiresome necessity because the parents have failed to socialize the pupil. Perhaps this is an example of the basic ambivalence of teacher toward parents and, more pertinently, an example of the way teachers define a situation to meet their own needs. The writer is uneasily aware that he has used parents as an excuse for his own failures with pupils, thus hampering the development of constructive relationships between home and school. In this way the pastoral system may be looked on the equivalent of a welfare agency, brought into being to compensate for the ineptitude of parents. If this happens the likelihood of a creative integration is diminished.

In his valuable discussion, Marland points out that the function of the pastoral system is that of helping the school attain its objectives, rather than developing a separate set of goals. It also has a central educative function not derived from other subjects. The present writer sees this as the development of young people who have integrated thinking and feeling in a way which leads to intellectual honesty and the capacity for concern for others, irrespective of their intelligence. The pastoral team can help to create and maintain standards of excellence by examining and sometimes changing conceptions of what certain groups of pupils *can* learn and what they *should* learn. The pastoral care system should continuously monitor the school organization and its influence on the performance of pupils.

All this sounds excellent, but it says nothing about how this can be done. Burdin and Hamblin (1974) and Hamblin (1974) draw our attention to the concept of critical incidents and how they may be used as the framework for pastoral care. A critical incident is a major task which emanates firstly from the organization of the secondary school and secondly from the adjustments that society demands of adolescents, and each one can be broken down into a number of smaller tasks which demand certain skills. If critical incidents are successfully resolved, then the adolescent can make full use of the resources of the school within the limits of his ability, but if they are evaded, the difficulties of adjustment will increase.

These tasks interact with the developmental tasks of adolescence. Pupils are asked to make the demanding adjustments to secondary school just when many of them are entering the pre-pubertal growth spurt which makes them feel clumsy and very visible. Some may be already experiencing a change in body chemistry which can lead to an upsurge of emotionality and a sense of uncertainty. They are then liable to feel overwhelmed in a new situation which expects them to cope with a sudden expansion of the number of people with whom they have to make working relationships.

Equally, we can see that the critical incident of choice of subject options comes when many pupils are preoccupied with the question, "Who am I?". They are struggling for a relatively stable and realistic sense of identity at the time that we ask them to choose options significant for their later plans in life. Subject options are closely related to the pupil's future identity, although his occupational aspirations may be far from clear. The pastoral team will have to develop a structured programme that aids wise subject choice, particularly for the less able pupil. This will facilitate the development of a positive identity as a learner, give him an added sense of purpose, and show the relevance of school to life.

Critical incidents provide a way of linking the pastoral and the curricular, and also allow the pastoral staff to exert a modifying influence upon subject teaching in an acceptable manner. The programmes of guidance often reveal in a constructive way the self-defeating elements within the school. Often people are partially aware of these but cannot deal with them because they fear destructive confrontations with colleagues. The idea of a team effort to construct a programme of activities is more likely to be acceptable because it is free from connotations of blame.

The critical incident approach uses scarce resources effectively

5

because it directs effort to crucial points. The following are examples of <u>critical incidents</u>:

   (i)   coping with examination anxiety
  (ii)   the stimulation of study skills at various levels of complexity to anticipate changes in learning style
 (iii)   induction courses for the sixth form
 (iv)   schemes of preparation for work or further education
  (v)   the development of decision-making skills
 (vi)   the decision to stay on at school or to leave for work.

Pastoral care programmes should always be concerned with the acquisition of new skills and the extension of current ones to allow a pupil to develop adequate coping strategies: therefore each incident must be clearly analysed. The diagram on page 18 gives an overall picture of this approach to pastoral care.

Distortion of the pastoral-care system

A visitor to a school, who had no knowledge of education might still suspect that the pastoral care system was malfunctioning. He might note that although the headmaster had given form tutors pastoral care periods, they were used by the pupils to do homework whilst the teacher talked to individuals. He could go away with the idea that pastoral care consisted of a somewhat vague attempt to "get to know the pupils", and be unable to describe the techniques used. Pastoral care, at least as much as any other activity within the secondary school, needs to be purposeful. Indeed I would argue that there is an even greater need for such periods to be well organized and stimulating, for they are concerned with personal development.

If pastoral periods are dull and unstructured, then we have failed at the basic level. When this happens, it seems to be due to the failure of initial courses of teacher-training to clarify the role of form tutor and the contribution of pastoral care to the efficiency of the school. Even if this is corrected the school still needs to provide its own in-service training by the heads of year or house, in conjunction with the trained counsellor. My own students, who are deliberately trained to train others within the school, pass on their skills of developmental interviewing; the use and development of games, simulations and role play; behavioural counselling; in recognizing factors which distort classroom interaction; and in group counselling, including relevant areas of sociology and psychology.

Sadly, there is a tendency to turn the pastoral system into a punishment system. There is an increasing tendency for staff to demand that heads of year and house should act as agents of punishment. But punishment is most effective when it quickly follows the act, when it is seen as just, and when the recipient has a working relationship with the person who is punishing him.

In some secondary schools, the function of the pastoral care system is conceived largely in terms of complaints, investigation of those complaints, and finally, of punishment. It is a moot point as to what the pupil is learning of the school as a caring community when this policy prevails. This trend seems to encourage the weak teacher to abdicate the responsibility for maintaining control during teaching. If the pastoral team accept the punishment role, then the tendency will increase, and it will prevent the pastoral system from performing a positive function.

The uselessness of the traditional resort to punishment is illustrated by the following case history—even if it is an extreme example. During his first week a first-year boy had a fight in the playground and received a severe warning from the head of year. The next week he kicked another boy in the face and was given "three strokes of the slipper". Next day he truanted. On his return to school he was insolent to a female teacher and received two strokes of the cane. The succeeding weeks were marked by continual incidents of bullying and truancy. Towards the end of term a subject master made a written complaint that he was insolent, refused to work and showed general insubordination. As a result, he was caned by two different people.

On returning to school after Christmas he was caned for fighting in the school yard. Three days later he was caught smoking and slippered. Two weeks later he kicked another boy in the face, seemingly without provocation. During the next fortnight he wrote obscenities in exercise books and increased his threatening and bullying behaviour, extorting money from other boys. And so the dreary progress continued. The point is that never did a single person stop to reflect upon the uselessness of punishment in this case or try to diagnose the difficulty and there was no attempt to seek additional help or investigate the home background.

Perhaps we tend to confuse punishment and discipline. The pastoral care team should be able to anticipate breakdowns in behavior

7

and investigate why a pupil fails to respond to the usual measures of reward and punishment. We should examine situations of this type in order to make constructive suggestions to the teacher whose poor classroom management may be contributing to these incidents. The pastoral team may help some of their colleagues who may not realize what they are doing to avoid destructive confrontations with pupils. We may also need to show how the physical arrangements of the school contribute to disorder. A badly positioned tuck shop, the toleration of lengthy and slowly-moving dinner queues which cause irritation and invite "pushing in", and the too frequent chaotic flow of pupils in both directions simultaneously along a corridor although alternative routes exist, give an idea of what is meant by physical arrangements. Halsall (1973) stresses the need for senior staff to anticipate the consequences of new routines before implementing them.

The major contribution to sound discipline made by the pastoral system comes from the creation of routines and clear procedures for dealing with crises and ensuring that immediate help is available to a pupil under stress. The system must detect pupils "at risk" as early as possible. Many pupils who become an intolerable nuisance in the fifth year could have been identified as potential problems in the first or second year and received help. Routine is essential if we are to achieve results economically. It reflects an old principle of criminology, that certainty of detection is more likely to prevent misdeeds than severity of punishment. Clearly understood and consistent methods of detecting pupils who show signs of emotional and behavioural disturbance in their first year will be more effective than sporadic attempts at dealing with these problems as they reach crisis-point. Although rewards work better than punishment, yet we must have routine and order, and inconsistent discipline at home should not be reinforced by a similar inconsistency at school.

Management of the pastoral system in our schools must recognize that each measure we take can create further complications. If we take steps to identify pupils who are vulnerable, we then have to make sure that we are not building a self-fulfilling prediction about that boy or girl. As we shall shortly see, the secondary school tends to allocate reputations to pupils, which then shape their behaviour for good or ill.

The pastoral team may consider it advisable to replace the concept of punishment, at least in part, by those of restitution and reparation. The forced apology, given unwillingly and with tongue in cheek, is not what is intended. If after discussing the problem, the pupil is led to make reparation and restitution in a way which emanates from him, this is likely to lead to moral growth through the acceptance of responsibility for misbehaviour. This restores the pupils self-respect. Reparation also includes the restoration of damaged relationships. It is the task of the teacher, as a responsible professional, to adjust to the needs of the immature pupil, rather than the other way round.

Somehow we are clearer about our punishments in the school than our rewards. What rewards do we offer a pupil when he tries to make amends or behave differently? Let us ask ourselves after a disciplinary encounter, "Have I strengthened this pupil's belief in himself as a responsible person or as good for nothing?". A pupil cannot have his reputation hammered daily into his head without something happening to his personality for good or ill. Our disciplinary task is to build up an ideal for pupils, sending them rewarding messages which enhance their sense of responsibility, rather than attempting to control by inhibition and checks.

The real failure of the secondary school

The poor quality of relationships between teacher and pupil in a secondary school compared with the primary school has often been criticized. But teachers and their pupils must be not only relationship-orientated, but also task-orientated. Concentration on the relationships and on the emotional side of the school may obscure the real failure of the secondary school in the field of learning. We then ignore the contribution which inappropriate teaching methods make to behavioural problems, and the even more serious under-teaching of certain pupils, even in mixed-ability groups.

The pastoral team are faced with the failure to move many pupils from what Piaget (1953) has called the stage of concrete operations, to that of formal operations. In the stage of concrete operations a pupil can deal with the world of surrounding objects but cannot pass to the world of logical possibility. The adolescent who has reached the stage of formal operations is able to reason deductively; he is no longer tied to the world of concrete reality but can deal with hypotheses. He is concerned with abstractions, and can examine things from a number of standpoints so that he can focus on the possibilities inherent in a situation, rather than the practicalities.

At the concrete level, the pupil allows a primitive theory to

9

emerge from his experiences in order to explain them, but in the adolescent who has reached formal operations the direction is reversed. The adolescent begins his problem-solving with a hypothetical model which implies certain relationships. He then applies this to reality. As Inhelder and Piaget (1958) say, "This type of thinking proceeds from what is possible to what is empirically true." Piaget and his colleagues are suggesting that pupils entering the secondary stage of education are losing the bonds that tie them to immediate perceptual experience in their thinking, although this is not true of all pupils. A large section of our school population does not achieve this transition at school, if at all.

In his discussion of counselling, Hamblin (1974) draws attention to the importance of Bernstein's (1965) work on language codes, implying that the school counsellor must adapt to the needs of the pupils with attentuated language skills. Bernstein's theory is that many pupils are limited because the structure of their language is closed, whilst they lack the ability to code messages in a way that is acceptable to those who use a more elaborate code. These pupils prefer visual to verbal learning, and also desire activity. Yet the major bias of the instruction they are given is towards the verbal and passive. We do offer them films and television, but they often fail to react to these in school, because they have become accustomed to non-participant experiences. We make very few attempts to present information diagrammatically or through carefully designed problem-solving situations which capture their imagination and integrate thinking and feeling.

Many teachers feel that the values reflected by our teaching methods are foreign to the needs and life-styles of many pupils. A reading of Hoggart (1959) suggests the dimensions of the conditions with which the pastoral care team have to cope in some sub-populations of the school. The underlying theme in the life-styles of those from deprived backgrounds is that of "us" against "them". In Rotter's (1966) terms they tend to see the world as dominated by luck and chance, and this reduces their belief that they can succeed through perseverance. They feel, underneath a veneer of toughness, that things are being done to them, and that they are the victims of forces they cannot control. Hence they become defensive, erecting barriers against communication, or taking such momentary pleasures as come their way.

The picture is extended by consideration of the work of Adorno *et al.* (1950) and Frenkel-Brunswik (1954). Many of the pupils who will

10

need the help of the pastoral team before they make better use of the resources of the school have been socialized in a way which creates an authoritarian personality. Their parents have insisted upon obedience without explaining the reasons for the commands; hence they adhere to the letter of the law rather than the spirit. These parents rely upon what Bernstein (1971) calls positional controls. Any attempt at dialogue between child and his parent about the rationale of an instruction ends up with "Why do it? Because I'm your father, that's why!". The pastoral team needs to identify the authoritarian pupil and then seek a remedy. This is not an easy task, as the following quotation from Frenkel-Brunswik shows. A girl who is authoritarian describes a good teacher as:

> Someone that is strict. If she asks for homework you have to get it done. Most teachers are not strict enough. If the assigned work is not given in then you should get zero. She shouldn't let the class get out of hand.

This shows that she relies on external checks and controls rather than upon self-control. Such a girl would be submissive in the face of strong authority, but would also be resentful of it and seek to outwit it.

The authoritarian personality has a strong tendency to divide people and events rigidly into categories of good and bad. No shades of grey exist for him. His world is dominated by the perception of threat—he anticipates it by defensive action, banding together with those of like mind.

Now, how does this relate to the academic life of the school, you may ask. Let me remind you that we are discussing a cognitive style—one which imposes immediate meaning upon a topic or situation. This is accompanied by a rigidity which causes authoritarians to adhere to their immediate definition of a situation despite contradictory evidence. Rokeach (1960) has shown that this reduces their efficiency at problem-solving. They fail to scan the evidence and analyse the problem.

Authoritarians tend to exaggerate the differences between the sexes. The males stress their physical strength and the superiority of what is masculine over the feminine. We are also beginning to see the emergence of aggression in the female authoritarian. Two problems arise from this. Joint roles which stress partnership and equality are becoming the norm in society, yet these boys and girls are ill-equipped to cope with these new roles. Equally, they are unlikely to react positively to informal methods of teaching and a relaxed approach by the teacher because they have been conditioned to misuse freedom and despise the tolerant as weaklings.

The pastoral care team will have to devise measures to help pupils who, through no fault of their own, have taken an anti-intellectual and intolerant stance. These are those in whom visual and physical attributes predominate over verbal ones; their way of thought is inductive rather than the deductive one of formal operations. They handle spatial concepts more easily than temporal ones, and are more concerned with immediate pleasures than long-term gains. They organize their lives along a relatively simple pattern in which the dimensions of weak versus strong, active versus passive, and, for the boys at least, masculine versus feminine play an unduly large part.

This approach affects their decision-making ability and their performance as learners. Their decisions will be based upon an almost automatic definition of the situation and they find it almost impossible to see alternative courses of action. This implies that the pastoral team will be concerned with teaching decision-making through realistic simulations. Dogmatism, or the tendency to be bound to rigid belief systems, is another problem described by Rokeach (1960). This again may appear within the family which stresses conformity and stifles the desire to explore ideas. Josephs' and Smithers' (1975) discussion of syllabus-bound and syllabus-free pupils demonstrates how this operates within the sixth form and influences the learning of young adults, although we, as teachers, must also question the ways in which we reinforce syllabus-bound pupils.

The task appears to be formidable, but it is possible to see that the description by Marland (1974), of the pastoral system as a device for helping the school attain its objectives, is one which can be given exciting shape. The team will be concerned with devising strategies and materials for overcoming such factors as those outlined above.

We must redefine our tasks to include the creation of an adaptive learning environment. The pastoral team must ensure an appropriate balance between task- and relationship-orientation, allowing for variations in the social backgrounds and ages of the pupils. For equality of opportunity to work, children from poorer backgrounds need not the same, but better, education and for this the pattern of relationships between teachers and pupils is very important. This means that we have to provide not only warm relationships, but also models of competence to a very critical audience of young people. We have to develop techniques and materials, creating a resources centre for pastoral care within the school.

The underlying processes

If the pastoral care team is to work effectively, then part of its task is the analysis of underlying constraints on teachers as well as pupils. Labelling as a member of a particular family rather than as an individual can unconsciously shape our responses to the challenge presented by some pupils. If we have had experience of children from that family we tend to anticipate the pupil's reactions, not seeing that we are calling out in him the very kind of reaction—positive or negative—which we expect. "I had his brother and I know what to expect, but this time . . . " is a familiar cry.

In understanding these processes it may be useful to think of the school as a gigantic signal system bombarding pupils and teachers with messages about themselves and their tasks. These messages incorporate a definition of the self of either teacher or pupil that is hard to reject. We become the kind of person that others tell us we are! The pastoral team should examine this situation. Are the messages which impinge upon a particular group negative or positive? Do they enhance self-respect or do they diminish the individual? Next, we can assess the discrepancy between the messages from the school staff and those from his peers, parents and the world outside. Many pupils react with chronic hostility when the messages sent to them within the school are incompatible with their responsibilities and roles at home, with what they consider suitable for their age, or with society's views of the adolescent. One need only think of the difference in signals of responsibility and respect sent to a girl of low ability who is coping with four younger siblings with an absent mother. At the age of fifteen she is of central importance at home, but at school she is constantly reminded that she is unsuccessful.

It is an adage in teaching that we get what we expect, yet at times we are unaware of the signals we ourselves send to pupils and how they interpret them. This can create a situation in the fifth year in which we find ourselves trying to do something about apathy, rejection of the values and aims of the school, disruptive behaviour of a pupil, and yet be oblivious to the possibility that they have been created by our own negative signals and sets of expectations.

Matza (1969) discussed the processes which precede the delinquent's or deviant's accepting his identity as such. The reactions of others and their attributions of intention and motive are crucial in building up a deviant identity. The first step in becoming deviant is that of *affinity*, which means that some individuals as a result of their circumstances are attracted towards activities disapproved of by society. This is not just a sub-cultural explanation, embracing all individuals from disadvantaged backgrounds. Affinity is therefore not the only condition; we must resort to the concept of *affiliation*, which is active rather than passive. Affiliation implies that a pupil is able to choose actively to reject school and then move towards delinquency or deviancy. I am aware that I have not defined deviance or delinquency carefully, but my purpose is to show that the process of becoming delinquent is not a completely predictable, socially ordained process. We must beware of such concepts as pre-delinquency in the secondary school.

The foregoing suggests that the individual still has to choose to be *converted* to the identity. This will apply to the situation that he is rejecting, just as much as to the one which he approaches. Becker (1953) shows that consciousness and intention are necessary for someone to become a marijuana user, for anyone can become one, but no one has to. It is the individual's conception of the behaviour of a user that is important, and delinquent behaviour can seem very attractive to certain adolescents compared with what we have to offer them. The individual must, as Matza indicates, begin to see himself as different from others, and must therefore change his perceptions of himself in relation to others. To help our failures and those who are disruptive, it is essential to identify which pressures in the school push pupils into defining themselves as different and produce a negative view of others, especially those whom they define as "snobs" or "ponces".

Next we have to ask what process crystallises the negative identity and makes it almost irreversible. This is what Matza calls *signification*, which is a strong form of labelling operated by those in authority. The pupils who suffer this are made conspicuous within the school by the public remarks of teachers, reinforced by overt disapproval, punishment and suspensions. Unfortunately, this not only derogates the individual who is being signified; it also provides him with an identity—one which is acquiring real significance. The years of difficulty in the secondary school are the middle years, and this is the very period in which adolescents are most unsure of their identities.

To be cast into the role of thief, slut, bully or an inadequate at this stage is liable to hasten the process of becoming the very thing.

The process of signification, together with our acts of punishment and disapproval, operate to exclude the pupil from other identities, so that his chances of seeing himself in a different way become progressively smaller. He then has little option but to seek out compensations and satisfactions in the role allocated to him. The pastoral team must see that the deviant identity assumes a central place in the pupil's life at school, simply because his teachers and peers constantly reinforce that identity.

Once a pupil has been allocated a reputation which has then hardened into an identity, people begin to treat him as if he were *nothing but* that identity. For certain individuals, sometimes for whole groups, a social process may be operating within the school which ends in allocating them a closed identity from which they have little chance, and eventually little desire, of escaping. This, strangely enough, should help the pastoral team, for once we understand these processes, we can take steps to stop them. Once we can see that what we have called corrective processes are actually feeding negative identities, we can examine and strengthen our reward systems, making them meaningful to pupils.

Responsible behaviour is the outcome of a positive picture of oneself as well as of the expectations of others. Examine the picture that pupils hold of themselves, and the model of the ideal pupil in the school. McKennell and Bynner (1969) writing on the self-concept of the smoker illustrate this. Adulthoodness and toughness seem to be salient components of the smoker's self-image, and his smoking reinforces and expresses this. To ask someone to give up smoking in adolescence may be asking them to identify with a group which they see as tied to the role of a schoolboy, and as "sissies" or "ponces". This is germane to the pupil's acceptance of his role.

The pastoral team may need to monitor and modify the image of the ideal pupil of the school, the relationships between staff and pupils and the transactions of the learning situation. These transactions often stress delayed reward and deferred gratification. It is also important to recognize that much classroom interaction is based on the assumption that a good pupil is one who is conforming and passive. Today, this is unacceptable to many pupils, girls rejecting it as strongly as boys. If streaming or banding is still used, we have to decide what the effect of being a member of a particular stream or band has on allegiance to the school and access to rewards

15

and status. In this way pastoral workers will gain valuable hints about how the school can function more adequately.

Alienation is more than a fashionable term, as Hamblin (1974) suggests. He investigated the way that some young people reject the identities offered by school, home and church as irrelevant, and their perception of many of the central rituals of the school, such as assembly, as trivia. Most sinisterly, he was left with the impression that although they were protesting, some were as apathetic about their alienation as they were about their commitment. The alienated seem to be responding to the fact that the school is basically uninterested in the true selves of the pupils. However, some aggressive pupils who may attack the fabric of the school as well as teachers and pupils, seem to be protesting vigorously about unintended and unrecognized attacks upon their self-concepts and self-respect.

The pastoral team may have to recognize that factors other than rational ones underlie educational decisions. Barker Lunn (1970) in her discussion of streaming in the primary school makes us aware of the way in which views and actions on a major educational decision were related to each teacher's personality factors, such as tolerance for noise, belief in the desirability of frequent testing and in the innate nature of ability. A pastoral care team which creates a climate in which colleagues can honestly examine these things is giving open-minded innovation a chance of becoming a reality.

Task-orientation and relationship-orientation have already been mentioned, and the team will need to work out their balance very carefully. A greater emphasis upon consistency of relationships may be needed with some groups from a disadvantaged background who are unable to adapt to frequent changes of teachers. There is a conflict between task- and relationship-orientation felt by the school staff. As teachers interact they begin to make relationships which support and satisfy them. If the sentient groups are related to the objectives of the school, all is well, but as Richardson (1973) points out, energy may be used to protect such a group rather than support the school as a whole. Coalitions, factions and near feuds will mar staffroom relationships, and it may need a well-integrated pastoral team to bring such conflicts out in the open and increase commitment to the task. If these sentient groups become more important than the task of the organization, then it is likely that innovation will fail.

The separation of the curricular and the pastoral has been condemned, yet the reader may still be unconvinced. We have already seen that the pastoral team will be giving deep thought to the processes through which pupils learn in the sometimes troubled period of development we call adolescence. The team should relate these processes to the developmental tasks of the individual, and to the possibilities for learning provided by the school organization. As all pastoral workers are subject teachers and most subject teachers perform some function in the pastoral term, the distinction between them is unreal.

If we accept that the pastoral system has an educative function, we can, I believe, successfully achieve this integration. It is useful to see the pastoral team as concerned with the production of what Sugarman (1974) has described as the morally educated person. Its task should be to produce an active striving toward an ideal taking shape during the identity-seeking period of adolescence. The pupil needs to commit himself to worthwhile tasks, and then there is no grudging measuring of involvement and effort. The morally educated person has developed the skill of standpoint-taking and of empathy, which also increases his intellectual competence. Again we can see that the two sides of school life are inseparable, for what is good for moral development is also good for intellectual growth.

Favourable attitudes towards oneself produce responsible behaviour towards others. Moral development includes the ability to read signals sent out by others; to present one's own views clearly and yet listen to those of others; to be ready to help rather than exploit the vulnerable; and to be able to make a positive emotional response when necessary. We may need to help pupils shed poor ways of coping with tension, which have often been acquired during childhood.

We can see that part of our pastoral task, which cannot be achieved by the pastoral team in isolation, is to facilitate the pupil's movement away from what Kohlberg (1963) has called orientation towards punishment and obedience, and towards the morality of individual principles of conscience. This is not easy. It is important to recognize that academic and moral tasks are related: to build skills in language is to increase the capacity for moral judgement and self-control. We must realize that the cognitive failure of the secondary school is

17

1. The diagram below shows the need for a long-term plan of pastoral care:

*Critical incidents in a comprehensive school for pupils
aged 11 years to 18 years*

Aims: 1. To isolate points at which pupils are likely to affiliate
with the school or dissociate from it.
2. To provide both the skills and perceptions which allow
pupils to deal with these incidents constructively.

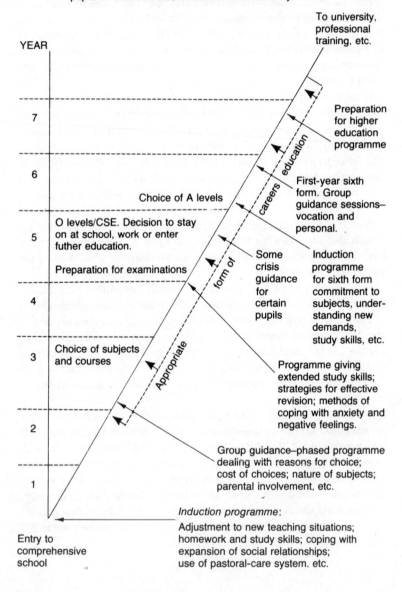

YEAR

To university,
professional
training, etc.

7   Preparation
for higher
education
programme

6   First-year sixth
form. Group
guidance sessions—
vocation and
personal.

Choice of A levels

O levels/CSE. Decision to stay
on at school, work or enter
futher education.

5

Preparation for examinations

Some
crisis
guidance
for
certain
pupils

Induction
programme
for sixth form
commitment to
subjects, under-
standing new
demands,
study skills, etc.

4

3   Choice of subjects
and courses

Programme giving
extended study skills;
strategies for effective
revision; methods of
coping with anxiety and
negative feelings.

2   Group guidance—phased programme
dealing with reasons for choice;
cost of choices; nature of subjects;
parental involvement, etc.

1

Induction programme:

Entry to
comprehensive
school

Adjustment to new teaching situations;
homework and study skills; coping with
expansion of social relationships;
use of pastoral-care system. etc.

careers education

form of

Appropriate

related to its failure as a socializing agency. There are teachers who confuse education with the passing on of information. A pupil's capacity to learn depends upon his ability to step outside an established frame of reference and suspend judgement until he has scanned the evidence; then to proceed to form tentative hypotheses. Such skills are also integral to moral judgement and behaviour, and fortunately, as Bramwell (1974) and Natale (1973) indicate, they can be induced through appropriate activities.

Integration of the pastoral and curricular stops us from looking outside the school for the sources of our problems with pupils. Consequently we have to accept that we are unwittingly creating some of these problems. Once this is accepted, we see the sense of making the pastoral task the production of open minds, of the capacity for commitment and of a creative belief in oneself and others. No easy task, yet a truly professional one.

REFERENCES

Adorno, T. Frenkel-Brunswik, E. Levinson, D. and Sandford, R. (1950) *The Authoritarian Personality*, New York: Harper.

Barker Lunn, J. (1970) *Streaming in the Primary School*, Slough: N.F.E.R.

Bazalgette, J. (1975) The transition from school to work: an organisational analysis, *British Journal of Guidance Counselling*, Vol. 3, No. 1.

Becker, H. (1953) Becoming a marijuana user, *Amer. J. Soc.*, Vol. 59.

Bernstein, B. (1965) A socio-linguistic approach to social learning, *Penguin Survey of the Social Sciences*, Gould, J. (Ed.), Harmondsworth: Penguin.

—— (1971) *Class, Codes and Control*, Vol. 1, London: Routledge & Kegan Paul.

Bramwell, P. (1974) *The Development of Standpoint Taking Ability in Boys*, Unpublished Dissertation: University College of Swansea.

Burdin, J. and Hamblin, D. (1974) Critical incident analysis, *Guidance Scotland*, Vol. 2, No. 2.

Frenkel-Brunswik, E. (1954) Further explorations by a contributor to the "Authoritarian Personality". In Christie, R. and Jahoda, M. (Eds.), *Studies in the Scope and Method of the "Authoritarian Personality"*, Glencoe, Illinois: Free Press.

Halsall, E. (1973) *The Comprehensive School*, Oxford: Pergamon.

Hamblin, D. (1974) *The Teacher and Counselling*, Oxford: Blackwell.

Hoggart, R. (1959) *The Uses of Literacy*, London: Chatto & Windus.

Inhelder, B. and Piaget, J. (1958) *The Growth of Logical Thinking*, London: Routledge & Kegan Paul.

Josephs, A. and Smithers, A. (1957) Personality characteristics of syllabus-bound and syllabus-free sixth formers. *British Journal of Educational Psychology*, Vol. 45, 1.

Kohlberg, L. (1963) Moral Development and Identification. In Stevenson, H., Kagan, J. and Spiker, C. (Eds.). *The Sixty-second Yearbook of the National Society for the Study of Education*, Chicago: University of Chicago Press.

Marland, M. (1974) *Pastoral Care*, London: Heinemann.

Matza, D. (1969) *Becoming Deviant*, Englewood Cliffs, New Jersey: Prentice-Hall.

McKennell, A. and Bynner, J. (1969) Self Images and Smoking Behaviour among School Boys. *British Journal of Educational Psychology*, Vol. 39, pp. 27–39.

Natale, S. (1972) *An Experiment in Empathy*, Slough: N.F.E.R.

Piaget, J. (1953) *The Origin of Intelligence in the Child*, London: Routledge & Kegan Paul.

Popper, K. (1973) *Objective Knowledge*, Oxford: Clarendon Press.

Richardson, E. (1973) *The Teacher, the School and the Task of Management*, London: Heinemann.

Rokeach, M. (1960) *The Open and Closed Mind*, New York: Basic Books.

Rotter, J. (1966) *Generalized Expectancies for Internal Versus External Control of Reinforcement*, Psychological Monographs, No. 609, Vol. 80, No. 1, Washington: American Psychological Association.

Sugarman, B. (1973) *The School and Moral Development*, London: Croom Helm.

CHAPTER TWO: KEY POINTS

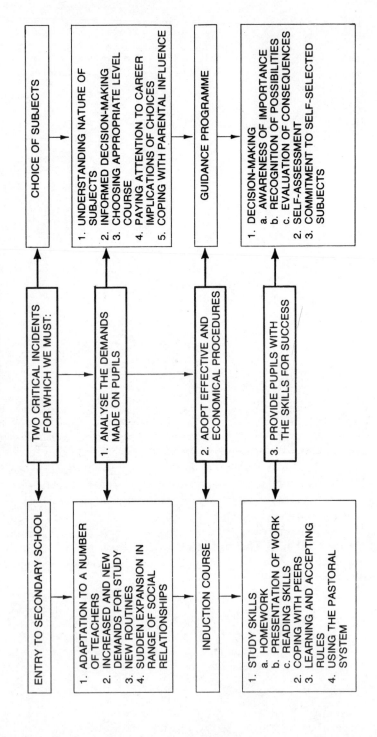

TWO CRITICAL INCIDENTS FOR WHICH WE MUST:

1. ANALYSE THE DEMANDS MADE ON PUPILS
2. ADOPT EFFECTIVE AND ECONOMICAL PROCEDURES
3. PROVIDE PUPILS WITH THE SKILLS FOR SUCCESS

CHOICE OF SUBJECTS

1. UNDERSTANDING NATURE OF SUBJECTS
2. INFORMED DECISION-MAKING
3. CHOOSING APPROPRIATE LEVEL COURSE
4. PAYING ATTENTION TO CAREER IMPLICATIONS OF CHOICES
5. COPING WITH PARENTAL INFLUENCE

GUIDANCE PROGRAMME

1. DECISION-MAKING
   a. AWARENESS OF IMPORTANCE
   b. RECOGNITION OF POSSIBILITIES
   c. EVALUATION OF CONSEQUENCES
2. SELF-ASSESSMENT
3. COMMITMENT TO SELF-SELECTED SUBJECTS

ENTRY TO SECONDARY SCHOOL

1. ADAPTATION TO A NUMBER OF TEACHERS
2. INCREASED AND NEW DEMANDS FOR STUDY
3. NEW ROUTINES
4. SUDDEN EXPANSION IN RANGE OF SOCIAL RELATIONSHIPS

INDUCTION COURSE

1. STUDY SKILLS
   a. HOMEWORK
   b. PRESENTATION OF WORK
   c. READING SKILLS
2. COPING WITH PEERS
3. LEARNING AND ACCEPTING RULES
4. USING THE PASTORAL SYSTEM

PROGRAMMES OF INDUCTION TO THE SECONDARY SCHOOL AND OF GUIDANCE ON SUBJECT OPTIONS

Summary

THE CENTRAL ARGUMENT

This chapter illustrates the way in which pupils can be given the skills required for success, through a programme of activities which have clear objectives. It is argued that pastoral periods, although short and sometimes not as frequent as we would desire, can be highly productive. Two key incidents are examined, and ideas for work in pastoral periods which have been tested for seven years, are presented. The activities outlined are intended to help pupils boost their performance in school by coping successfully with the major transition of entry to secondary school and by wise choice of subjects in the third year. The materials produced by a team effort for such programmes form the nucleus of a resources centre for guidance and pastoral care within the school.

THE INDUCTION COURSE

This aims at giving pupils a good start in the secondary school, utilizing their keenness, whilst improving their capacity to cope by giving them the essential skills, including those of study and homework. The major difficulty of adapting to the demands of many teachers rather than relating to a single one as in the primary school is given constructive attention. The aim is to aid maturation rather than protect pupils unduly. The basic foundations for constructive discipline are provided by activities which teach pupils the school rules and their rationale, the procedures for dealing with absence, bullying and other difficulties, how to look after their property and use the pastoral system constructively. The programme should also contain activities which emphasize the rewards and opportunities offered by the school. A successful programme presents the school as a caring community and ensures that maximum opportunities for affiliation are offered.

TO HELP PUPILS MAKE A WISE CHOICE OF SUBJECTS

A three-phase, activity-based programme is put forward to modify the situation in which parents are more influential than the teacher in shaping the pupil's choices. Many pupil's express dissatisfaction with the choice of subjects a year after choosing them, which, combined with existing tendencies towards alienation, causes rejection of the school's demands. Such a programme has great significance for the less able, for girls with unduly low aspirations, and above all for pupils in the middle-ability range. Such pupils may well be taking only two or three subjects at O level, and the choice of these has long-term consequences which the pupil does not recognize without guidance.

In the first phase, the programme creates awareness of the factors underlying choice, buildings up the capacity to make a considered decision of taking or not taking a subject and of its career relevance. The second phase highlights parental involvement through discussion groups led by form tutors. A minimal third phase then deals with individual difficulties. Attention is given to communication with parents and the self-defeating nature of some current practices.

The purpose of these programmes

It has been argued so far that our primary task is the integration of the pastoral and curricular within the school in a way which facilitates

24

the growth of positive identities of the pupils as learners, and which encourages them to associate with the aims of the educative process. Next, we must ask what is the most economical way of doing this. One way is to construct programmes of guidance which focus on critical points in the pupil's school career. Such an approach uses the teachers' skills to the best advantage. If a trained counsellor is available he can co-operate in the construction and presentation of the activities—for these are activity-based programmes—so that he can communicate his skills and attitudes to his colleagues. Marland (1974) was making a crucial point when he said that pastoral care cannot be conducted in a vacuum.

These programmes are part of the long-term aim of developing a resources centre for guidance and counselling within each school. The resources will include tape recordings, questionnaires, simulations and games, all devised by those with intimate knowledge of a particular school. Spirit duplicators allow the production of durable colourful material, for thin manilla card can be used in these duplicators and if covered with self-adhesive plastic film, not only is it pleasant for pupils to handle, but remains clean. Incidentally many parents are prepared to help with such tasks, and the art department can give invaluable help with general presentation. Each programme should involve the year tutors in workshops where the activities are devised and the apparatus prepared, so that they are actively involved from the beginning.

Entry to the secondary school

Industry spends large sums of money on induction courses for young workers, but the transition from primary to secondary school is equally severe. It is a discontinuity of experience, where some pupils, if they cannot cope, will begin to dissociate from the school, either by truanting, under-functioning or failing to become actively involved in school life. Often these are the over-protected and the anxious, who are prevented from successful adaptation. But we are concerned with giving all pupils a good start in the secondary school, showing them the rewards and the facilities which we have to offer, demonstrating our understanding of their needs and that the secondary school is a caring community.

Several years ago, the writer, with the help of his students, collected almost two thousand confidential reports of pupils' perceptions of their difficulties on entry to the comprehensive school. A small selection is given below.

"I was really scared about coming to . . . because I had heard so much about the fights and things getting stolen. About a month later I met some of the boys who were supposed to be the hard boys but really they're a good lot of guys if you know them."

"Before I came down here one or two of my friends said it was terrible down here and of course I believed them. I was shown around the school, it was to me massive and I wondered how I could remember which way to go and which classroom is which."

"They do ask you for money and threaten you but if you're careful you can avoid being asked. But never never give the boy any money because they come back again and again for more."

"The first day I had to come to . . . I was scared as I thought some of the boys would beat me up. When I got there things were much different than I though they would be, no boys started on me and I was pleased they didn't. I was still a bit nervous as I had not met the teachers who I thought would be hard. Now and again boys started on me saying give me 5p or I'll beat you up. I was scared at this as the boys were older so I gave the money."

"I noticed a lot of bullying by some of the boys because most of them were all over 5 feet and as strong as about $1\frac{1}{2}$ boys and some of the teachers were like sergeants in the army."

"After I had been in school for a while say about a month, I began to love it then. I did not have any worries, the bat now and then, but that didn't worry me."

These extracts reflect the themes found, although one source of anxiety in some schools was a fear of being pushed downstairs. The way negative responses to some teachers can be created is illustrated by the following extract:

"What's it like? Who are the teachers? These are what I thought every night for weeks before I came to . . . Then I kept talking to boys who came last year and they said 'It's all right but watch some of the teachers—keep out of the way of so and so.'"

26

A few examples seem to reveal some failures which we should strive to eliminate.

"My first ever lesson was French and it seemed it would never end. After the first day I thought I would never get through the term."

"It is half way through the first term and only four teachers know my name and that's not including my form tutor, he don't know my name yet. I say if they don't know you they can't help you."

"I was told it was OK but it started to be a drag, the teachers get on your nerves. You had to do this, you had to do that, if not you get hit."

Perhaps this has given the reader some insight into the ways pupils react to entry to a comprehensive school. Myths and fantasies have been built up, and in some cases confirmed. Certainly the state of anxiety revealed by these pupils gives us cause for thought because it is fertile ground in which negative attitudes can develop. Amongst the sources of anxiety were fear of the apparatus in gym and of getting hurt in team games, but it was surprising to see the number of pupils who found the experience of school dinners and guarding their dinner tickets a cause for worry. Now let us examine the induction programme.

Planning the induction programme

Many readers will already have established liaison with their feeder primary schools, but these programmes need to be extended. It is useful for pupils to visit the secondary school before they come. The information gathered by the year head or first-year tutors about children at risk is extremely valuable, but there should be other links between primary and secondary schools. Two examples suffice. In one school the teachers visit the primary schools in the spring term and, with their colleagues there, undertake a survey of attainment in reading and mathematics. The results are fed back into the secondary school, allowing subject teachers a whole term to plan their strategies. Adaptation to the needs of pupils in these crucial areas can do much to reinforce pupils' positive attitudes. It is worth recalling that Sumner and Warburton (1972) found that one of the factors

27

which distinguished the industrious group they studied, from those who were allergic to school, was the attitude towards mathematics. Teaching which is based on a pupil's attainment rather than an arbitrary norm is likely to give him a sense of success rather than of inadequacy.

In another school the headmaster allows first-year teachers to talk to pupils in their primary schools when they are working on a special project during their final term. These projects are completed in the secondary schools, and give a sense of continuity.

Induction programmes should be planned and all the duplication completed before the end of the summer term. As many of the first-year tutors as possible should take part in the planning sessions, and the head of year or house should play a major part. He must take responsibility for co-ordination of effort, organizing the planning meetings with clear objectives in mind, ensuring that material is produced and distributed, and monitoring the programme once it is under way.

The first meeting is intended to gather suggestions, evaluating ideas from first-year subject teachers who are not form tutors, or even from first-year pupils. Teaching notes clarify the objectives of those conducting the programme and should be produced as a matter of course.

After an initial brief introduction, the material is handed out and pupils begin to work in small groups of three or four. They are set problems and encouraged to think of ways of coping with them. If we get pupils who may be feeling isolated on their first day interacting in small groups, we shall dispel their anxiety and build up real communication between them and their peers. The form tutor then reintegrates the class as a group by ending with a discussion of the experience or answering their questions. This reversal of the teacher's usual role seems to stimulate positive interaction between pupil and teachers, whilst the small-group activities create an emotional climate in which they are receptive to the teacher's remarks. A hopeful approach towards the problems of adjustment is established.

It is useless to bombard new pupils with a mass of details on the first day. They need repetition of each topic, so that they can consolidate their ideas about the best ways of coping. Urgent matters such as bullying should be dealt with as soon as possible. Get rid of the fears and fantasies, and move on to more positive ideas of study skills and the rewards offered by the school.

Most schools use about twenty to twenty-four periods for the induction course, spreading them over the first four or six weeks of term. Many use the normal pastoral periods, taking care that the time is not dissipated by passing on routine administrative instructions. An example of the way one school presented the topics is given below.

This programme worked very well over three years, although it could be criticized for giving insufficient time to study skills, the presentation of homework and the rewards offered by the school. Yet it helped pupils make a successful adjustment, and certain difficulties found in the first year of this school almost disappeared. Some schools allow new pupils to plan a social evening at the end of the induction course. This marks the individual's integration into a new status in the school community. Sixth-form pupils often act as helpers in this, permitting the first formers to do the work, but only offering advice when asked and acting as resources upon which the new entrants can call.

Parents, first-year pupils, head of year or house, form tutors and the sixth-form pupils who have helped with the preparations, attend the social evening. During the evening important information about pupils is often given to the pastoral team by parents—not merely by mothers, for fathers attend this function. The major benefit, however, is the positive picture of the school that parents take away with them. Parents gain immensely from talking to sixth formers about the school; indeed this may be one of the most valuable parts of the exercise.

There is more opportunity for flexibility in the timetable in the first year than later on, but if the induction programme is found too difficult to fit in, then one can have an introductory week of special activities which include the major elements of the induction programme. There is no single way of running an induction programme; merely different approaches which are more or less effective within the context of a specific school and type of intake.

INDUCTION PROGRAMME FOR FIRST-YEAR PUPILS

Timetable

(a) To commence on Tuesday, 3rd September.

(b) The usual form periods will be used by the tutors for the activities.

TOPIC	Week 1	Week 2	Week 3	Week 4	Week 5	Week 6
Teaching Styles		TUES	TUES			TUES
Classrooms	TUES			TUES	TUES	
Homework	WED		WED		WED	WED
Bullying	THURS		THURS		THURS	
Gym and Games		WED		WED		
Welfare and PE		THURS		THURS		THURS

Notes

1. The six topics are spread over six weeks. Pupils cannot assimilate all the information and deal with the problems quickly—time is necessary.
2. Each topic has been repeated three times on the same day. This has been done deliberately to allow you to:
   (i) develop discussion and exploration of the topic;
   (ii) reinforce the pupil's positive attempts at coping with the problem at regular intervals.
3. The core of this programme is you in your role of form tutor—you are the one who will provide the first step in a pastoral care programme which will cover the pupil's whole school career.
4. Regular briefings will occur at 1.30 pm for the first six Fridays of this term. We will discuss the current week's work and prepare you for the next week. Notes will be taken in order to modify the programme for next year's intake.

Very clear signposting of corridors, lavatories, medical room, dining hall and assembly hall is a first practical step. The pupils have stressed the sense of being confused and lost. The anxious child feels exposed, grossly insecure and afraid of ridicule. Situations of transition inevitably increase a sense of vulnerability and make new pupils perceive threat where none is intended.

Some schools have placed a clear staff and pupil timetable at strategic points in corridors, its height and position such that it can be seen easily and that pupils grouping around it do not cause inconvenience to others. And why not give pupils a duplicated timetable, with spare copies for each form and subject teacher? Teachers in some schools wear badges showing their names and the form for which they are responsible. To have to talk to an adult whose name you do not know is intimidating.

None of this is unnecessary coddling of pupils, for our aim is to build up their confidence in the first few days. The induction programme will then have maximum effect on new entrants.

Bullying

Many fears of bullying are unjustified, yet they can persist if they are not dealt with quickly. There will always be a few unfortunate incidents which confirm a nervous child's fantasies, creating reactions which may harden into school refusal. The aim is to build up his ability to cope and make him aware of what he does which can attract bullying. A child who responds to teasing by crying, tantrums or blind attack is likely to initiate a labelling process amongst both his peers and his teachers. Our task is to develop his skills and help him act in a mature manner.

One simple device is to record on tape a simple extract lasting about one and a half minutes. Two pupils are heard approaching a teacher and one says, "Miss, Robert Jones has been taking my crisps in the playground, and now today he asked me for five pence". His friend adds, "That's right, Miss, he's asked me too". The teacher then says, "Well, I suppose I can do something about it and I will if necessary, but what do you think you can do?". The form then discuss this in small groups, after which the teacher writes some of the ideas on the blackboard and looks at viable strategies, showing the positive and negative consequences of some of the proposed actions.

In some schools simple questionnaires of the type illustrated on pp. 43 and 44 have been produced. This helps pupils become aware of the characteristics of those who attract bullying or hostility and then asks them to assess themselves in a simple way. Note that it would include a final positive task: to discuss how they would help someone being bullied, and what advice they would give this boy or girl. Such indirect approaches prevent a pupil labelling himself as someone likely to be bullied, and yet they anticipate the situation helpfully if it does occur.

Cartoons are very useful in dealing with bullying. These can suggest more useful ways of using strength in physical education and games, drawing attention to the idea that another kind of strength is the determination to do something well—maybe something which seems difficult at first. Pupils respond to the idea that it is part of growing up to gain the strength to help people.

Activity is essential, and simple role play or semi-simulations provide it. "The New Football Boots" is an example of a situation around which a simulation can be built. New possessions of which pupils are proud often act as the focus for bullying. Therefore pupils need to be taught not to provoke incidents and how to cope with them if they cannot be avoided. A good simulation allows them to choose between several possible solutions, for we are suggesting possibilites rather than a single way of behaving.

Even in cramped classrooms pupils can discuss the situation at their desks, before one group performs it. This may be an advantage, for some pupils find role play difficult at first. The teacher's role is to make the salient points clear once the pupils have had the vicarious experience. When using activity methods fears of disorder can be exaggerated, but it is true that they reveal weaknesses in our classroom management. The lesson has to be conducted vigorously and to a time schedule, and by the end of the period the class must have worked through the material and the teacher should be the focus for the pupil's attention.

A good introduction to the topic of bullying is to compare their entry to school with other new situations, such as their move from infant to junior school and the way they coped with this. The reminder that they have already coped with such situations, and found them to be different from what they thought, increases their

32

sense of being in control. Never give more time to bullying than is strictly necessary, for this is obviously counter-productive. What one must aim at is to make them realize that we all have to face threatening experiences and that we usually do it successfully.

The rules of the school

Obviously school rules, if they are to be kept, must be known by pupils. The evidence from the developmental psychology of adolescence, Conger (1973), Wenar (1972), suggests that adolescents will accept rules provided that their function is made clear. A formal written statement of rules should be supplemented by discussion and explanation by the form tutor, who will have to intervene when normal disciplinary measures are not working. Experience suggests that pupils learn rules best in the form group, using a small group of three of four as a basis for the activities.

An introductory activity is the "Desert Island Game". Some survivors from a ship have landed on a lonely island, with supplies needed for existence. They will, however, not be rescued for eighteen months. What rules will they need to maintain their well-being? The teacher can add any conditions he likes, the aim being to show that rules function to create an orderly and safe community. The school rules are then presented from the viewpoint.

Irritation and exasperation are felt by many heads of the first year or form tutors when they have to spend time dealing with parental complaints about lost or stolen property. This can be prevented if in the induction programme we train pupils to look after their property. Some come from disorganized homes, and an orderly approach to life is unfamiliar; others have been over-protected. We need to show these pupils the importance of labelling P.E. kit, overcoats and other personal belongings, and to help them recognize when things are likely to get mislaid. Activity methods can be still used, and this part of the programme might well begin by deciding what advice they would give a new pupil who might lose his belongings. The teacher can then show what precautions are essential. If we are to avoid "protection" or "extortion rackets", a sensible first step is to make them realize the inadvisability of bringing too much money to school and displaying, too openly, pens or sweets.

Every teacher knows about these aspects of school life, but we do little to bring them under control or provide pupils with ways of

"WHAT DO I DO IF . . . ?"

In a new school there seem to be so many things that puzzle you. In a few months you will have forgotten them, although they were important at first. It is useful to think about these situations and discover that you already have a good idea about coping with them.

You can work with a friend. Make your answers as precise as possible—say exactly to whom you would go or what you would do.

THE SITUATION	WHAT YOU WOULD DO
1. You have been sent on a message, but you cannot find the person for whom the message is intended. What do you do?	
2. You have fallen in the playground and hurt your wrist. It is not very swollen, but it is very painful. What do you do?	
3. You have lost your new duffle coat. Your name is clearly marked in it, but it is not on the hook when school ends. What do you do?	
4. You have been asked for 5p by a boy in the playground. He asks you every day. He has not threatened you at all. What do you do?	
5. You have been having fun rushing around with your friends. Suddenly, there is a noise—your friends laugh —your trousers have well and truly split! Well, what are you going to do?	
6. Your bus was late. It wasn't your fault. The registration period is over. What do you do to get your mark?	

dealing with them. This section of the programme will also teach pupils what to do when they are absent from school: they must know where to bring the absence notes and understand that illegitimate absences will be followed up. How they can get first aid should be made clear, for the basic question in a pupil's mind is, "What do I do if . . . ?" This can be dealt with through questionnaires as well as by direct teaching—an example is given on page 34.

We need to make explicit, and to teach deliberately, much that we have taken for granted. Pupils should be taught the functions of the form master or mistress: their responsibility for progress reviews; the help they offer with difficulty in studies; their readiness to listen to personal difficulties in an understanding way. If this is not made clear we, on the one hand, may feel that pupils have no problems, whilst pupils, on the other, may feel that nobody is interested in them. Equally, we should teach pupils how their parents can arrange to meet the form tutor or year head and what support they can expect from them. To do this successfully needs a clear job specification for the first-year form tutors.

The major adaptation

The new entrant to the comprehensive school is faced with a new problem, that of being taught by a number of teachers. He has to adapt to varying the styles of teaching, demands and mannerisms, often moving from classroom to classroom and using unfamiliar equipment. Some primary schools and home backgrounds will have prepared children to do this with confidence, but others may not have done so.

Some pupils may not have previously been taught by male teachers and are intimidated by the normally more powerful masculine voice. Variations of speech rates, demands on the pupil for neatness, for signs of attention, can create stress in those pupils whose margins of adaptability have been restricted by personality or environment.

The initial discussion could develop from a handout which draws pupils' attention to these points in an amusing way: there is no need for pastoral care to be dreary. The example given below is adapted from a booklet which supplements the induction course in a South Wales school. Form tutors can discuss the differences between adults so that the fixed ideas some pupils have about teachers is modified.

The focus moves quickly to what pupils can do to present a good picture of themselves in different situations and how they can cope with subjects they dislike or find difficult. This is done through the help of activities and questionnaires which give the pupil's responses salience. Added motivation is given by the emphasis on these adaptations as essential components of becoming mature.

MATERIAL ON TEACHING STYLES TAKEN FROM THE HANDBOOK FOR PUPILS SUPPLEMENTING THE INDUCTION COURSE IN A SOUTH WALES SCHOOL

You have probably noticed lots of things that are different in your new school.

Perhaps the first difference you saw was that this school is a lot bigger than your old school: but you have probably also realised that you have many more teachers to teach you the different subjects:

In your junior school you had one teacher for your class

Now in your new school you have lots of teachers—teaching you different subjects: all teaching you in different ways.

By now you have probably met all your teachers who are going to teach you in the different subjects. Maybe you have realised that no two lessons are the same! Let's have a look at some different lessons and see what they are like—

In this lesson—

talking

In this lesson?

laughing and joking

In this lesson?

hands up to answer

In this lesson?

writing and writing

In this lesson?

very strict

In these lessons, did you notice that the pupils were behaving in different ways?

You see, all people look different—this is what makes us individuals.

People have different ways of wanting things done—you could see in the drawings that the teachers all had different ways of teaching in their lessons.

Some teachers like you to wait outside the classroom before they arrive and other teachers would want you to go into the classroom.

People speak at different rates—some more quickly or slowly than others.

People have different sorts of voices—some soft voices, some LOUD.

People dress differently.

People walk, sit or stand differently.

People ARE different.

So in the same way naturally the new teachers you've met are all different but the one thing that they have in common is that they *care about you* personally and want to help you get on and grow up and be successful in school and in life.

You will be behaving differently in each lesson—you will be adjusting to suit each teacher.

MATERIAL ILLUSTRATING THE INDUCTION PROGRAMME OF A SOUTH WALES SCHOOL

Teachers' notes on classrooms, the geography of the building and the form tutor's functions

1. *The building*

Investigation has shown that the physical size of comprehensive schools with their tall buildings, many classrooms and the distances which have to be travelled from part to part tend to disorient pupils. They not only get lost, but frequently lose their property. They can develop acute feelings of losing their identity and become reluctant to come to school. The following points will help.

(a) Second-year boys are available on the first day as guides.

(b) Draw attention to the notices indicating room numbers.

(c) Use the map provided to look at the main features—especially lavatories, medical room and dining hall.

(d) Make quite sure they are familiar with the lower school.

(e) Explain that the form room is a base for registration etc.

2. *Your function as form tutor*

Explain this carefully, stressing the welfare aspect of your role, e.g. lost property, free meals, absence notes. In other words, try to reinforce the link between your role and that of the primary school teacher. We have to bridge this gap by showing that you as Form Tutor are concerned about every pupil.

3. *General points about classroom procedures*

(a) Explain the need to mark *all* books and clothing with their names.

(b) Emphasize the fact that they should not bring too much money to school.

(c) Explain the main school rules which will impinge on them. Give the reasons for the rules so that they do not seem arbitrary or stupid.

People—and the sort of picture they give

You've been at .... Comprehensive School a short time by now and you've probably met nearly all the teachers who will be taking you in the different subjects. You've probably worried a bit before coming to the school as to what these teachers would be like. Well you've probably realized that like all human beings the following things are true about them.

All people look differently, that is what makes us individuals.

People walk, sit or stand differently.

People speak at different rates, some more quickly or slowly than others.

41

People have different ways of wanting things done.

People have different sorts of voice—some have soft voices, some loud.

People dress differently.

So in the same way naturally the new teachers you've met are all different, but the one thing that they have in common is that they *care about you* personally and want to help you get on and grow up and be successful in school and in life.

NOW—You make a list of at least 5 things you can do in school which will give a GOOD PICTURE of yourself to people.

1. ....

2. ....

3. ....

4. ....

5. ....

NOW—write also what sort of things do you think will give a BAD PICTURE of yourself.

1. ....

2. ....

3. ....

4. ....

5. ....

Finally, place a tick (√) in the box in answer to the question.

Which picture do you want to give people?

A good picture ☐   A bad picture ☐

GOING SOMEWHERE FOR THE FIRST TIME

You have just come to a large comprehensive school for the first time as a pupil. Going to anywhere which is new can be a bit frightening. So can you think back to when you were SEVEN YEARS OLD and going from the Infant school to the Junior or 'big' school. Can you place a tick in the box you think best describes how you felt then.

Going to the Junior School	Like me	Not Like me
1. I was looking forward to it.	☐	☐
2. Afraid of bigger children.	☐	☐
3. Wondered what the teachers would be like.	☐	☐
4. Wondered if the work would be too hard.	☐	☐
5. Looking forward to doing new things.	☐	☐
6. Being with my friends.	☐	☐
7. Good at my work.	☐	☐
8. Making new friends.	☐	☐

(a) Will you now put a ring around any of your answers you think still describe how you feel on entering this comprehensive school.

(b) Now work in groups of 4 and draw up a list between you of the things that you find the most frightening in coming to this school.

(c) Discuss in your small group what you can do to make a good start in this school.

At the secondary school we should be steadily building up the pupil's ability to make considered decisions. There is a place for this in the first few weeks of the induction course. The programme can include among others, situations such as those given below. These decision-making activities incorporate the principle of evaluating alternative courses of action to modify a situation, the need to look at the costs of certain responses, and, above all, the realization that remedies exist for situations which can escalate into negative attitudes to learning. When we do these things, we are building up in pupils a methodical approach to problem-solving, a sense of potency and a habit of industriousness.

Decision-making situations

Jane cannot always remember exactly what she is supposed to do in her homework. She tries to remember, but she sometimes wastes her time by doing the wrong thing. Which of the following actions do you think will be the most helpful to Jane in putting the situation right?

(a) Carefully write down the instructions in a special notebook.
(b) Check with her best friend.
(c) Ask the teacher after she has done her homework.
(d) Ask her mother what she thinks the teacher wanted her to do.
(e) Ask the teacher as soon as the instructions have been given, if she thinks she has not understood.
(f) Wait until the lesson is over and then ask the teacher.

Now discuss the answers in your small groups. Is there any reason why your solution may not work?

* * *

Jack wants to get on in his new school, but he sometimes gets into difficulties because he has not got the right books or has left something at home. He is thinking of what he can do to stop this happening and has made the following list of ideas. Which do you think is most likely to help him?

(a) Try to stop the teacher from noticing him.

(b) Apologise to the teacher when it happens.

(c) Check his timetable last thing at night and see that he has everything he will need next day.

(d) Leave it until the morning and then check what he will need.

We can tackle problems like this in different ways, as Jack's list shows. Some are more likely to be successful than others. In your small group discuss the one you chose and try to find out if there were some snags that you had not seen.

* * *

This part of the programme leads into a consideration of the pupil's attitudes towards homework and his possession of adequate study skills. Banks and Finlayson (1973) in their study of under-functioning demonstrate the critical importance of good attitudes towards homework in the able pupil who is functioning adequately. This will apply to other pupils. Some pupils have little experience of homework and receive little support at home.

First teach pupils how to present homework clearly, showing them the importance of headings and a logical structure. Subject teachers should draw up a model for the presentation of a typical piece of homework in their subject for the first year. These models can be supplemented by exercises which give the main headings, but present the content in each section in a muddled order. Pupils can then discuss the logical order of the material with a partner and re-arrange it. Their attention is thus directed towards the need to think about the structuring of notes in homework without unthinking reproduction of the text. Jacobs (1974), in her study of sixth-form pupils who had failed A levels and were repeating them, found that, even at this level, they lacked the skill to present their answers to questions in a logical manner. The school is more likely to attain its academic objectives if the foundation for these skills is built systematically from the moment of entry.

The old game concerned with instructions can teach pupils a lesson that they will not easily forget if it is used in the induction programme. They are presented with a sheet of paper headed, "How to follow directions", which tells them that they have only three minutes to complete the test. The first instruction asks them to perform some simple task, and the second to read all the questions on the paper before proceeding. Usually most of the class have responded to the tension created by the idea of a test and time limit, and are frantically dividing, adding, drawing circles and performing other specified tasks. A few look smug and self-satisfied and are doing nothing. At the end one of these pupils will reveal that question seventeen said, "Once you have read this, do the first three questions and nothing else". This form of learning lasts longer than countless admonitions by teachers.

Homework offers pupils a chance to work on their own and think things our for themselves; yet we cannot assume that pupils will see it in this light. Only by making this clear and using our powers of persuasion can we prevent pupils seeing it as an imposition and dreary chore. It is important to mark homework quickly and thoroughly, for immediate knowledge of results can be a powerful motivator.

Even so, many pupils still attempt to do homework in a crowded room or with the television on. One programme opens this up for discussion by asking pupils to say which of the following they agree with. They are then asked to select the five statements most likely to ensure rewarding homework.

1. It's best to do homework as soon as possible after it has been set.

2. Homework should not be done in a rush.

3. You should think hard about what your teacher wants before you begin the homework.

4. Homework should be carefully planned so that it can be done properly, and you can then have some fun.

5. It's a good idea to discuss your homework with your parents if you're not sure about it.

6. It's all right to listen to the radio while doing homework.

7. It's a good idea to get books from the library to help with homework.

8. It's all right to copy homework from someone else in your class.

9. It's a good idea to go out and play and then do your homework.

10. Homework should be handed to the teacher on time.

Discussion of these points can be very helpful, for most pupils desire to do well and value the teacher's approval at this stage in their school career. The same programme offers pupils the following tips in the booklet around which the induction course is based:

1. Read through your work when it is completed.

2. Isolate the main facts.

3. Check with the teacher if you are not sure that you understand exactly what the homework is.

4. Ask your parents or older brother or sister to scan the homework when you have finished.

5. Allocate your time for each subject; decide whether you will do the easiest work first or start on the difficult piece at once.

The point about tackling the difficult or easier subject first can be developed into a decision-making exercise. There is no right answer, but some pupils spend so much time on the difficult subject that they become dejected and get to dislike it more, neglecting the subjects they are good at and doing less well than they should. The anxious pupil may, however, find himself unable to deal with other subjects whilst the difficult one remains undealt with. So it is important for each pupil to draw up his own timetable for homework. Obviously, if a pupil dislikes a subject and is constantly predicting failure, additional help is necessary from subject and form teacher. Otherwise the dislike for one subject is likely to spread to other similar subjects.

Perhaps it may be felt that too much emphasis has been given to homework, but we must remember that homework is often a major source of tension between the pupil and his parents, sometimes between the parent and the school, and sometimes between all three parties. It is sensible to try to induce in pupils a sense of commitment to the activity, anticipating difficulties before they arise. It may come to light that there is no unified plan for the allocation of homework in the first year. Pupils may be getting three difficult assignments on the same night, and then feel overwhelmed by the load. Such a situation is rare, but it reflects a failure in co-ordination. Unnecessary sources of threat and pressure can gradually arise if vigilance lapses.

To ensure affiliation to the school, it is helpful if heads of department and other teachers present their subjects to pupils in a way

47

which shows their relationship to life and the rewards they bring. Enquiry One (1968) has shown that pupils and parents have very definite ideas about those subjects which are useful. Schools sometimes have merit award systems or privilege schemes, which should be clearly presented to the pupils. Before you respond to a reward system you must know what it is. Even more important, the rewards must be not only attainable, but meaningful to those whom they are intended to motivate. Success in academic work and the security of knowing that one is spending many of one's formative years in a caring institution is often more influential.

Physical education can be extremely rewarding, although many pupils are anxious about it. They may have fears of apparatus or dislike changing if their physical development is in advance of the majority. Physical and psychological maturity are not identical. A friendly chat from the P.E. master and mistress will remove these anxieties in all except pupils who have a deep-seated aversion to physical activity. These pupils will sometimes have other anxieties which may indicate the need for some special help.

This programme has been designed to allow the form tutor to detect pupils "at risk". It is important that once a pupil is so considered, information about his reactions should be gathered from as many sources as possible. Subject teachers may feel that the pupil is responding well in the learning situation, hence we need to suspend judgement.

A final meeting of the team should record any suggestions for improvement, and someone should be clearly charged with the responsibility of implementing these the following summer.

SUBJECT OPTIONS

The resources of the pastoral team should next be centred on subject options. The thorough research undertaken by Reid *et al.* (1974) has confirmed the views of teachers that much more needs to be done to help pupils with this. It is a point at which important decisions are made, it cannot be separated from other forces at work within the school.

Unless our pastoral system is developing pupils' power of making thoughtful decisions, we may be forcing them to make choices when they have little knowledge of themselves, their aptitudes and goals, and so do not understand the implications of their choices and the nature of the examination system. Hence the argument put forward here is for a programme to provide essential knowledge and, particularly with the less able, stimulate the capacity for making good decisions, in the year preceding the choice of subjects.

We may need to invest more conscious efforts to solve the special problems of girls, for, career aspirations of girls seem to rank lower in importance than those of boys, and, sadly enough, girls themselves tend to accept this, as the work of Wheeler (1974) demonstrates. Fortunately the climate of opinion is changing, and the pastoral care team can do something to change this negative situation, for the finding of Hutchings (1970), that girls consciously lower their sights, is still relevant. The tag of "unfeminine" still has a compelling quality. In the vocational counselling of girls I have found that they feel that emotional pressures discourage them from choosing careers traditionally dominated by males. It is little wonder, then, that the female engineer is still a rarity.

Major problems have to be faced by the pastoral team in the choice of subjects. Here the curricular and the pastoral interact closely, for adequate subject options depend upon the school's skill in constructing courses which satisfy pupils' needs. It may be difficult to provide enough flexibility to allow a pupil who experiences a genuine change of interest to take up a new course. Certainly the problems of co-ordination are great, and we need to make sure that form tutors understand the implications of subject choice and the procedures attached to it. Our role as form tutors is to provide concerned and objective guidance for each pupil. And this may cause some anxiety. Yet as professionals we should be able to deal with them in a constructive manner.

Reid and her colleagues reveal that pupils, when considering options, stress interest, liking for and ability in the subject, and its relevance to their careers. This is not a teacher's commonly held view. This report demonstrates how little influence we have on the choices made. Less than fifteen per cent of pupils, in any of the schools studied, attributed the most important help received in a crucial educational matter to a member of the school staff. Between fifty-eight and seventy per cent cited their parents as the most important influence, and twenty-five to thirty-three per cent considered that none of their teachers played an important part in helping them to decide. Yet parents often have little knowledge of modern educational practice, and often build up an inflated estimation of the ability of their child, sometimes as a result of our system of reporting. Then comes the moment of subject choice and tensions erupt. Parents who have held these false assumptions for some time, need wise handling if they are not to feel a sense of grievance for the remainder of their child's school career.

The schools investigated in the study had made real attempts to provide guidance; yet the results were disappointing. The methods were superficial and casual, and therefore could not counter-balance other influences upon pupils. It seemed that a pupil's chances of obtaining adequate guidance varied and was a result of the form tutor's willingness to be involved. This again raises the question of a clear task specification showing the form tutor's responsibility. How to provide adequate training within the school has to be faced by the senior management.

Schools seemed to be less successful in diagnosing and meeting the needs of the less able, than they were with the able pupils. This means that the pastoral team must diagnose and meet the curricular needs of certain groups of pupils. The study did show that nearly forty per cent of pupils were in fact being taught in groups which did not correspond to their capabilities in two or more subjects. It is likely that a particular pattern of misplacements develops unwittingly in a school and that this crystallizes over the years. The pastoral team may need to search out such a pattern, trying to detect the reasons for it and then correcting it.

As one would expect, the able pupils were more satisfied with their choices than the less able. Is the range and content of subjects offered to the less able inferior to those offered to the able pupils, or are they less appropriate to their needs? Or is their choice less adequate because they lack the skills of decision-making? If so, the remedy is partially in the pastoral team's hands. Our programme of guidance should contain decision-making exercises specially devised to help the less able where the results of certain choices are discussed.

Earlier in this book we stated our concern with the processes through which pupils associate with the school or dissociate from it. Is there a connection between satisfaction with subject options and attitudes to school? Reid and her team are again helpful, detecting a strong association between pupils' feelings that their options had been well chosen and a positive attitude to school. Those who felt that their options were faulty viewed school as a constraining and purposeless community, but the dissatisfied were probably less committed to school by the third year, before they made their subject choices, and this influenced their reaction to courses which they themselves elected to take. However, the research comforts us by indicating that although over half the pupils felt that their teachers did not really help them with subject choices, they still had favourable attitudes towards teachers. We can build on this.

A programme of guidance on subject options

The objectives of this programme might well be to inculcate decision-making ability; to develop the skill of accurate self-assessment; to relate the subjects to the pupil's purposes and career orientations if these have developed; to develop understanding of the demands made by the later stages of a subject; and to highlight the salient reasons which should shape choices of subject, including awareness of the long-term consequences of choices and, possibly, of omissions. The principle that could underlie this programme is that of intelligent anticipation through planned guidance sessions over the preceding twelve months.

The research on which I have heavily relied above draws our attention to failure in dealing with the less able, but I would argue that subject choices are even more important for pupils in the middle ranges of ability in the comprehensive school. In a curious way, they occupy a marginal position, despite their numbers, and deserve better guidance than they often get, for we may pay too much attention to extremes of ability.

If parents influence subject-options so strongly, it seems sensible to build up first a stock of sound ideas and skills in the pupils. The programme is therefore presented in three phases, the first giving pupils basic skills and information, the second continuing this, but bringing in the parents, the third concerned with difficult cases with special problems.

Self-assessment and decision-making

Self-assessment is difficult for many pupils, for their background has not encouraged them to think about themselves. We can take the idea of "getting on in life" as the basis for an introductory activity. Ideas about qualities necessary for this are collected and written on the blackboard. Pupils are then asked to select and put in order the seven that they think most important. They discuss their choices in small

51

groups. Next, they try to assess which qualities they possess and which they need to acquire, again discussing their choices in their small groups. As usual, the class rejoins for a final discussion led by the teacher. Many variants of this type of activity will spring to mind.

A next step could be to ask them to work out, in groups, the qualities that they believe are demanded by certain subjects. I have found it useful to present two very unlike subjects such as metalwork and history. Once they have isolated these qualities, a class discussion follows to extend their ideas. They then assess themselves. this is the equivalent in vocational guidance of comparing occupational qualities with psychological qualities. The teacher can produce simple questionnaires which explore the following: what am I good at; why am I good at it; what do I like doing and why?

Decision-making can be introduced in a number of ways. We must ensure that we hold pupils' interest in these activities. A simple, exciting situation based on caving is presented. One of the members of the party has broken his leg and received other injuries. He is lying at the bottom of the chamber indicated in the drawing. The sketch shows that there is a farmhouse twenty kilometres away where help will be available. Another house is marked, but the party does not know if it is occupied. The four members of the party came by bicycle. There is also an outbuilding, made of wooden planks, about two kilometres away. The party has an adequate supply of ropes. The critical fact is that the cave in which the injured man is lying will flood in an hour and a half. What should they do? This predicament makes them think about the selection of alternatives, the degree of risk in a decision and the need to scan a situation carefully. It may sound naïve stated so baldly; yet pupils learn much about decisions and their costs and consequences.

A BALANCE SHEET

You are about to choose the subjects which you will study during the next two or three years. A poor set of choices can make you feel very dissatisfied and give you unnecessary feelings of failure. To make your choices after careful discussion will mean that you are taking real responsibility for yourself and your future.

Please answer each section as fully as possible.

Section One

1. Make a list of the subjects at which you do well.

2. Now try to decide why you are good at them.
   Is it because you like using words and writing, or are you good at figures and drawing diagrams? Are you particularly good at using your hands?

Section Two

1. Now list below the subjects at which you feel you do not do well.

2. Examine this list and see if it contains any subjects which you feel will be important to you in the future.
   [You may need to discuss these with your form tutor. It is surprising how we can improve our performance if we make plans to do this.]

Your Balance Sheet

This is a four-cell balance sheet which will make you think hard. Discuss it with your form tutor.

1. Subjects in which I do well which are important to my future.	2. Subjects which are important to my future, but in which I need to improve.
3. Subjects at which I get little success.	4. Subjects which give me pleasure, although they do not seem to be important for my future career.

POT-HOLING ADVENTURE. A SIMPLE DECISION-MAKING EXERCISE

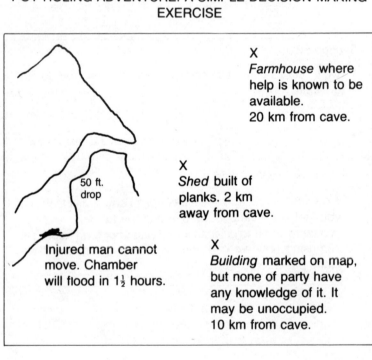

X
Farmhouse where help is known to be available.
20 km from cave.

X
Shed built of planks. 2 km away from cave.

50 ft. drop

Injured man cannot move. Chamber will flood in 1½ hours.

X
Building marked on map, but none of party have any knowledge of it. It may be unoccupied.
10 km from cave.

Many pupils have some experience of helping out in part-time jobs, and the following situation has stimulated interest in decision-making in the less academically orientated pupil.

THE GARAGE

1. A boy is working on the forecourt of a garage when a customer calls to collect his car. He needs it urgently, and the garage manager assured him that it would be ready.

   The boy goes to the mechanic who says that he hasn't even begun to work on the car. When the mechanic is told that the manager promised that the car would be ready, he gets very angry and tells the boy to clear off. The boy is left with the customer, who also gets angry when the boy tells him politely that the car is not ready. What should he do?

2. Should he:

   call the manager;

   make up a story which might satisfy the customer;

   be rude to the customer who has got angry;

   have a word with the manager and quietly ask him what to do;

   give up his part-time job?

3. Discuss the situation in your small groups. Try to work out what would happen if he did what you have suggested.

Such a simple exercise contains the essence of decision-making theory, and pupils assimilate the principles automatically, although we can usefully suggest ways in which they can be used in their everyday life. Here is another situation of this type.

MAKING MISTAKES

1. You have just taken up your first job in an office. Yesterday, you had some new invoices to deal with. Your boss did explain how to fill them in, but suddenly as you are doing them today, you realize that you have made some mistakes in the first batch which have been sent on to the next office.

Do you:
> take a chance by keeping quiet about it;
> explain to the supervisor what has happened;
> try to get them back and correct the mistakes;
> have a row with your boss because you feel he did not explain it properly?

2. Split your small group into pairs. One is the supervisor and the other the invoice clerk. The invoice clerk tries to explain what he has done to the supervisor. Then change round—if you were the supervisor, now play the part of the clerk.

3. Discuss in your small group the best way of putting the mistake right. Can you find a way to do this, without feeling stupid?

The form tutor will try to explain certain key elements in the decision-making process. It is through these concrete activities that we can begin to help pupils from disadvantaged backgrounds to acquire the skills of abstraction. Each one of us has a habitual style of decision-making which incorporates a fairly constant level of risk. At the extremes we either adopt a "safe-bet" style or habitually "take a chance". Observation shows that styles of decision-making are often well established in the third-year pupil. They can, however, be modified through activities followed by structured discussion. The competent decision-maker learns to avoid excessive reliance on impulse and, when he is faced by a dilemma, scans the situation to detect the alternatives available to him. Some of our pupils, however, find this difficult.

It is possible to analyse the reasons for choosing a subject by giving pupils a list such as the following:

> my best friend is taking it;
> I like the teacher;
> it is new to me;
> it will be useful when I am at work;
> it is interesting;
> I am good at it;
> my parents say that I should take it.

Small group discussions then follow, which alert pupils to the limitations and negative consequences which can follow from reliance on some of these reasons. Later the form tutor can select those reasons which he feels are relevant to the group and explore them through further activities. With some groups, for example, it may be especially important to highlight the way they transfer responsibility for decisions to their friends or parents.

The first phase of the programme, in which pupils are given information, is crucial. It is also important that pupils are told about the later stages of a subject. The style of thinking, the rewards and the career relevance of a subject should be spelt out objectively.

If booklets for the information of pupils and parents are produced for this critical point of subject choice, they should be carefully planned, attractive to look at and, above all, written in a style that can be easily understood by the potential readers. The commerce and art departments can be involved, application of their skills eliminating the situation in which an attractive cover conceals poorly typed and presented information.

The second phase

The aim of the first phase was to give to pupils realistic and accurate information about the nature of options and to build up their capacity to make wise decisions. The second stage brings in parents, with whom contact can be highly productive or can reinforce negative attitudes and narrow prejudices. Parents have been embittered by experiences at open evenings, which they have left feeling they have been "talked at" if not "got at", that they have had to stand in a long queue for a short talk about their child. In one school the norm for interviews attempting to deal with subject options appeared to be five minutes, and the most skilled interviewer would be unable to do anything constructive in such a short time.

Urgent attention to the interviewing skills of form tutors must be given if productive links are to be developed between the school and the type of parent who feel rather inadequate, and come to a subject-option interview from a sense of duty to their child, needing to be set at ease. Such skills are built up through discussion, simulation and interaction, using the resources of the school. The trained counsellor, if there is one, will obviously play a major part in in-service training, but there are other members of staff with appropriate skills.

Group discussion with parents is more useful than talks. Discussion should be conducted by the form tutor with the parents of the pupils for whom he or she is responsible. The senior members of the team can systematically prepare the tutors for the task. Videotapes can be used, or a ten-minute tape-recording of interaction with a parent or group of parents. The writer's students have constructed videotapes showing the difference between a negative interview and a positive one with the same parents. This proved a useful kind of training material.

The discussion can be introduced with some visual material, such as charts or slides. Then, as far as possible, the parents should be allowed to talk freely, the tutor intervening only to clarify the discussion or bring it back to the point. Parents will begin to bring out their doubts and anxieties in these discussions. They will perhaps see that they have unrealistic aspirations for their child or are working out their own frustrated ambitions through him.

This work with parents may be more important than some other activities. In practice, two discussion groups at this point are sufficient, provided that they are long enough. It takes time for ideas, feelings and standpoints to emerge. A two-hour discussion period with a short break for tea or coffee is not too long. If the parents of pupils within a form are divided into two groups, then we have a manageable number, for not all will attend. The form tutor will therefore be responsible for four discussion-group sessions, two in the spring term and two early in the summer if subject choices are made in the summer term.

In this way, the form tutor does not take on an undue burden, although it is likely that these meetings will stimulate requests from parents to meet the form tutor and year heads. This, after all, is one of our objectives.

The third phase

If there is doubt about what courses the pupils should follow, then there should be some system whereby pupils' choices, parental desires and teachers' recommendations are co-ordinated. Where necessary, there can be an *informed* interview between the year or house head and the pupil. More rarely, there may be a need for an interview between the parent, pupil and the year or house head, together with the form tutor. These interviews should be relatively infrequent. When they do occur, our aim will be to demonstrate that we do try to tailor courses to meet the needs of pupils rather than

expect pupils to adapt willy-nilly. This final phase is largely administrative, and each school has its own approach.

It is hoped that if the programme of guidance for subject-options,
as described above, is carried out then the situation described by Reid
and her colleagues, where the teacher is seen by the pupil as playing
little part in his decisions, will be changed for the good.

REFERENCES

Banks, O. and Finlayson, D. (1973) *Success and Failure in the Secondary
School*, London: Methuen.

Conger, J. (1973) *Adolescence and Youth*, New York: Harper and
Row.

Hutchings, D. (1970) *Factors Affecting Choice of School Subjects*,
Mimeo, Department of Education, University of Oxford.

Jacobs, V. (1974) *A Study of the Effect of Counselling on Pupils
Experiencing Difficulties with A-Level Work*, Unpublished D.S.C.
Dissertation, University College of Swansea.

Marland, M. (1974) *Pastoral Care*, London: Heinemann.

Oppenheim, A. (1966) *Questionnaire Design and Attitude Measurement*,
London: Heinemann.

Reid, M., Barnett, B. and Rosenberg, H. (1974) *A Matter of Choice*,
Slough: N.F.E.R.

Schools Council (1968) *Young School Leavers: Enquiry 1.*, London:
H.M.S.O.

Sumner, R. and Warburton, F. (1972) *Achievement in Secondary
Schools*, Slough: N.F.E.R.

Wenar, C. (1971) *Personality Development*, Boston: Houghton
Mifflin.

Wheeler, H. (1974) *The Career Aspirations of Able Girls in Secondary
Schools*, Unpublished D.S.C. Dissertation, University College of
Swansea.

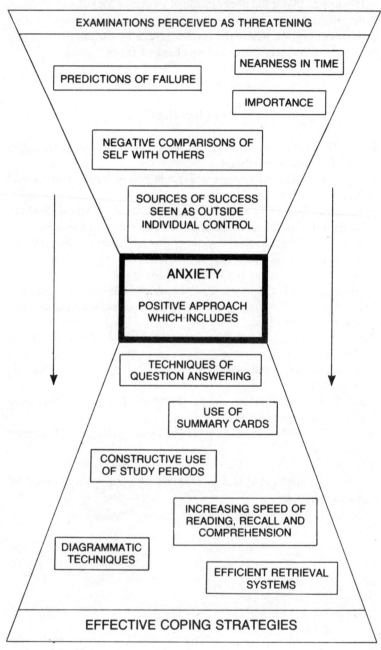

CHAPTER THREE: KEY POINTS
COPING WITH EXAMINATION ANXIETY

EXAMINATIONS PERCEIVED AS THREATENING

NEARNESS IN TIME

PREDICTIONS OF FAILURE

IMPORTANCE

NEGATIVE COMPARISONS OF SELF WITH OTHERS

SOURCES OF SUCCESS SEEN AS OUTSIDE INDIVIDUAL CONTROL

ANXIETY

POSITIVE APPROACH WHICH INCLUDES

TECHNIQUES OF QUESTION ANSWERING

USE OF SUMMARY CARDS

CONSTRUCTIVE USE OF STUDY PERIODS

INCREASING SPEED OF READING, RECALL AND COMPREHENSION

DIAGRAMMATIC TECHNIQUES

EFFICIENT RETRIEVAL SYSTEMS

EFFECTIVE COPING STRATEGIES

EXAMINATION DIFFICULTIES AND STUDY SKILLS

Summary

THE CENTRAL ARGUMENT

The assumption behind this chapter is that both pupil and teacher may not gain their just rewards for hard work unless examination anxiety is dealt with constructively and pupils' study skills methodically developed. These skills should include the techniques of preparation for examinations, the constructive use of unsupervised study periods and of homework.

ANXIETY

A simple threefold analysis of anxiety is presented:

individual differences in susceptibility;
the situation arousing anxiety;
the learned and habitual mode of response to anxiety.

It is argued that the pastoral team can do little, if anything, about the first element, but can deal with how pupils perceive a situation which causes them anxiety. One can help pupils develop better ways of coping with stress and increase their sense of being in charge of their lives. Anxiety is basically presented as a danger signal, implying that the teacher must help the pupil locate the real source of threat, and take realistic measures to deal with it.

STYLES OF THOUGHT

Rigidity of thinking is discussed, and the unreceptivity to new ideas on academic achievement. It is desirable to help pupils develop intrinsic motivation, recognizing that the source of control over their actions should be internal rather than external, and that it is possible for them to modify their behaviour, succeeding where previously they failed. The restrictions on independence and the stunting of maturity derived from a view of the world which sees causality as outside the individual's control, are brought home to the pupil through the various activities.

THE MAJOR DIFFICULTIES AND REMEDIAL ACTION

These difficulties are systematically analysed, and suggestions made as to the ways in which they can be tackled with maximum chances of success. There is a programme to tackle the three major elements of study skills.

Reading: speed, recall, comprehension and the generation of new ideas.
General organization of study: note-taking, answering written questions and essay-writing.
Effective homework and revision: techniques, self-evaluation, the development of a retrieval system.

A self-help questionnaire is incorporated into the chapter, to structure the guidance sessions. The principles of behaviour modification are applied to eliminate unproductive habits and to allow pupils to build the skills of target-setting and self-evaluation. This is associated with suggestions about how friends can provide mutual support, ensuring that what often reinforces negative attitudes is transformed into interaction which raises the level of performance.

Although examination results are far from the most important factor in assessing the success of the school, we must recognize their significance for the school, and for the pupils and parents in a modern society. To deny this is to deny reality.

Teachers are usually deeply concerned when some pupils fail to get results commensurate with their apparent ability, the hard work they have put in and the effort of their teachers. The good teacher is uneasily aware that the pupil's failure may be the teacher's own failure, although they would be hard put to analyse this in detail. It seems that we need to anticipate difficulties in examinations in a more systematic way.

Relative failure in examinations may stem from destructive anxiety, a lack of study skills in certain key areas, and habitual patterns of coping which are both costly and unviable. The pastoral team will need to analyse the contributory factors. As usual, one should anticipate difficulties and build up skills, and not just supervene in an emergency with certain individuals. The programme of guidance developed at the beginning of the fifth year is most significant when carefully related to what has been done by the pastoral team earlier in the child's school career.

Anxiety

Anxiety is not necessarily a bad thing; nor is it possible or desirable to eliminate anxiety completely. The crucial element is the pupil's reaction to anxiety. The discussion will not treat the complex phenomenon of anxiety in depth, but the reader who wishes to pursue the topic will find Levitt (1968) a sound introduction. The limited objective here is to help the pastoral team pose questions and seek answers which allow pupils to develop better coping strategies.

The first discrimination to be made is between *trait anxiety* and *state anxiety*. Spielberger (1966) has edited a useful volume in which this distinction is explained. Trait anxiety refers to the extent to which a person has a predisposition to that type of response which we call anxiety. He may also habitually try to avoid stressful situations.

For the pastoral team, the relevance of this is that there are a few pupils who find a wide range of situations potentially threatening, because anxiety is a marked personality trait in them, often reinforced by an over-protective mother who is anxious herself. These pupils therefore respond to such situations with a degree of anxiety that most pupils would consider disproportionate. This minority will react very strongly to examination anxiety and need individual help from form tutors.

We must learn to recognize and respect this anxiety, referring the pupil for specialist treatment if the condition is severe, although we still have to support and help him to cope. This is no easy task, for trait anxiety is accompanied by a proneness of guilt, a tendency to be embarrassed and suspicious of other people's motives and intentions. Pupils who are highly anxious also feel inadequate and helpless, and this makes it hard for them to believe that they can succeed.

State anxiety is a response to a situation. It is transitory and varies between individuals: some will respond intensely; and some will scarcely react; others will feel exhilarated and stimulated to positive action. There will be a wide range of reactions to examinations in a specific group of pupils. Anxiety can energize as well as inhibit, and the form tutor has to detect how each pupil responds to the situation.

We live in an achievement-orientated society which emphasises success and regards failure as reprehensible. It is therefore likely that the approach of examinations which have important implications for the pupil's access to further education and choice of careers will arouse complex reactions in susceptible pupils. The effect of anxiety upon examination performance is not easily predictable. Writers such as Ruebush (1963), and Gaudry and Spielberger (1971), stress the positive as well as the negative aspects of anxiety. There is a complex relationship between anxiety, attainment and intelligence, making hard-and-fast statements impossible, yet there is often a connection between high levels of anxiety and the deterioration of performance in strictly timed situations, of which the examination is a major example.

Examinations are associated with highly emotional elements in a pupil's life: their parents' expectations; their own expectations; feelings of being compared, evaluated and coerced. What can the pastoral team do?

The first step is to orientate ourselves to the problem in an open-minded way. It is therefore essential to see anxiety as an intervening condition which triggers off certain behaviour, and at the same time as a product of some perceived threat. This threat may vary in individuals faced with the same situation, and so has to be detected. We must learn to distinguish between the conditions which arouse anxiety and the manoeuvres which some pupils use to reduce it.

Endler et al. (1962) produced a Stimulus-Response Inventory of Anxiousness which may help the pastoral team. They show that three factors are involved in anxiety: the susceptibility to anxiety of the individual; the situation which provokes anxiety; and how the individual responds to the signal of anxiety. The question is then which of these factors is most significant. Endler's research shows that the learned mode of response of the anxious individual was the most important, while the threatening situation followed. This suggests that the teacher's expertise can help to resolve the problems created for the pupil by anxiety.

The pastoral team and examination anxieties

As teachers, although we cannot deal with trait anxiety directly, we can help pupils develop more effective coping strategies. We can also build up their study skills whether or not they seem to be anxious in the year preceding the examination, reducing the likelihood of disruptive anxiety. A number of my students have found that the two-pronged programme, which deals with perception of the situation and provides added tools of effective study, rewards both the pastoral team and the pupils.

Cattell (1966) postulated that anxiety is, to a large degree, dependent upon the uncertainty of reward, and also, related to the magnitude of the anticipated deprivation. A pupil's doubt of his ability to cope may develop into a firm prediction of failure, which may lead to avoidance mechanisms, such as sickness or failure to attack revision with determination. To build up false self-confidence is foolish, yet we must not erode their confidence. This means that we may have to reconsider our practices when we assess mock O-level papers. It is probably best to mark as objectively as possible, with the form tutor supporting individual pupils.

The keynote of the guidance programme at this point is to allow the pupils to take an active part. Rotter (1966) and Rotter et al. (1972) have shown that pupils can feel that sources of control lie in the environment, rather than in themselves. Spielberger (1966) pointed out that factual information about the environment and the tasks to be accomplished alleviates anxiety and allows students to cope with them more effectively. In several schools known to the writer, first-year sixth-form pupils have joined in the small discussion groups with fifth-year pupils discussing their own experiences and indicating the measures they took to overcome anxiety.

Simple case histories can be presented to pupils in these sessions, which indicate how the individual coped with the source of anxiety. The small groups discuss this, and then decide whether or not the strategy has relevance for them. Any experienced teacher can write such histories although every precaution must be taken to ensure that the individual cannot be recognized.

Heads of year or houses can take a group of pupils for unstructured discussion on anxiety and the circumstances which arouse it. The range of materials which emerges can be very wide:

> the feelings of being under continuous surveillance by both teachers and parents;
> the conflict between going out with friends and studying, when they wanted to do both;
> the irritation produced by mothers who say one day that all they want is for their child to be happy, the next day that they expect him or her to do well;
> the feeling that effort doesn't matter, for it is all a matter of luck or how you happen to feel on the examination day;
> the feeling that you can't remember anything;
> having to do a subject that makes you feel a hopeless failure;
> the feeling that you have to do the same as your elder brother and/or sister;
> the inability to make a start on homework and on revision;
> not understanding what the question is about.

Anxiety makes many pupils in the period preceding O levels, adhere to inappropriate methods of study, such as trying to learn everything off by heart, preventing them from seeing these as the cause of failure. The form tutor must be aware that for the anxious pupil that which is familiar appears safe, whilst anything new is threatening. How can this be overcome? One step is to tell pupils in plain language about the impact of anxiety upon performance. Such a discussion is always accompanied by practical suggestions for overcoming anxiety and improving performance.

The principles of behavioural modification can easily be applied. Pupils are asked to think about three situations in their work where they wish to improve, and to rate them in order of difficulty. They then discuss the easiest situation with a friend in the class whose job is to be helpful, making concrete suggesions about what his partner could do. Each helps the other in turn.

A simple diagram is then drawn on the board.

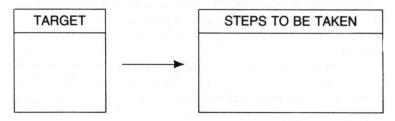

Each pupil fills this in for himself, after discussing it with his partner. They are then asked to try to carry out as thoroughly as possible the strategy that they have devised, until the next pastoral-care discussion period, when pupils report to each other their progress. If they feel ready, they can proceed to the next task. There is no compulsion to progress at the same rate. The form tutor acts as consultant, giving suggestions when asked, but otherwise not intervening. This type of activity reinforces the fact that pupils are in charge of themselves and that there is much that they can do to overcome sources of threat in the learning situation. They also learn how to co-operate and communicate learning difficulties to a friend in a constructive way.

Pupils need further experience at problem-solving. In one method the form is given a duplicated sheet containing a brief problem about examinations, such as the following:

> It is about three months before the O-level examinations. Phil is bright and has done well in school, but finds that he is unable to settle down to his homework in the evenings. He has a room of his own with a desk, but when he goes upstairs, he either starts playing records or doing something else. If he does start, he soon finds he is beginning to day-dream.

> How do you think Phil could change his behaviour? He really wants to succeed.

After ten minutes' discussion in small groups, the teacher suggests that it might be helpful if they pooled their ideas. The aim is to get as many ideas as possible for use in the small groups, so these are written on the blackboard. After a further ten minutes, each group is asked to write down their suggestions in an orderly fashion, meticulously evaluating their probable outcome. The session ends with a brief discussion of ways of coping with such a problem.

The perception of a situation is crucial in the production of anxiety, and it is helpful to discuss examinations in a positive way. It is even more useful to show pupils how their predictions shape their behaviour.

The writer has sometimes done this very simply by discussing a boy who predicts that if he asks a girl for a date she will turn him down. On tape he is first of all heard approaching a girl in an arrogant way, compensating for his sense of insecurity. She reacts adversely to his over-emphasised masculinity by brusquely telling him to disappear. He is then heard approaching her in a way which is perhaps best described as "wet". The girl remarks after she has dismissed him, "I wouldn't go out with him—my friends would think I was hard up for a boy". Next he approaches her in a way which suggests that he is indifferent. The girl gets the impression that he is ambivalent. She is not going to risk being stood up, and so refuses his request. By this time, the message is clear. Whatever he does, he will probably make his prediction come true.

Next, try giving the class a duplicated list of the possible variations in the behaviour of a boy who predicts that he will experience failure and difficulty in mathematics. These include:

> going into class in such a tense state that he cannot take in what the teacher is saying;
> forgetting his books or some essential item of equipment so that he is unable to do the work;
> being a nuisance so that the teacher ejects him from the class.

The class is then broken into pairs to discuss the situations when they predict that they will fail. Do they do anything which makes this happen? Pupils begin to appreciate that the responsibility for success and failure is in their own hands, and not controlled by external forces. This gives them hope, and they are further helped by discussing methods of analysing anxiety and techniques for coping.

Examination anxiety begins to appear in the February preceding the June examinations. The programme tries to anticipate this by dealing with anxiety in the autumn term. Without this pastoral effort some pupils will not make full use of the Christmas and Easter vacations for consistent and methodical study and revision.

In our schools we are becoming increasingly aware of the risk that a sense of alienation may develop in some pupils, incorporating a feeling of separation and of powerlessness. This can be an unintended by-product of our approach to examinations, although it can also be a defence against a pupil's fear of failure and feeling of inadequacy. If our guidance programmes at this point concentrate on the development of effective modes of coping; provide more positive ways of dealing with anxiety; and reduce the sense of unpredictability; then we are also lessening the likelihood of resort to ritualistic performance and the growth of alienation.

Work with individual pupils

The guidance programme is always concerned with detecting those in need of special help. This minority will be dealt with by the form tutor or head of year, either individually or in groups. The advantage of the group method is twofold: it takes less time; and allows pupils to help one another deal with their anxieties while acquiring new attitudes.

Behavioural methods permit us to avoid the trap of allowing pupils to talk repeatedly about their feeling of anxiety. We need to analyse situations which produce these reactions in a way which will suggest the steps to be taken to overcome failures in learning and cope with the sources of threat.

The teacher therefore gets the pupil or group of pupils to try to answer the questions set out below. The answers form the basis of the guidance.

(a) Which behaviour may have to be reduced in frequency and intensity?
(b) Which behaviour should be increased in frequency and intensity?
(c) What new behaviour will have to be learnt?
(d) What factors in the home or school may make it difficult for the pupil to modify his behaviour?
(e) What supports can help the pupil successfully to change his behaviour?

In this method of pastoral work, the skills required are those used in the presentation of subject material in the classroom:

(a) the ability to set meaningful targets adjusted to individual capacity.
(b) the skill of breaking down a long-range goal into intermediate ones;
(c) methodical analysis and teaching of relevant behaviour.

Diagrams and other visual methods can show the connections between the steps. This offers pupils a clear framework for tackling difficulties and indicates how they can acquire new skills. A diary can be kept in which steps taken and stresses and successes undergone are described. This can become a useful source for evaluation of progress and for self-observation by the pupil.

Through the diagrams, discussions and the setting of targets, one is helping someone restructure a problematical situation both cognitively and practically. Role-play can be used as a form of imaginative rehearsal; decision-making games can be employed; and peers can act as counsellors for one another. A vital part of the activity will be teaching pupils to reward themselves for effort. This means that they check on themselves and decide if they deserve the reward, whether it is watching a favourite television programme; an extra cup of coffee; playing a special record reserved as a reward. Experienced counsellors have found that pupils can be trusted to monitor their own behaviour and to apply rewards only when deserved.

This is again a point at which it may be useful to work closely with parents, if the pupils desire it. If parents are to be involved, it is important that the type of participation and the strategies should be explained to the parent by the teacher in the presence of the pupil.

Study skills

The focus for the pastoral team in the fifth year is a businesslike examination of the conditions of success and failure for O level and C.S.E. The development of better reading skills and the acquisition of more effective study habits are the surest method of increasing the potency of the individual and eliminating any incipient avoidance of the demands of this stage of school.

The main causes of ineffective study and of poor results

1. Inability to cope with anxiety.
2. Rigidity of thought and study habits.
3. Inadequate reading skills.
4. Unplanned and sporadic attempts at study.
5. Low rate of productivity, resulting in inability to complete work in the set time.
6. A lack of structure in written work and thinking, including a logical structure.
7. The inability to develop an argument in a reasoned and coherent way.
8. Failure to use the teacher's comments.
9. Poor note-taking.
10. Inadequate retrieval plans.
11. Inadequate strategies for tackling examination papers.
12. No methodical plans for revision.

Inability to cope with anxiety

Study skills played an important part in the induction programme designed to give pupils a good start in the secondary school, and were probably reinforced during the second and third years. The fifth-year programme should boost vigorously all pupils' study skills during the first and second terms of this crucial year rather than isolating those who are at special risk. If special provision is necessary for these pupils, it is better for them to receive this in a small group.

We often seem unwilling to make our pupils partners in the educational process, explaining to them openly what we hope to achieve with them and how to do it. Hamblin (1974) described the transactions of face-to-face counselling as "status-equal" transactions, and it is likely that it is this type of interaction which produces real co-operation. We can reduce the distance between pupils and teachers by acquainting pupils with our objectives, and sharing the knowledge of the principles of our pastoral work. We may begin the programme for the fifth year by explaining the nature of anxiety and the impact it has on the individual's performance, as suggested earlier in the chapter. Many adolescents who procrastinate or put on a mask of jollity are defending themselves against anxiety. Bringing out into the open the fact that worry which is not faced can lead one into "putting off" study or working in a half-hearted manner produces an unwilling groan from some pupils or a heartfelt sigh of relief from others.

Discussion of anxiety might well be followed by an inspection of pupils' attitudes towards study and homework. The suggestion will be made in this section, based upon the work of Festinger (1957) and Brehm and Cohen (1962), that the best method of changing long-standing attitudes is to involve pupils in new behaviour with the minimum of coercion and the maximum of voluntary engagement. The main elements in attitude-change are the credibility of the source of exhortations towards change, the difficulty of the tasks involved and the relationship of the changes to the values of the person and his or her friends. Let us also remind ourselves that many pupils as well as their teachers cling to the theory of the impossible task: that too much is being asked of them and that the changes suggested are beyond their capacity.

In one sense, attitude-change is about decision-making, for once one has acted upon the decision and engaged in certain behaviour, then one tends to see the new behaviour in a positive light and the behaviour that one has rejected in a negative light. Decision-making is also part of personality-development, for the ways in which a pupil learns to make decisions at school during adolescence will stay with him throughout his life. These, together with the kinds of decisions he makes, will influence the kind of person he turns out to be. Hence, study skills are an integral part of the developmental process.

The most effective step to tackle attitude-change is to create conditions within the pastoral-care period under which pupils can examine the costs and utility of their attitudes, look at alternatives, and select a new way of tackling study within the context of a supportive group of peers and through activities and experiences.

Through this experience, pupils can allow themselves to recognize the ambivalence in their attitudes which creates the simultaneous desire to tackle study and evade it; a quandary which we tend to ignore and they feel unable to resolve. The writer has also found simple sentences stimulate discussion in small groups, making the pupils aware of typical excuses and willing to do something about avoidance behaviour. Such sentences would include:

"I would study, but it's all my mother's fault, she keeps irritating me by nagging about homework."

"I come in from school meaning to get started on my work, but somehow I can't."

"There seems so much to do this year that it gets on top of you, and then you just can't decide what to do first and end up doing nothing."

"If you did everything the teachers want you to do, then you would not have any life of your own."

Through such simple devices, much that has been evaded by both teacher and taught can be brought into the pastoral period, increasing the possibility of changes in behaviour. A particular source of difficulty, however, are those pupils who, either from upbringing or personality or both, tend rigidly to adopt techniques of study which are unproductive and self-defeating. They deceive themselves by looking everywhere for a cause of failure, except to their own study habits.

Rigidity of thought and of study habits

Rigidity has become a highly emotive term, today often used as an accusation which those against whom it is directed should refute at all costs. Rokeach (1960) offers some evidence that those who are dogmatic and rigid take longer to solve unusual problems than those with open minds. He seems to be saying what every teacher knows: that a pupil may have the ability, but personality qualities negate it. The rigid individual has, other things being equal, more difficulty in combining new facts and beliefs with those they already have, to form new concepts or detect new routes to a problematical goal.

Rubenowitz (1963) found that rigidity was a personality factor more closely connected with the emotions than the intellect. Hence the intelligent can still act rigidly despite their ability and educational level. Not only did the rigid resist change; they tended compulsively to do the "done thing" in an unquestioning way; their imagery and modes of thought were concrete rather than abstract; and they were over-concerned with questions of prestige. Rigidity influences people's reactions to unconventional music and art. Not only did the rigid dislike the new, but they tended to make disapproving or condescending statements about the composers and artists as well as about their works. The pastoral team should realize that this type of immediate and closed judgement, accompanied by the tendency to reject those who produce innovations, must be tackled, for it reduces the efficiency of such pupils in discussion and problem-solving, and makes it difficult for them to accept new activities or curricular practices.

The impact of rigidity on the capacity to learn is illustrated by a study conducted by Leach (1965), with pupils of both sexes around the age of entry to the secondary school. They gave little thought to questions of motive and intention; they were slow to change their original orientation in problem-solving and classification tasks; they could not tolerate ambiguity, resolving it by making up their minds very quickly and suppressing expressions of doubt; they experienced great difficulty in classification tasks when they had to hold several considerations in mind at the same time. As the demands of the secondary school increase, those who are rigid are likely to react by retreat to ritual performances, applying limited techniques to difficult situations. Anxiety often leads to avoidance, but when rigidity is present, this is supplanted by modes of study which emphasise unthinking activity.

We can try giving pupils interesting extracts from various disciplines to read and then discuss within a small group what they think the writer has omitted from his argument or what would be a counter-argument. Discussions like this seem to capture pupils' interest, helping the rigid to explore possibilities without making them feel under threat. Pupils were asked to appraise the validity of the following arguments as part of an introduction to a study-skill course in which, among other things, it was hoped that they would learn the art of appraisal of evidence.

1. Sir,

I am writing to express my gratitude for "Quiskip". These salts are marvellous. Every day for forty years I have taken a spoonful before breakfast (yesterday I celebrated my ninetieth birthday). I am as fit as a fiddle—I walk three miles every day. I attribute my long life to "Quiskip". I heartily recommend it to all your readers.

Yours faithfully,
L. G. Summers

2. Why not buy Triple Z oil? It was used by the world champion in the Monaco Grand Prix. Every winner since 1973 has used it. Why not buy it for your car? Then see the difference.

3. I believe that schools are becoming too permissive. They allow long-haired layabouts to come and go as they please. It's discipline they need. There was none of this nonsense in my day. I had many a clout when I misbehaved and it hasn't done me any harm. Too much freedom is bad.

In helping pupils to free themselves from ineffective study habits, I have encouraged them to condense what they have learned into a simple diagram. In this way the structure of the topic becomes clear and the salient features are isolated. Many pupils anyway prefer the visual modality in learning. First let them see several diagrams which present information concisely, and if they are then allowed to work in groups, helping one another to construct their own diagrams, the gains are likely to be considerable. Their understanding of the basic structure of the topic is increased, so that they can write about it more confidently.

Reading skills

Skills in reading need to be continuously boosted. Many pupils feel that they read far too slowly, and this is often a correct self-diagnosis. Lack of speed may spring from faulty eye movements or the seeing of words in isolation. Discussion of the need to read more quickly, and practice in this, are useful. Let them begin by reading as quickly as possible for five minutes and then making notes on what has been read. Gradually the time is increased, and a record is kept by the pupil of how much he reads and whether he is satisfied with the amount that he recalls.

Two major types of comprehension exist. The first is recall of what has been said and the capacity to present it in logical and chronological sequence. The second, more important type of comprehension requires the reader to speculate in an intellectually disciplined way about the passage and its implications, and to develop new ideas and questions on the basis of what has been read. It is useful for the secondary pupil to train himself to ask what the writer has left out of the argument or what he is protesting against. Perhaps the greatest need is to teach pupils the art of appraisal rather than of criticism, for appraisal involves an all-round assessment of a position.

During the last two years the writer has been developing a study–skills questionnaire as a self-diagnostic instrument for the brighter fifth-form and sixth-form pupils. It is intended to help pupils at this level to develop strategies for more competent use of their time. The questionnaire treats pupils as mature individuals who desire to do well and who are searching for ways of raising their level of performance. The questionnaire is in three parts, and the first, which deals with reading skills, is given below. It has also been used in several schools as the basis for pastoral periods concerned with study skills.

Study-skills questionnaire

INTRODUCTION

This simple questionnaire is intended to help you undertake a self-analysis of your study skills and then to develop a plan for improving them in conjunction with a friend or your form tutor. If you develop such a plan, either on your own or in co-operation with your form tutor, not only do you raise your chances of success, but you are likely to develop skills which increase your independence and maturity in the learning situation. The study habits you develop now will transfer in a helpful or unhelpful way to situations where you may be required to study on your own with only minimal guidance.

INSTRUCTIONS

1. Two basic assumptions underlie the approach taken in this questionnaire:
   (a) that you desire success in your academic work;
   (b) that you have realized that as a mature individual you should pay attention not only to the *content* of what you learn, but to the *processes* by which you learn—not only *what* but *how* you learn is crucial for your success.

2. Read the introduction to each part of the study-skills questionnaire. When a section is completed, you can then begin to

76

set your goals for improvement in this area of learning and develop a strategy for achieving your targets. To modify your study skills in a systematic way it will be necessary for you to make an order of priority of tackling any difficulties.
3. There are no traps or tricks in this questionnaire. The significance of the items has been deliberately made very obvious. The items on the left represent skills which are associated with effective study in most people. The items on the right are those which may be reducing your efficiency as a learner.
4. Please read each item carefully and then put a tick in the box beside the item which *most closely represents what you tend to do* when studying. A rough guide is whether:

(a) you feel that this is having an important effect upon your study;

(b) you think you behave in that way for more than half of the time.

If you are uncertain, then tick the middle box. There may be certain items or subjects in which you experience a particular difficulty. If this is the case, make a note underneath.

Why bother with this? We can all read! You may be surprised that you are asked to begin by thinking about your reading skills, but the ability to read difficult material, extracting the meaning from it quickly, and using what you have read in an intelligent and creative way, will be crucial for your academic success. Some of the skills which are of importance to you are:

speed of reading;
recall of what has been read, both immediately and over a period of time;
ability to go beyond the actual passage which has been read to make inferences and develop new ideas;
taking a critical but balanced view of the material you read;
making meaningful and organized notes from your reading;
locating and using additional sources of information about a topic;
distinguishing between what is central and what is subsidiary information.

The strategy used in this section.

You are asked to think about your behaviour rather than about attitudes—the assumption is that identification of behaviour is necessary before you can develop ways of improving your study skills. This section is divided into four parts:

a brief section on the mechanics of reading;
a section on the development of recall;
a section on developing inferences and new ideas;
finally, some items on the use you make of your reading.

SUB-SECTION A   The mechanics

1. I usually read quickly enough to finish all the set reading.

   I read rather slowly and quite often have difficulty in finishing the set reading. 1.

2. I usually look carefully at any diagrams and tables.

   I usually take little notice of any diagrams and tables. 2.

3. If the reading set is rather long, I make a start on it as early as possible.

   If the reading is rather long I often put off starting for as long as possible. 3.

4. I have carefully examined my reading skills.

   I have never carefully examined my reading skills. 4.

5. I usually check the meaning of unfamiliar words in my dictionary or in some other way.

   I usually pass over unfamiliar words without finding out what they mean. 5.

6. I usually make notes as I read.

   I very rarely make notes as I read. 6.

7. ☐ I can read with concentration for fairly long periods. | ☐ I find it difficult to concentrate and can only read a few pages at a time. | 7. ☐

8. ☐ I usually note difficult sections and go back to them once I have got the general meaning of the passage. | ☐ When there is a difficult section I go on reading, but I usually do not go back to try to understand the difficult section. | 8. ☐

SUB-SECTION B Recall of what you have read

9. ☐ i usually recall main points when I have finished reading. | ☐ I frequently find I have forgotten the main points when I have finished reading. | 9. ☐

10. ☐ I usually look at the chapter and section headings before I begin to read. | ☐ I usually begin to read without noting the chapter or section headings. | 10. ☐

11. ☐ I scan a chapter or passage very quickly to get the main ideas and then begin to read carefully. | ☐ I usually begin reading a chapter or passage without scanning it first. | 11. ☐

12. ☐ As I read I make a list of key words or phrases as an aid to my memory. | ☐ I do not regularly make lists of key words or phrases as an aid to my memory. | 12. ☐

13. I test myself by jotting down the points I can remember and then check them against my notes.

    I do not often test my recall of a passage as soon as I have finished reading. 13.

14. I usually look out for words like "first" or "second" which indicate the main points.

    I usually seem to miss this kind of word in my reading. 14.

15. I always arrange my notes to give a brief, logical summary.

    I rarely have the time to arrange my notes in this way. 15.

SUB-SECTION C   Stimulating comprehension

16. Once I have understood the passage I often make a list of questions about it.

    Once I have checked I can remember the main points of a passage I go on to something else. 16.

17. I quite often go to the library and look up other books or articles on the topic.

    I usually rely solely on the references about a topic which are given by the teacher. 17.

18. I usually begin by assessing what I already know about the topic.

    I do not usually think about the topic before I begin reading. 18.

80

19. When I finish reading I always ask myself what the writer has left out of his argument. | I do not usually evaluate the reading for omissions or bias. | 19.

20. I find it useful to compare what different writers have to say on the same topic. | I usually rely on the point of view given by the recommended author. | 20.

21. I often look for reviews of a book, which help me assess its value. | I have never searched for information of this type about a book. | 21.

22. I usually try to make a list of careful criticisms of what I have just read. | I usually concentrate on making sure I can recall the main points of the reading. | 22.

23. I usually try to assess the weaknesses and strengths of a particular argument. | I do not assess my reading in this way unless I am told to. | 23.

24. I usually re-write the main points in my own words. | I usually copy out sentences used by the writer for my notes. | 24.

SUB-SECTION D   Using your reading

25. When I have read something I usually talk about it with someone. | I do not usually talk about what I have read unless I have to. | 25.

26. ☐	I sometimes try to create a counter-argument to what I have read.	☐	I usually reproduce the argument as it was put forward in the reading. 26. ☐
27. ☐	Whenever possible I use what I have read in my written work at the first opportunity.	☐	I rarely refer to what I have read in my written work unless I am asked to do so by the teacher. 27. ☐
28. ☐	When I finish reading for an essay I arrange my notes in an organized way before I begin writing.	☐	When I finish reading I usually begin to write at once without organizing my notes. 28. ☐

Using this analysis of your reading skills
1. You can now develop a strategy for improving your reading skills, if you feel this will improve your academic work. Select the items which you feel are the most important for you. It will be helpful to discuss your plans with a teacher, counsellor, your parents or a friend.
2. Go through each sub-section and enter the skills you would like to develop in the box below. You can, of course, include any which were not mentioned in the questionnaire.

Sub-Section A   The mechanics

Sub-Section B   Recall of what you have read

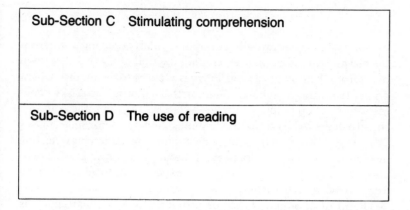

Sub-Section C   Stimulating comprehension

Sub-Section D   The use of reading

3. The next step is to arrange them in the order in which you would like to deal with them in Box 1 below. You can see that it would be very difficult to deal with them all simultaneously. Therefore a planned approach is essential. Discussion of the way you hope to develop the skills is important, because this opens up alternative ways of achieving your goal. When you are clear, write in Box 2 the steps you intend to take. Finally, set yourself a time target for the achievement of your aim.

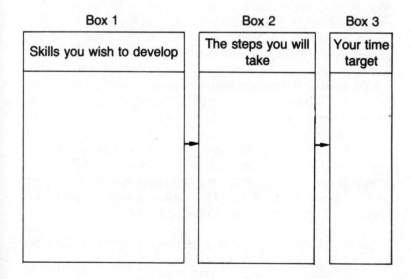

Box 1	Box 2	Box 3
Skills you wish to develop	The steps you will take	Your time target

83

In many schools one can still see pupils regularly copying notes from the blackboard rather than developing the skill of making their own notes from their own reading. There is a failure to distinguish salient points from the peripheral. Suggest that coloured asterisks could identify the key points or that a "skeleton" of the topic could be constructed. We have to teach pupils first to think in terms of "headlines", and then to identify the logical connection between one headline and the next. Note-taking should never be a passive process, but we can encourage pupils to experiment, to allow them to find out what suits them.

The most common source of problems and eventual failure is random and unplanned study. The pupil so characterized is often the extreme extrovert who responds easily to any distraction, lacking the blessed singlemindedness which marks some introverts. Hence a pattern of study and a controlling framework have to be developed, first for them, later by them, in order to compensate for personality tendencies.

Random methods of study often lead to a failure to orientate accurately to the task. To attack a task systematically which produces the results desired by the teacher is a skill which has to be learned. Without it, a pupil is liable to waste much time. Many undergraduates fail examinations because they have written, not a poor answer, but an excellent answer to the wrong question.

Closely related to failure in orientation is the pupil's reaction to the appearance of the work. Students who are marginal in both ability and sense of purpose are easily influenced by the look of a piece of work. This avoidance reaction should be openly discussed with pupils.

Conceptual and organizational difficulties reduce the level of performance of some pupils who, despite good ability, consistent application to work and the desire to do well, find it hard to get the hoped-for results, mainly because they find it difficult to write an essay with a clear logical structure. It may be because pupils lack the experience of discussion and of how ideas should be explored and put to the test. The basic intellectual approach that is needed is put well in Magee (1973), who, while discussing Karl Popper's ideas about the nature of scientific method, remarks:

For all of us, in all our activities, the notions that we can do better only by finding out what can be improved and improving it; and therefore that shortcomings are to be actively sought out, not concealed and passed over; and that critical comment from others, far from being resented, is an invaluable aid to be insisted upon and welcomed, are liberating to a remarkable degree.

Appraisal in the way suggested above is just as essential for us as teachers when we are examining the processes of learning and study, as it is when we are thinking about the content of what we teach. And the pastoral teacher should help their pupils to develop this attitude. Obviously those who write without a logical structure lack the skill of quickly constructing a framework for a piece of written work, to ensure that they keep to the point.

The development of general study skills

If these pastoral periods devoted to the stimulation of study skills as part of preparation for examination are to have real effect, then they must impart to pupils the sense of urgency, vigour and commitment that is the hallmark of the good student. Planning is crucial. It is self-defeating to deal half-heartedly with study skills. Teaching methods will utilize communication and activity in small groups designed to allow members to appraise one another's approach to study.

The first step is to demonstrate to pupils how productive they can be. Pupils are often almost disconcerted by how much they can produce in fifteen-minute mini-examinations on topics of interest. The stress is on speed and concentration without loss of coherence. In pastoral work in school care and control should go together, and carefully adjusted, but none-the-less real demands must be made upon pupils.

Jacobs (1974) devised a series of exercises for sixth-form students when investigating the study habits of those who had failed A level or who their teachers thought to be likely failures. One of these activities illustrates the point about urgency and precision. The aim of the exercise was to increase skill in analysing the meaning of a question, and therefore students were required to look at the implications of each word. The allocation of time for this activity was as follows.

Explanation of objective	2 minutes
Ideas bank—the contribution and recording of impressions of what the writer of the question required from candidates	5 minutes
Intensive discussion with a partner about the meaning of the question	10 minutes
Making a schema or skeleton outline on which to base the answer	5 minutes
General discussion	8 minutes

The objective was not to write an answer but to modify old approaches and develop new skills. The habitual approach was at least temporarily modified by exposure to new ideas from others and intensive discussion with a partner. The students were completely absorbed and felt that they had learned some extremely useful things about their capacity for analysing a question.

There are a number of variants of peer counselling in which pupils support one another. Kelly (1955) describes a technique which he calls fixed role therapy. It is productive to present to fifth formers simply written case histories describing the steps that other adolescents have taken to solve their learning difficulties. These steps are discussed in small groups, focussing on viability, costs and economy. This experience increases the sense of being in control of one's own destiny and the belief that it is possible to make an impact on the world through skill and perseverance.

The next step is to get pupils to analyse their difficulties in a subject which concerns them. This is started in the pastoral period, but completed at home. The pastoral aim is to deal with general difficulties, but pupils should be encouraged to discuss special difficulties with those who teach that discipline. The pupil should go through his notebooks and essays to detect areas where he is uncertain of meaning, and to discover trends in his teacher's comments. He then begins systematically to diagnose his difficulties, with a friend to check and make suggestions. The final step is the construction of a plan for improvement, which incorporates clear targets and spells out strategies.

In building up the plan of action, pupils should be taught to use two simple principles of behaviour modification: the art of constructing a hierarchy of tasks in order of difficulty; and the need to provide themselves with some reward for effort. The pupil will usually agree that it is sensible to begin with the easiest weakness and cope with it before proceeding to the next one, except when something is urgent or a source of great anxiety. The most important rewards come from recognition that one is beginning to improve and the approbation of friends and teachers.

The activity outlined above is one that requires an adolescent to take real responsibility for himself; although it is an activity rooted in mutual help, for peers help each other. The form tutor has constantly to assess pupils' reactions and provide stimulating activities. He must also ensure that pupils become more aware of the relationship between their own behaviour and the results of study, by a careful mixture of discussion, comment and activity.

Another development in study skills will include the tough task of persuading pupils to process what has been read and translate it into their own terms, rather than using the writer's words. This is helped by outlining the argument to a fellow pupil before writing it down, after which together they can construct a counter-argument, which prevents them blindly accepting what has been written.

If pupils are to acquire the skills of independent study, then we have to train them in self-assessment. A simple schedule which they apply at intervals to their work, discussing the results with the form tutor or subject teacher, could include:

clarity of expression
development and structure
appraisal of weaknesses and strengths
the use of evidence
the use of references
originality
clear conclusions

Any teacher will be able to devise a relevant self-assessment form, which develops ways of tackling deficiencies.

Study-skills questionnaire

SECTION TWO ORGANIZATION AND PLANNING

Do we need to organize and plan? The school sets a routine. The answer to this lies in the need for growing independence in your study as you progress towards higher education. This section will help you investigate the general organization of your work outside the classroom, the way you take notes, answer examination questions and write essays. Everyone has to develop a method of study which works for himself—we are all different!

The skills which influence these aspects of your study are very wide, and so cannot all be included, but amongst them are:

development of the skill of logical presentation;
methodical note taking which also stimulates new ideas;
development of critical thinking;
acquisition of the skills of answering questions;
avoidance of over-reliance upon memory;
orientation to problems and tasks;
development of the ability to construct a clear framework as the basic structure for an essay or answers to questions;
ability to discriminate between what is salient and what is of marginal importance;
presentation of work.

The strategy adopted in this section.
The items fall into four groups:

general organization of study;
note-taking;
answering questions;
essay-writing.

They will draw your attention to some sources of difficulty which may reduce your level of performance. A number of items in the section on reading skills are related to note-taking, and so this sub-section is brief.

SUB-SECTION A   Organising myself

1.	When I finish homework I usually check to see that everything needed for next day is in my bag.	I often seem to forget my books or something I need.	1.

2. Although memorising plays a part in my study skills, I usually try to think about the topic.

My study methods seem to rely on learning things off by heart when this is possible.

2.

3. I usually take a pride in presenting my work attractively.

I often find I do not have enough time to present my work attractively.

3.

4. I usually read through my work carefully and correct any mistakes before I hand it in.

I often get low marks because my work contains mistakes which I did not correct before handing it in.

4.

5. I usually plan the use of my time more carefully if I am feeling worried about my work.

If I am worried about my work I often put off doing it for as long as possible.

5.

6. I have definite times for studying at home to which I usually stick.

I usually do my study at home when I feel like it rather than work at set times.

6.

7. When I find my work is deteriorating I try to sit down and draw up a plan of action.

When my work begins to deteriorate I usually do not take any steps to deal with the situation.

7.

8. I usually begin working as soon as I get to my bedroom or the place I study.

I often seem unable to make a start on my homework.

8.

9. □ I try to rewrite a piece of work with which I am dissatisfied. □ I usually hand in a poor piece of work and hope to do better next time. 9. □

10. □ When I am in difficulties I admit that I need help and will ask for it. □ If I am in difficulties with my work I seem to avoid asking for help. 10. □

11. □ When I am in difficulties with my work I set out to discover why or try doing it in a different way. □ When I get into difficulties I sometimes seem to lose heart and give up. 11. □

12. □ I usually try to ensure that I have understood what is required of me in the work that has been set. □ I quite often find I have misunderstood what I am supposed to do and have wasted my time and effort. 12. □

13. □ If I get a free period I usually try to use it for private study. □ If I get a free period it seems to be most often spent in talking to friends. 13. □

SUB-SECTION B   Efficient note-taking

14. □ I have developed a system which allows me quickly to locate a piece of information in my notes □ Quite often I find I have to waste time hunting for a piece of information in my notes. 14. □

15. I sometimes con-
struct a diagram
which contains
essential informa-
tion as part of my
note-taking.

☐

I mainly rely on my
notes just as I took
them down.

☐

15.

☐

16. I underline or mark
the key points in my
notes so that they
stand out.

☐

I do not usually make
sure that I can
identify the key
points in my notes
by underlining or
marking them.

☐

16.

☐

17. When I have made
notes from my
reading I usually try
to rewrite them in
my own words.

☐

I very rarely rewrite
the notes from my
reading in my own
words.

☐

17.

☐

SUB-SECTION C Answering questions efficiently

18. I usually try to read
the question care-
fully to make sure I
know exactly what
is being asked.

☐

Sometimes I begin
to answer the
question and then
realize that I have
misunderstood it.

☐

18.

☐

19. I usually make quick
notes which act as a
framework for my
answer before I
begin to write.

☐

I usually begin to
write immediately
but find I tend to
wander from the
point.

☐

19.

☐

20. I usually try to be
critical in answering
questions but I
always give reasons
for alternative
points of view.

☐

I usually seem to
repeat what I have
been taught or have
read without being
critical.

☐

20.

☐

21. ☐	I usually plan to leave a little time to check my answers for errors.	☐	I usually continue writing the answers until I am told to stop.	21. ☐
22. ☐	I try to train myself for writing good answers by constructing brief outline answers as a regular part of my study.	☐	I often find it difficult to put down my ideas in a clear logical way when I answer questions.	22. ☐
23. ☐	If I have not understood the instructions I usually ask the teacher.	☐	If I do not understand the questions I usually do not ask the teacher.	23. ☐

SUB-SECTION D   Writing essays

24. ☐	I usually begin planning an essay by making a list of questions and points I will raise.	☐	I often find that I have no clear idea what I am going to say when I begin to write.	24. ☐
25. ☐	I usually make a list of sources of information which I will consult.	☐	I sometimes find that I have ignored important sources of information.	25. ☐
26. ☐	I always make a plan which briefly indicates the content of each paragraph.	☐	I find it rather difficult to construct a plan for my essays.	26. ☐
27. ☐	I try to ensure that all my ideas are related to the main theme of the essay.	☐	I rarely seem to find the time to examine the ideas in my essays.	27. ☐

28. I usually pay special attention to the first and final paragraphs of an essay.

☐ I usually seem to begin writing and let the essay take its own shape. 28. ☐

29. I develop my own ideas in my essays although I take care to avoid rash statements.

☐ I usually seem to repeat in essays more or less what my subject teacher has said. 29. ☐

30. I usually try to ensure that each paragraph leads on to the next one.

☐ I usually pay little attention to the way in which a paragraph is related to the next one. 30. ☐

Using this analysis of your organisation and planning

Select any points you wish to deal with and proceed as in the previous section on reading skills. If there are a number of points which you feel need attention you will have to plan very carefully.

Sub-Section A   Organising myself
Sub-Section B   Efficient note-taking

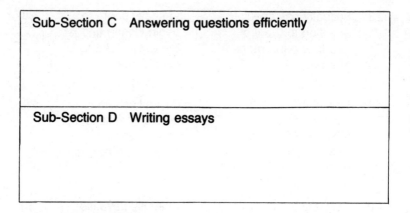

Sub-Section C   Answering questions efficiently

Sub-Section D   Writing essays

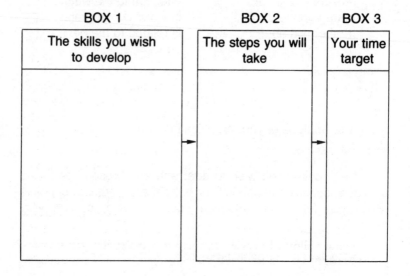

BOX 1 | BOX 2 | BOX 3

| The skills you wish to develop | The steps you will take | Your time target |

Strategies of revision

The majority of pupils work hard before an examination, but not necessarily systematically or efficiently. We can begin by helping pupils organize a good working environment. The importance of order, the availability of books and being able to locate the papers one wants, is underestimated.

Let us not impose our ideas upon others. Some people can work best with background music and others cannot. A regular pattern has to be created, and must allow the adolescent time to do other things. The planning of a revision timetable is essential. The basic principles of good planning include the balance of time given to strong and weak subjects, the final decision being a product of the importance of the subject to the pupil's plans, the degree and type of difficulty, and the relation to the rest of his work of a subject at which he is particularly poor.

Some thoughts must be given to retrieval systems. Many pupils use notebooks alone to store information, and it is surprising how often a key notebook gets lost. One simple method of retrieval is to construct an outline of the main points of a key topic—thinking in headlines—and enter this on a 200 × 125 mm record card. These cards can be stored in a shoebox with clear markers so that any topic can be selected at a glance. The same can be done with key sketches or diagrams in subjects where these are important. Notebooks can be arranged in alphabetical order, and stored in a box so that they are readily available.

The sense of being in control needs to be built up in other ways. It is useful to encourage pupils to build up lists of questions and ideas related to particular topics. These personal ideas are stored with the summary card outlining a particular element of a subject. In this way, we allow someone to replace the sense of self that has been unintentionally eroded through the stress of examination preparation.

The principle of anticipation is prime in planning for revision. It is helpful if pupils who cannot work to time are encouraged to learn this skill by answering questions at home, strictly timing themselves to the period allowed in the examination. In planning the revision programme for the Easter vacation the pupil should be cautioned to leave time for fun and activities with his age-mates. A key point is the repetition of topics and the narrowing down of study into salient areas without indulging in limited "question-spotting". A balance should be established by each individual between study activities in which he or she is basically assimilating material, and those which are primarily productive, such as answering a question. The sensitive alternation and balance of these activities prevents fatigue and distaste for study.

During the preparatory months weaknesses are revealed. The form tutor should be aware of anyone who has been away for a considerable period during the fourth year or in the first term of the fifth year and take special care with them. Often, only minimal help is required to overcome deficiencies.

The final section of the study skills survey brings the difficulties of the revision period into the open. Note that it ends by asking the pupil to stand back and report on himself in as objective a way as he can.

Study-skill questionnaire

SECTION THREE HOMEWORK AND REVISION FOR EXAMINATIONS

I know what I have to do. I'm organized. This section may help you organize your work during the year preceding major examinations. It is possible to work hard and conscientiously and yet be unaware that many of our strategies are unproductive or even working against our own aims. Even if this is not the case, there may be simple techniques which can raise our level of performance.

The strategy adopted in this section.
The items deal with two broad areas:

> general organization of homework;
> revision techniques.

During the period before examinations it is normal to feel under pressure, but this can be used creatively if you see it as an opportunity to develop your own coping strategies and powers of independent study. Some of the items therefore deal with your reactions to pressure. Perhaps the old-fashioned phrase, "willpower and determination", is relevant to this section.

SUB-SECTION A   Organisation of work

1. I have a carefully
    planned timetable   I have not con-   1.
    of homework to   structed a planned
    which I keep.   programme of
                               homework, but fit
                               it into my other
                               activities.

2. ☐	I record the date an essay or assignment is due and hand it in in time.	☐	My teachers are often chasing me to hand in essays or assignments.	2. ☐

2. ☐ I record the date an essay or assignment is due and hand it in in time. ☐ My teachers are often chasing me to hand in essays or assignments. 2. ☐

3. ☐ I keep my books and papers tidy so that I can begin work at once. ☐ I often seem unable to find essential books or papers. 3. ☐

4. ☐ I usually plan my work to give myself a few minutes break between each subject. ☐ I usually try to get through my home-work as quickly as possible by doing it all at once. 4. ☐

5. ☐ I do not allow myself to be dis-tracted by noises and what other people are doing. ☐ I am easily distracted by noises and what other people are doing. 5. ☐

6. ☐ I keep a record of the work I do at home. ☐ I do not have a record of the work I do at home. 6. ☐

7. ☐ I usually explain my feelings of stress to my parents in a calm, rational way. ☐ I sometimes accuse my parents of "nagging" or have a row with some-one when I feel under stress. 7. ☐

8. ☐ When I am tempted to put off a difficult piece of work I usually decide to get on with it according to my plan. ☐ I put off a difficult piece of work and then find myself doing it hastily at the last moment. 8. ☐

97

9. I evaluate my progress at intervals and modify my study plans as a result of this.

I usually rely only on the teachers and examinations as a guide to my progress.

9.

SUB-SECTION B   Effective revision

10. I have already made a careful plan for revision.

As yet, I have not made plans for revision.

10.

11. I have already devised a clear index system for my notes.

I have not yet developed a way of quickly finding the information that I want.

11.

12. I am building up a set of summary cards for each subject for use in my final revision.

As yet I have not thought out my techniques for final revision.

12.

13. I have already made a plan for the constructive use of the next vacation or term.

I have not yet made any plans for the use of the next vacation or term.

13.

14. I carefully break down my own notes into sections with clear headings.

I do not break down my own notes into sections with clear headings.

14.

15. If I get behind I make a definite plan for catching up and understanding the work that has been missed.

If I get behind I do not take any special steps to catch up and understand the missed work.

15.

16. I usually allocate my time carefully and anticipate the points at which more time is needed for a difficult topic or assignment.

I often spend time on a difficult subject or assignment without planning so that I do not have time to do justice to something at which I am good.

16.

17. I have a carefully-thought-out plan for increasing the amount of study and the frequency of revisions in the last term before my examinations.

I have not yet made a careful plan for revision and additional study to prepare for the examinations.

17.

18. In my revision plan I have carefully allocated the time given to each subject on the basis of its importance to my future and my strengths and weaknesses.

I had no particular considerations in mind when I drew up my revision plan.

18.

19. I am building up a list of critical questions and ideas for each subject for use in essays and questions.

I often find I am short of relevant ideas and criticisms for essays and questions.

19.

20. I am anticipating the stress of examinations by answering questions set in them within the same strict time limit.

I have not yet taken any positive steps to prepare for writing under examination conditions.

20.

Two important items

21. I try to do each piece of work better than the previous one and use this as my measure of progress.

I judge my achievement by comparing myself with other people.

21.

22. Even when I am depressed or upset I have the will-power and determination to tackle my homework.

I sometimes get into moods and then I do not do my work.

22.

Using this analysis of homework and revision skills. This section has great relevance if you are taking your examinations in the next twelve months, although the earlier you think about your study skills the more confident you will become. It may be helpful to do the following.

1. List in the box below your strengths and weaknesses.

STRENGTHS	WEAKNESSES

2. Now imagine that you are someone writing a report on you as a pupil. The writer is concerned with your study skills and is making

100

realistic and *practical* suggestions about the techniques you could adopt to give you the best chances of success. Write the report *as he would write it* below.

3. From the suggestions made in the imaginary report above select any that you wish to carry out. List them below.

A FINAL NOTE

This study-skills questionnaire can help you if you think about it and then discuss the results with someone. It is only of value if you begin to examine your study skills and then act on the basis of your discoveries.

AN AFTERTHOUGHT

It may be useful if the writer confesses that it took him some years to realise the need for study skills. As someone who believes in the creativity of education, he under-valued this aspect of the educational process. *What* and *why* were allowed in his early teaching to obscure the *how*; yet absence of the *how* in the field of study creates many barriers which unfortunately operate most strongly with those pupils whose environment is less than optimal. Study skill-programmes are not only a part of education, but a part of compensatory education which makes more sense of the phrase "equality of opportunity".

REFERENCES

Banks, O. and Finlayson, D. (1973) *Success and Failure in the Secondary School*, London: Methuen.

Brehm, J. and Cohen, A. (1962) *Explorations in Cognitive Dissonance*, New York: Wiley.

Cattell, R. (1966) Anxiety and Motivation, in Spielberger, C. (Ed.) *Anxiety and Behaviour*, New York: Academic Press.

Endler, N., Hunt, J. and Rosenstein, A. (1962) *An S—R Inventory of Anxiousness*, Psychological Monographs, Volume 76, No. 17, Whole No. 536.

Festinger, L. (1957) *A Theory of Cognitive Dissonance*, Stanford, California: Stanford University Press.

Gaudry, E. and Spielberger, C. (1971) *Anxiety and Educational Achievement*, Sydney: Wiley.

Hamblin, D. (1974) *The Teacher and Counselling*, Oxford: Blackwell.

Jacobs, V. (1974) *A Study of the Effect of Counselling on Pupils Experiencing Difficulties with A-Level Work*, unpublished D.S.C. Dissertation, University College of Swansea.

Kelly, G. (1955) *The Psychology of Personal Constructs, Volume I and II*, New York: Norton.

Leach, P. (1965) *Social and Perceptual Inflexibility in School Children in Relation to Maternal Child-Rearing Habits*, unpublished Ph.D. Thesis, London School of Economics, University of London.

Levitt, E. (1968) *The Psychology of Anxiety*, London: Staples.

Magee, B. (1973) *Popper*, London: Fontana/Collins.

Rokeach, M. (1960) *The Open and Closed Mind*, New York: Basic Books.

Rotter, J. (1966) *Generalized Expectancies for Internal versus External Control of Reinforcement*, Psychological Monographs, Volume 80, No. 1. Whole No. 609.

Rotter, J., Chance, J., and Phares, E. (1972) *Applications of a Social Learning Theory of Personality*, New York: Holt, Rinehart and Winston.

Rubenowitz, S. (1963) *Emotional Flexibility—Rigidity as a Comprehensive Dimension of Mind*, Stockholm: Almquist and Wiksell.

Ruebush, B. (1963) Anxiety. In Stevenson, H., Kagan, J., and Spiket, C. (Eds.) *Child Psychology, Sixty-second Yearbook of the National Society for the Study of Education, Part I*, Chicago: University of Chicago Press.

Siegman, A. (1956) The effect of manifest anxiety on a concept formation task, a non-directed learning task, and on timed and untimed intelligence tests, *Journal of Consulting Psychology*, 20 pp. 176–178.

Spielberger, E. (Ed.) (1966) *Anxiety and Behaviour*, New York: Academic Press.

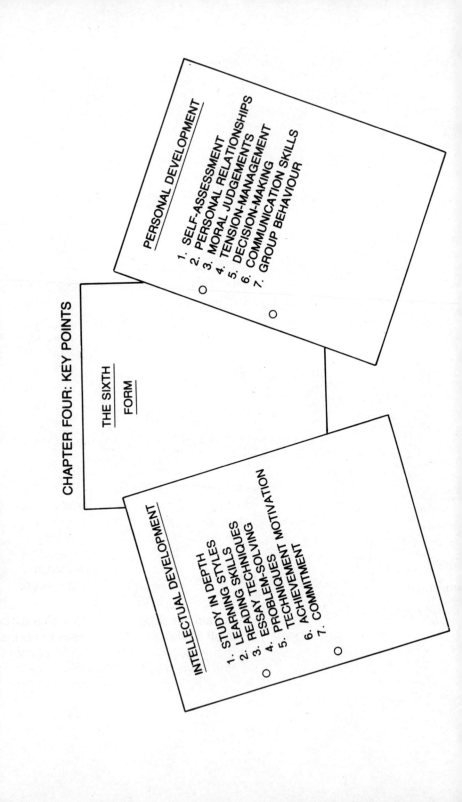

CHAPTER FOUR: KEY POINTS

THE SIXTH

FORM

PERSONAL DEVELOPMENT

1. SELF-ASSESSMENT
2. PERSONAL RELATIONSHIPS
3. MORAL JUDGEMENTS
4. TENSION-MANAGEMENT
5. DECISION-MAKING
6. COMMUNICATION SKILLS
7. GROUP BEHAVIOUR

INTELLECTUAL DEVELOPMENT

1. STUDY IN DEPTH
2. LEARNING SKILLS
3. READING TECHNIQUES
4. ESSAY TECHNIQUES
5. PROBLEM-SOLVING TECHNIQUES
6. ACHIEVEMENT MOTIVATION
7. COMMITMENT

THE GUIDANCE NEEDS OF THE 16–19 AGE GROUP

Summary

THE CENTRAL ARGUMENT

The theme of this chapter is the need for more appropriate guidance and counselling for the 16–19 age group. Evidence from recent research indicates that is would be generally welcomed by the sixth-form student. Suggestions are made about methods reflecting the intellectual orientations that should be present in sixth-form activity.

It is recognized that the sixth form contains those future members of society who will work with others in a responsible and involved way. Such people need the skills of communication, of understanding the standpoint of others, of recognizing what determines their own reactions to those to whom they have to relate, and of man-management in the best sense.

The sixth former's style of thought, mode of problem-solving and learning method is as important as the disciplines in which he exercises his cognitive skills.

INDUCTION COURSES

Evidence suggests that some sixth-form pupils find intimidating the new demands for study in depth and expression of opinion, unless they are simultaneously helped to acquire these skills. Without this, some pupils in the first term in the sixth form acquire negative attitudes to themselves, teachers, subjects and school. These will have detrimental effects on their later performance at A level.

The structure and content of a basic induction course is provided. This anticipates these difficulties and equips students to develop viable coping strategies. They are also alerted to the causes of failure in higher education, and advised of the steps that they can take to eradicate them. Such an induction course will also reinforce the student's sense of commitment to his chosen subjects after further examination of his reasons for selecting them. Standards of excellence are endorsed, and the sixth-form student is encouraged to take up a truly responsible attitude towards himself and his school.

PROGRAMMES FOR PERSONAL DEVELOPMENT

These programmes must incorporate real intellectual content and be relevant to the student's future career. They should involve the subject teachers who will draw from their particular discipline in a creative way. Topics such as fear of failure, attitudes and attitude change, interpersonal perception and judgement, will form part of this course. Analyses of problem-solving, of the student's style of thought and reasoning, and of intrinsic motivation, are some of the key elements. The need for intellectual integrity in the organization and development of such programmes is stressed.

The background to the guidance of this age group

The success of the sixth form in British education is amply witnessed by the remarkable growth in the last two decades in the number of pupils receiving full-time education after the age of sixteen for the vast majority receive this in the sixth form. Taylor *et al.* (1974) draw attention to the increase in the number of sixth-form students and suggests that the traditional prestige and social advantage gained from membership of the sixth form has diminished.

If we are to provide meaningful guidance, then these changes in the composition of the sixth form must be taken into account, together with an evaluation of our examination system and the concern about standards. Most sixth forms now contain pupils taking a combination of O and A level examinations, C.S.E., or no examinations at all. We cannot conlude automatically that pupils will spend two years in the sixth form, and so the guidance offered to some pupils needs to be intensified. Certainly the costly nature of small sixth-form groups is being questioned in an age of economic uncertainty. Keniston (1972) has postulated that education has to deal with a new stage of development which he calls youth. In this stage the individual is preoccupied with the relationship of the individual to society, the choice of vocational and social roles, and discovering a satisfactory life-style. Sixth-form students will benefit from forms of guidance which help them develop to the level where they can cope with social reality, without passively accepting it or automatically opposing it with a revolutionary fervour. A guidance programme for the sixth form must have real intellectual content and incorporate the extension of skills of communication and inter-personal relationships. Such a programme is likely to produce in the students what O'Brien (1972) has called the "suspecting eye", as they learn to assess their sages and slogans critically and to look at their own motives and ideas of authority and society from a different perspective.

General studies have fared badly in the sixth form, but I would argue that a well-planned programme of guidance incorporated into the general studies programme can add much to the interpersonal skills and intellectual development of those whose minds are mastering the process of abstract reasoning. We are, after all, educating those who will be our future professionals, who will be required to work with others in a way which demands integrity, empathic communication and the skills of man-management.

The need for guidance

The pastoral team have to ask two questions about the sixth form. First, does guidance need to be improved or are we already carrying out our functions adequately? Second, is there any evidence whether young people feel the need for more guidance? The answers indicate that the sixteen to nineteen age group would actively welcome more guidance and counselling, although it may have to differ from what we have conventionally offered.

Fogelman (1972) undertook a study of pupils in the second year of the sixth form in October, 1967. These individuals were contacted again in the spring of 1971, and invited to comment on the adequacy of the guidance received at school in the light of post-school experiences. From the 9,400 replies received a random sample of 1,000 was selected as the basis for the report.

Only one person in the sample who did not go to university or some form of higher education was complimentary about the guidance received at school. The respondents felt that teachers were over-preoccupied with their own profession in giving guidance, and stressed that opportunities had been missed because schools lacked knowledge about the new courses available in the polytechnics, and about alternatives to the traditional routes through tertiary education. Most seriously, the erstwhile pupils felt that often the advice they received was misleading, reflecting a lack of knowledge of modern technology. One hopes that the greater availability of specialist careers officers for the sixth form has done something to modify this situation.

The responses suggest that even when pupils were going to university, the information offered them was inadequate and that they were told little about the nature of university teaching and life. These comments indicate the need to prepare students systematically for the transition from sixth form to higher education or work.

Bailey (1972) conducted a study, based on a small sample of a hundred, randomly selected pupils after they had taken A levels, which is at least suggestive. Evidence of a poor choice of A level was found. Choices were sometimes made on the basis of O level results rather than on considered and balanced criteria which included their plans for the future. Yet Bailey found that they still looked forward to their university courses with optimism and hope.

In analysing the results, Bailey found that pupils' decisions in choosing A level subjects were largely determined by four groups of factors:

academic factors such as O level qualifications and how parents and friends reinforce good or poor performance in a subject.

technical factors which included the availability of courses, the likelihood of acceptance for a particular course at university and the history of A level success in that subject within the school;

personality factors of which the most important seemed to be the self-concept that the pupil was developing and the implications of the choice of subject for long-run identity;

guidance factors, especially the advice of significant people in the pupil's life and the information available within the school.

This study shows the need to explain to pupils some of the underlying issues and forces which affect choice of subject at A level. The period of development from sixteen to nineteen may include a radical redefinition of identity, especially in the vocational and philosophical aspects of the self. Many sixth-form students question the set of values still commonly operating in our society which categorizes males as primarily specialists in objective and logical tasks and females as preoccupied with the expressive and social. At the same time, some pupils are vulnerable to pressures to move towards the pole of this fallacious dichotomy that is traditional for their sex.

Bailey also found evidence that forceful and prudent parents were intervening in the choices made by their children: the professional father, in particular, seemed to be exercising strong persuasion, if not actual control, over his son's or daughter's choice of A-level subjects; a point worth remembering when planning a guidance programme.

Girls may be in especial need of guidance in the selection of A-level subjects. Wheeler (1974) is one investigator who found that the career aspirations of girls were lower than desirable when academic records and evidence of aptitude were considered. The girls were asked to imagine that they were married and successfully launched upon a career. The husband had the opportunity of moving to gain promotion, but this meant that the girl would have to give up her job and accept an inferior one. The majority of girls felt that they should give up their job to facilitate their husband's career. In the reverse situation only a very small minority felt that they had the right to expect the same of their husband.

The need for better guidance about subject choice is strikingly brought out in Bailey's intensive study when she reports that twenty per cent of girls and seventeen per cent of boys *after* taking A-level would, in retrospect, have added a subject to those that they took or would have replaced one of their subjects by another. Six per cent of the boys and the same percentage of girls stated that they would study entirely different subjects if they could begin A-level again. It seems likely from the evidence that this dissatisfaction was due to the fact that expediency and pressure, rather than personal inclination, unduly narrowed their choices. Small sixth forms often create this situation, and it seems essential that we urgently seek remedies for it.

Lack of purpose is found in some of Bailey's subjects, for although forty-eight per cent of her sample made a choice of university course with a definite career in mind, twenty-four per cent had no clear idea about their future. This means that a sizeable minority of young people embark upon a higher-education course which may seriously limit their career possibilities, or, at the very least, that they will spend three critical and formative years without contributing positively to building a career which embodies a satisfying life-style. Even more alarming, twenty-nine per cent of Bailey's respondents stated that they would take up something quite different from the course on which they were about to start, if they had the necessary qualifications. Added evidence of the confusion and anxiety of first-year undergraduates is provided by the insightful accounts of Newsome *et al.* (1973). All this shows that the onus falls on the school or sixth-form college to provide guidance of an informed and creative type as a prophylactic measure.

The foregoing gives some hint of the urgency of the need for adequate guidance in the vocational and educational field. Now let us look at the answer to the second question which asked if students recognize the need for more guidance, and if they do, are they prepared to take advantage of it? King *et al.* (1974), in a study of post-compulsory education in Western Europe, found that fifty per cent of British students in the sixteen to nineteen age group endorsed the need for "much more" guidance and counselling, whilst seventy per cent of Continental students felt the need for this. These workers found evidence of the need for new groupings of subjects and the development of new perspectives within these disciplines. This was paralleled by an equally strong desire by the students for such changes.

This report highlights the urgency of modifying the pattern of relationships between this age group and those who teach them in a way which constructively fosters self-awareness and independence. This might influence their interaction with others outside the school setting. The report also insists that we accept that part of the educative task consists of the preparation of youg adults for a lifetime of relearning, accompanied by increasingly complex decision-making.

Wankowski (1973), in a meticulous exploration of the links between academic achievement, motivation and temperament, threw light on the guidance of this age group. His research indicates that we must adapt our teaching to the student's personality giving special attention to his degree of introversion or extraversion, providing special supports for those who show extreme tendencies of either type. In his research on undergraduates, Wankowski found that many had been ill prepared for the more independent methods of study which form the core of university education. Others were unable to deal with the more complex and demanding pattern of social interaction. Such students are at risk. His work appears to endorse the suggestions and findings of King and his fellow workers.

An unpublished study by Buckton (1971) explored the problems of the sixteen to nineteen year old in a traditional grammar school, a comprehensive school and the first year of a college of education. The focal points of anxiety were relationships with teachers and peers, examinations, careers, and doubts about personal identity. Twelve per cent of this sample were prepared to state that they were "very worried" about the future, whilst the large majority indicated that they would welcome guidance and help, so long as it was free from overtones of directiveness and paternalism.

My own experiences with various age groups in the secondary school seem to coincide with the general trends of these studies. In the third and fourth years, problems connected with parents and difficulties of meeting their expectations loom large in the lives of many pupils. But most sixth-form students pass successfully through this stage, perceiving their parents realistically. They have learned that they can be different from them, and maintain the bonds of affection and communication without losing their personal integrity.

Personality and developmental needs

It is scarcely surprising if we sometimes fail to take account of the underlying preoccupations of our students; yet incomprehension of these can make our interaction with them unproductive and even self-defeating. The identity crisis of earlier adolescence still reverberates in them, but many will have embarked on learning to make a truly intimate relationship which is of complete integrity and will not threaten their personal boundaries and integration, as Erikson (1968) describes.

Intimacy does not necessarily mean sexuality although it may lead towards a full sexual relationship. It is a matter of maintaining one's personal boundaries whilst allowing another to become aware of our hidden aspirations, fear and doubts. Each of us has an inner core of privacy which he cherishes, and the prospect of allowing another entry into it fills one with apprehension. Allowing another to become close to one is a matter of learning to accept him for what he

111

is—imperfections and idiosyncrasies as well as strengths—and then possessing the courage to reveal oneself with honesty.

The stage of young adulthood often brings an awkward self-consciousness in which doubts centre on the individual's capacity to relate to others, ability to convey his views and intentions accurately, and competence in the field of learning. A sense of inadequacy in these areas may be hidden under nonchalance and bravado. It is sometimes hard to detect this, but it is even more difficult when doubt about sexual identity is present. This means that they are uncertain of their sexual self. They may feel that they cannot live up to the sex roles displayed by the mass media, which, although they affect to despise them, still have a compulsive quality for many young adults. Here condemnation is feared and there is undue sensitivity to the comments of others.

In social interaction some of this age group experience problems which they are reluctant to discuss except with a close friend. They feel they do themselves less than justice; that interaction which they earnestly desire to have a positive outcome turns out to be sterile. They know that they tend to precategorize others in a way which inevitably leads to conflict, yet find themselves powerless to change this. Many have accepted that words are the major tools of communication, and then, in key areas, discover that words in their hands are blunt or double-edged tools. In a few cases, sometimes those of the very intelligent, there is a sense of being trapped in a situation where the signals they send to others are counter-productive or distort their original meaning.

The reader may feel that this is unduly dramatic. In fact, I lack the skill to convey the intensity of feeling and near-despair that many sixth-form students experience. One device in group guidance is the writing of a character sketch in which the individual is asked to look at himself as objectively and honestly as possible. He is asked to write in the third person. The following extracts from a character sketch indicates the sensitivity to psychological processes. It has been selected because it was written by a stable and successful student. It speaks for itself.

GARETH

Gareth is an intelligent young man, who is successful in school and is very proud of his success, as well he might be. He does not, perhaps, have the quickest of brains but he has a fairly good capacity for understanding provided he is not rushed.

Gareth is tall, slim, one might almost say thin person, but is nonetheless quite muscular. He is not exceptionally good looking but he considers himself to be fairly good looking and reasonably attractive. Like most people he occasionally has nagging doubts about his appearance, which is important to him. He sometimes wishes that he were not quite so slim and that he could be rid of the acne which blemishes his skin. He occasionally worries about his appearance, but is able to shrug off his doubts quite easily.

He sometimes gives the impression of being carefree, and tries to belittle the importance of some things, such as examinations, which other people consider vitally important. His friends know, however, that he does care, and that they are very important to him. He does occasionally become depressed, for no apparent reason; this he puts down to the pressure of work and the general monotony of everyday life; he may be right. This depression is, however, nearly always short-lived, since he will not allow himself to remain depressed he will usually make a conscious effort to raise his spirits, and nearly always succeeds.

He seems to have a fairly complex character, and his moods are variable. He sometimes appears shy and retreating and silent, whereas at other times he is lively and gay and not the least bit shy; the latter is nearly always the case, however, and he is very easy to get along with. When in a crowd, or even in a small group he will always join in the fun and get into the spirit of the occasion without being at all self-conscious. In these situations it is almost impossible to believe that he can be very shy. He is very easy going and this probably helps him when he makes friends, which he does very easily. If asked to perform in any way on his own, he is very embarrassed, even in front of his closest friends, and finds it very difficult to do so. He blushes very easily when confronted with seemingly trivial situations and usually does so when speaking with people whom he does not know very well. This is, however, usually overcome when he gets to know the person a little better. He will never speak up for himself in an argument with people he does not know very well and is usually too embarrassed to ask questions in meetings or after lectures. He is a lively person and an outward sign of his joyful character is probably his love of singing, dancing and running, and the fact that he is quite energetic generally.

Gareth often finds it difficult to make up his mind about what to do in a situation, which may be of considerable and obvious importance, or may be completely trivial. His mind becomes very confused, and concerted attempts at arriving at a logical decision are usually frustrated, leaving his mind in a worse state of turmoil than before. To him, no decision is trivial enough to be taken unthinkingly; everything needs careful deliberation. This slowness in decision making tends it irritate some of his friends, but their pressure does not usually succeed in making his brain work at a faster pace, perhaps it cannot. When under pressure in examinations, however, his brain does work at a very fast pace, and he seems to thrive on pressure. This may be one of the reasons for his successes in examinations. He does not enjoy the preliminary work for examinations, but enjoys the atmosphere of the examination room; the tension and the strained laughing. Outwardly he does not seem to be nervous, and even within he is not usually nervous; this may also be a factor in his success. Another source of embarrassment for him, somewhat paradoxically, is his examination success. Although to succeed is vitally important to him, for self-satisfaction if nothing else, he becomes embarrassed if mention is made of his success, as it often is. This is particularly true of his ordinary level success, which is still mentioned even though it occurred nearly two years ago. Although he himself cannot easily forget that he has passed so many "O" levels, he would prefer other people to forget it.

Gareth is a bit of a dreamer. He daydreams quite often, and his mind often wanders. When he is reading a book of some kind, he can usually concentrate quite easily, but his mind sometimes wanders; a smile may appear on his face as he recalls something which has happened and he may look up from his work. If this happens, then he usually has to pull himself together in order to concentrate on his reading again. His daydreams are based on a number of things; some, but by no means all, of them are sexually based but in others I imagine that he projects himself into fantastic situations, in which he would not normally find himself. In his dreams he might see himself as a strong and powerful person, both physically and mentally, who is admired by all people and is supreme among his friends. Of course, he realizes that this will never be, but he sees no harm in allowing his mind to get out of control in this way; he is, however, a little ashamed of this tendency. Perhaps he sees himself as a warrior, a hero, respected.

Tensions such as those described must impinge on the achieve-

114

ment of those who possess them. It is not by chance that group-guidance sessions often lead to discussion of an imposed identity and a superficial or "shell" self. This creates a discomfort which has to be relieved. Sometimes the blame is projected upon others, and an attempt to compensate for inner insecurity is made by attributing negative intentions to those who teach them. Pupils search for signs of inconsistency and hypocrisy, and look at the new relationship between them and their teachers with cynicism. Opinion-leaders suggest that sixth-form councils are intended as tension-reducing devices, to give the appearance of responsibility and participation without the substance. Effective guidance has to look at the reality of such viewpoints whilst also directing the suspicious glance back to themselves.

Of course sixth formers are adult in many ways, but it is also sensible to realize that the sixteen to nineteen year old who remains in the educational setting can demonstrate some of the egocentrism of adolescence that Elkind (1970) describes. Here the adolescent behaves as if his actions and motives are the object of close scrutiny, and are as important to others as to himself.

A sixth-form student who is particularly susceptible to the comparison process scans the behaviour and achievement of others, comparing himself with them negatively. He feels that others are more successful than he is and, very significantly, that they achieve those successes with comparative ease. He may often feel that he alone has to work hard. Such sensitivity is, in some anxious sixth-form students, associated with stress and the sense of failure. We can bring this out into the open in the guidance session, although as teachers we must always check on our classroom behaviour to ensure that it does not contradict what we say and do in our pastoral role.

The sense of occupying a marginal position in society is strong during the sixth-form period. The sixteen to nineteen year old in full-time education may overestimate his adulthood, but is still in a position of financial dependence. This sense of being on the edge of life causes some to search for signs that they are being treated in a manner which denies their maturity and intelligence.

Something that we often miss at this stage of development is an acute awareness of time and a fear of lack of progress and personal change. I often find that those who come for counselling have a compelling fear of stagnation, which comes from a sincere desire for change, but their self-expectations are unrealistic, indeed almost self-punitive. The result is that the individual loses hope.

It was stated in Chapter 1 that one of the objectives of the pastoral system was to aid the development of the truly moral individual. If the school has been successful in this, some sixth-form pupils will have reached the final stage in Kohlberg's (1969) sequence of stages in moral development. Such students make their moral judgements on the basis of general principles gradually internalized after considerable thought: the individual adhering to them not because he fears punishment from external sources or to win the respect and approval of others, but primarily to avoid self-condemnation. The range of maturity in moral development is as great as in social and emotional development: indeed all three are intimately linked. Within the same group of sixth-form students there may be the occasional student who has reached the level of post-conventional morality based on principles which can bring him into conflict with traditional codes.

To work with these people may be stimulating but discomforting, for they challenge those of us who have ceased to examine critically our assumptions about moral behaviour. During counselling I have found that such individuals generate unease because their freedom from imposed codes has created an unwilling awareness in me of my underlying rigidity and intolerance of standpoints dissimilar to my own. In pastoral work with these young men and women one must be prepared to look at oneself critically and suspend judgement.

We will not find many who have reached this stage in the sixth form. However, none of the above denies that there are some sixth-form students who, for reasons of romanticism and rebellion, not only challenge the existing moral order—if one can still talk about this in a pluralistic society—but also reject the social structure. This is not true post-conventional morality; instead it often turns out to be a bid to gain identity through opposition. They adhere to a blind, unthinking ideology which stunts their intellectual and moral growth. It is often held together by utopian conviction and fervour which hide the emotional needs for security. If we try to get them to examine their postulates critically, we are liable to arouse an extremely defensive reaction and be cast either into the role of an enemy or as lacking in understanding. Pastoral work with this type of student can only be productive if one reaches the underlying emotions which sustain the ideology and disrupt the behavioural mechanisms which accompany it. Has the teacher the right to do this?

116

Curriculum development in recent years has ignored, except incidentally, the processes by which pupils learn. There is now a refreshing shift towards giving priority to active methods of acquiring and understanding knowledge, and of subsequently utilizing it in a way which extends the student's comprehension of its significance. Good teaching, aimed at extending the student's autonomy and his capacity for critical thought, takes as its first principle the desirability of ensuring that he grasps the nature of the thought processes encapsulated in the subject.

Most of us would agree that one of our major aims in the secondary school is to produce a well-informed mind with the capacity to renew itself continually; yet it is possible that failure to pay attention to the more mundane aspects of learning may sabotage our attempts. There is no necessary conflict between the provision of demanding and stimulating content in our teaching, and the insistence that we must help pupils analyse their basic style of learning. Our intellectual task can be simply put as follows.

1. The production of a trained mind which works efficiently because it has grown out of the student's idiosyncratic learning style which he has consciously extended.

2. The development of the student's capacity to engage in a discriminating way in a variety of mental performances based on the nature of the problem, and to apply relevant information competently.

3. To provide the student with the skills of detecting the salient aspects of a concept or topic, and of proceeding to manipulate them in order to extend his understanding.

This suggests that our curricular task should be directed towards the production of students who have *consciously* acquired a range of intellectual techniques together with a system which gives them the power of applying them to relevant situations.

The development of the sixth form, of which we can be justly proud, has, however, brought unintended consequences which may interfere with these objectives. The heterogeneous population of the sixth form, although it is to be welcomed, can lead to a sense of division amongst the students. This can depress the non-traditional-sixth-form student because he feels inferior compared with the academically more competent. It seems clear from research such as that of Swift (1973) that for the sixth-form student who is marginal in his attitudes towards learning and his own capacity, the presence or absence of positive and favourable signals from the school can be of crucial importance. For those sixth-form pupils who receive little active encouragement from their homes, support from the sixth-form teacher and tutor is a vital factor in their success.

Newberry (1974) investigated adjustment to the sixth form in two schools for girls, one of which was a traditional grammar school and the other a large comprehensive school. The increased demands for study in depth were uppermost in the girls' minds, and the relevance of new modes of thinking was appreciated. But this had not been anticipated, and therefore came as a shock. Stress associated with this was arousing negative attitudes towards school and academic work, and causing some girls to question their ability to continue with the sixth-form course. Such reactions should not remain unmodified.

Discussion and the expression of opinion were felt to be a source of threat which they strove to avoid, as was the move to the analytic and critical style they were being urged to adopt. This research shows the need for well-planned guidance and a carefully designed induction course in which the new style of thinking is methodically introduced.

We know that we are asking new things of sixth-form students, but may not comprehend the full impact of this upon vulnerable individuals until behavioural difficulties or alienation manifest themselves. Heavier and more intensive work-loads are an inevitable part of the academic sixth-form student's existence, yet at the same time we require them to take responsibility for planning their independent study, a task which some cannot manage without training and temporary supervision. To do something about this does not mean "spoon-feeding". But we should take measures which detect the sixth-form student who is at risk in the first months of his course. Such pupils will be those who find it difficult to discard earlier modes of study and thinking, or who take an inflexible approach towards problem-solving. Others may still depend excessively upon approval and be bound to the concept of the single right answer. We must intelligently anticipate and apply our professional skills at the most effective point.

Over-reliance upon memorization is a common source of dif-

118

ficulty in the first year of the sixth-form. Another hazard, less frequently recognized, is the inability to search out relevant information. This should be dealt with as quickly as possible. Many students have a passive approach to the reading of texts, marked by the failure to appreciate the intelligent use of indices; the importance of skimming to check that the located passages are germane to the issue. Without these skills, the student reads carefully, taking notes, only to discover that he has been wasting his time. Teachers need to give these students exercises in searching out information, showing, in note form, the sources they would use if they were to write on the topic. Constant reinforcement of these basic skills is necessary during the first two terms, so that the habits become deeply embedded.

Many of the first-year sixth experience a conflict between their desire for freedom of expression and the associated striving to communicate, and the fear of losing face with their fellows by voicing ideas in groups. Some skilled guidance and understanding are called for with such individuals if they are to engage in the exchange of ideas.

Perhaps we too easily assume that all our students wish to succeed; yet it is not impossible that some of them fear the implications of success. In my work with sixth-form groups I have found that once they trust me, they sometimes discuss their fears that a display of prowess would open up an apparently endless vista of expectations which they would not be able to meet. Anxiety is not the prerogative of those who are struggling with their academic work. To those who have not yet come to terms with themselves, success may be fraught with threat. We should try to help such individuals deal with their underlying sense of insecurity. It is helpful to face the fact that irrationality still plays a part in the sixteen to nineteen age group and that the sixth form needs at least one tutor who has sufficient intuition to accept such feelings without condemning those who have had the confidence to express them.

Perhaps we still need to learn that it may be better for both teacher and taught if, instead of haphazardly urging higher achievement upon students, we provide them with an analysis of the factors influencing achievement which they can apply to themselves. Achievement is the product of interaction between the relatively stable motives and personal characteristics of the individual, and the learning situation. Associated with this is the application of some standard of excellence to classroom work, discussion and writing. The student's interpretation of the learning situation and its subjective and evaluatory nature provide a starting point for understanding which leads to greater autonomy.

Next we can tackle the concept of the level of aspiration, showing that this is based on the reaction to success and failure. The desired level of future performance is compared with past performance. One aspect is personal, measuring the student's past performance; with the other the standard for assessment is external. Perception of the degree of discrepancy between the student's own performance and those of the people with whom he compares himself can be distorted and its significance for future performance can be over-estimated.

Sixth forms contain those who tend towards neuroticism and hypersensitivity, and these people react strongly to the cumulative effect of minor frustrations or failures. In isolation, each incident may be trivial, but they are being woven into a pattern of self-assessment which can have far-reaching effects upon their predictions about the outcome of their sixth-form work. The impact of unexpected failure can be severe, and can cause a radical shift towards a negative perspective of themselves that could have serious consequences, which could not be ignored.

Achievement motivation is surprisingly subjective once it is analysed, as the work of Atkinson and Feather (1966) and Weiner (1974) demonstrates. The student's perception of the probability of success seems to be crucial. If predictions are negative, then behaviour is shaped in a way which reduces the chances of success, for there is little point in striving when the only outcome appears to be almost certain failure. Conversely, predictions of success are likely to be backed by sustained effort and, we hope, by intelligent strategies of study.

Persistence brings success, it is said, and James and Rotter (1958) and Rotter (1968) argue that persistence in a gruelling task is strongly related to the person's sense of being in control despite difficulties. When a pupil feels that a solution to problems is internal and can be found by the exercise of his own wits, success is perceived as dependent upon individual effort, and failure as temporary. The learner then refuses to opt out, because this would mean a loss of self-respect, and leaves him with the more palatable alternative of revising his actions and, if need be, acquiring new skills.

Equally logically, when the source of control and success is seen as external, attempts at mastery will be either sporadic or rapidly extinguished. The self-selection which underlies the decision to continue education on a voluntary basis will ensure that most sixth-form pupils are not of this type. But it is possible that some may, under pressure of the demands of the sixth form, revert to a passive view of the world and of the learning process. They then react by self-pity or, more healthily, by blaming their teachers or courses.

Birney *et al.* (1969) show that some of the students about whom their tutors are concerned turn out to be those who work not for the active enjoyment of success, but to avoid the pain of complete failure, although unfortunately that is what they get. These pupils often come to the tutor's attention because they engage in voluntary learning tasks in a way which makes it evident that they are not really trying: they fail to orientate themselves purposefully; they respond apathetically to encouragement or sanctions, and yet still make the motions of working. The research suggests that if success comes their way, they lower their level of aspiration, and tend to raise it when they meet failure. This is, of course, the reverse of the usual response. In my experience such students may work harder for a short time after failure, but I have never detected any raising of the level of aspiration. However, some have been too ready to lower their sights when they were successful, even if this was only relative to their previous performance. This reaction to success may be an indicator of the problem of avoidance behaviour based on fear of failure.

Self-respect and its maintenance seems to be at the back of their approach to learning, self-respect which has to be preserved despite its fragility. They boost their esteem by relying upon their teachers and peers taking the approach that "they could do better if they wanted to" or that "they are really better than they appear to be". These are the pupils unsure about their reasons for entering the sixth form, a point which has obvious implication for the preliminary interview between the pupil and the director of the sixth form. They find vocational choice difficult, if indeed they can be induced to think about it sensibly, for they tend to avoid learning about themselves and the requirements of a job.

In practice, there are many variants of pupil marked by fear of failure and avoidance strategies. One of the most difficult for a tutor to deal with is the one who resolutely devalues himself to avoid taking on responsibility. If such pupils receive reassurance, they refute it steadily, ending by exhausting the teacher's patience, which they take as further evidence of their uselessness. Why? The self-derogation allows them to evade improvement of their learning skills. Their viewpoint is: they are like that; it is not their fault; and there is nothing that anybody can do about it. With another of his ilk, where each reinforces the other, they effectively insulate themselves against the disquieting impact of the tutor's efforts.

How can the pastoral team cope with these problems? A tutorial should include a methodical examination of the nature of achievement and the factors which influence it. For those with special problems of avoidance and fear of failure, group counselling is essential. The common theme will be the extension of study skills, training in problem-solving methods, stress on organization, and, crucially, developing the ability realistically to set their own targets. A behavioural approach which stresses self-reinforcement, self-observation and the acquisition of skills has yielded the best results. If support from peers is built up systematically, then the outcome seems even more positive. It would be dishonest to pretend that pastoral care is likely to provide any real solution to the problems of the sixth-form student just described in whom the mechanisms are strongly established. At best, we may do something to alleviate them. Unless such patterns of behaviour are detected early in the secondary school before they have crystallized, many pupils will under-function later in their school career.

The pastoral and the curricular have identical aims, one of which is the development of intrinsic motivation in pupils. Certainly this should be a central theme of guidance in the sixth-form. Intrinsic motivation has been described by White (1959) as the behaviour in which a person engages so that he can feel competent and self-determining in relation to his environment. The person who has developed intrinsic motivation has acquired patterns of behaviour which are ends in themselves: these include the manipulation of ideas, the habits of problem-solving, and a questioning approach to life; prerequisites for commitment to a discipline or profession. It may be better to teach students about the value of commitment and give them an analysis of the skills of thinking rather than tell them what they should be committed to and dictate the content of their thoughts, if we are seriously trying to produce intrinsic motivation.

Tardiness in responding to the changed needs of an age group is probably a self-defeating strategy. We have learned that it is better to reward our pupils than punish them. But is there not a risk that a pupil's over-reliance upon extrinsic rewards, including the approval of parents and teachers, can reduce his intrinsic motivation? The sixth-form students should be discarding the idea that learning is undertaken for the sake of external reward. Tangible rewards should become subordinate to the pleasure which comes from an increased sense of mastery and competence.

How, then, can the sixth-form tutor assist this? Much can be done in tutorial periods by encouraging students to examine their general style of learning. The use and misuse of deductive and inductive thought can be discussed, relating this to the particular subjects. We may see intellectual inquiry as a process of conjecture and refutation, under-pinned by a process of analysing information into its components or the opposite process of synthesising facts into a complex picture. In a learning task one or other of these may predominate, or one may be followed by the other. Many students will not have learned to apply the appropriate process to the task, and do not break their goal down into manageable steps, tackled in a logical order.

Sixth-form students respond well to the invitation to analyse their learning style if one provides them with an elementary structure. The following framework can be useful.

ASSESSING YOUR STYLE OF LEARNING

---

1. Would you say that your style of learning tends to be either thoughtful or impulsive? A thoughtful style of learning is one which looks not at the content alone, but at its implications and possible applications. This approach to learning can leave you with as many new questions in your mind as answers. An impulsive learning style is one where you get on with a task without bothering about such issues.

2. It is useful to ask how you orientate yourself to the learning task. You may begin by saying, "it all depends", but if you think about it, you may detect a pattern. Do you, for example, try to put a task into the context of what you have learned already, asking how this task relates to past ones? Do you try to look at different ways of tackling it and then select the one that you feel best? Do you find that the amount of reading or the appearance of the task is an important influence on your attitude towards it?

3. Do you look for as much evidence as possible and keep an open mind until you have surveyed the facts and arguments. Is it possible that your learning style is one where, if the topic is open to speculation, you make up your mind quickly and then set out to "prove" that you are right? Can you see any

need to learn to think in terms of tentative propositions which have to be either supported conditionally or denied, if you are not a scientist?

4. In a learning task do you fix your attention on the separate parts of it or do you remind yourself about the purpose of the task and relationship of each part to the whole?

This illustrates the form of approach to study skills in sixth-form pastoral groups. Discussions can touch upon the initial categorization of tasks and the influence this has on the steps taken to deal with them. It is useful to discuss the reaction to a faulty start, distinguishing between unthinking rigidity and intelligent persistence in problem-solving. This leads to exploration of the ways in which we can modify our tactics when the original attack has not yielded results.

Many of us will have felt puzzled and irritated when a student's performance is erratic. This is one of the situations where we need diagnostic skill. In each case, the factors contributing to variation in performance will differ; yet it may be useful to highlight two possibilities. These students tend to be intuitive thinkers, leaping ahead to conclusions which are often valid, although they seem unaware of how they arrived there. I would suggest that intuition is unverbalised insight. Some thinkers habitually make these leaps, but proceed to validate their conclusions through examination of the evidence or questioning the tenability of their argument. This attempt at refutation is lacking in some pupils whose performance is unpredictable. The obvious remedy is for the tutor to teach them the skills of examining the evidence, the basics of logic, and, above all, to put their ideas into serialistic form before they begin to write.

Able students coming from a background where there is little understanding of academic work may begin to display weaknesses in logical thinking. Words for them are tools not fully under their control, because in early years they were deprived of the emphasis on reasoning provided in the home where the parents justify and explain their demands. Their hold on language is precarious, therefore the style of thinking required for advanced academic work makes demands which they either do not appreciate or cannot meet without temporary help. The deficiency will be corrected eventually if things go well, but there is the danger that they may begin to under-rate themselves and feel they have taken on too difficult a task.

BASIC PLAN

INTRODUCTION

Summarising what I propose
to do in this essay

CONTENT

Definition ⎫
Various forms ⎬ of advertising
Its purpose ⎭ Style of communication

EVALUATION OF THE STATEMENT

EVALUATION OF ADVERTISING PRACTICES

TONE + CONTENT

Language used
Emotive words
e.g. indulges,
endangers etc
How the tone affects
the content

ADVANTAGES + DISADVANTAGES

Mention specific products and
techniques used
Possible or intended reactions
of consumers

**IMPORTANCE OF EXISTING CONSUMER
ORGANISATIONS**
Question the availability of their
findings to a FULL RANGE of the public

Importance of EDUCATING THE PUBLIC
about the TECHNIQUES of PERSUASION
used in the various forms of advertising

CONCLUSION

A summary of what has been said, emphasising
my main idea that education ABOUT the techniques of advertising will provide AN EFFECTIVE
MEANS OF CONTROL for the consumer.
Start at school

FINALLY . . .

This involves making "A
FREE AND RATIONAL
CHOICE", and the skills
can be used by us in OTHER
AREAS where we are ex-
posed to high-powered and
financed propaganda. e.g.
VOTING AT ELECTIONS

Such pupils often write their essays through a blind process of associative thinking, almost as if they waited to see what emerged because the outcome was beyond their control.

What can we do? Intensive training in tutorial periods over about six weeks has given the necessary impetus to development in many cases. The training has consisted of practice in constructing outlines of essays in which the logical structure of the argument is made clear. This is backed by post-writing assessment. When one has finished an essay, one often wants to start again because the limitations and weaknesses are clear. The student can make use of this reaction if he writes comments on his essays in a notebook immediately after finishing them, together with the subject specialist's comments. He can refer to these before writing the next essay. To construct a diagram is useful for pupils who tend to think visually and spatially, although the fundamental purpose is to help them build up an explicit model for the analysis, appraisal and exposition of a specific topic. An example of one such diagram (see page 125) will, I hope, show its potential value for the student in writing the essay.

SIXTH-FORM ESSAY TOPIC

The advertising industry indulges in a dishonest practice which endangers the right and ability of the consumer to make a free and rational choice of goods on the market. Its blatant attempts to brainwash the public should be subject to far stricter control."

Consider the content of this statement, and the way in which opinion is expressed. In discussing the validity of the opinion, express your own views on the work of the advertising industry.

1,500–2,000 words

The induction course for the sixth-form

Just as the induction course for first-year pupils is the first step in a structured programme of guidance for the next five years, so does the sixth-form induction course direct the subsequent pastoral effort. Timing of the course will differ from school to school. In some, it is held immediately after O levels; in others, where the tradition of a mass exodus to temporary work is established, for

126

reasons of expediency it is held in September. There are many arguments in favour of holding the induction course at the beginning of the autumn term, the main one being the opportunity for the natural development of pastoral work out of the material of the course. One headmistress, who has built up a systematic approach to guidance and counselling, finds that a hiatus exists in the fifth year after mock O levels, during which the sixth-form staff give an induction course to all fifth-year pupils. The advantage is that all have the opportunity of finding out about sixth-form work, not only those who have already made up their minds to enter. Some readers may consider a more general informational course at this point, followed by a carefully designed intensive course in September.

Without clear objectives, the induction course, like any other pastoral activity, is likely to lose the sense of urgency vital in maintaining pupils' interest. For the sixteen to nineteen age group, it is doubly important that we share these well-defined objectives with the students. Evaluation of the course is as much their right and responsibility as it is ours.

OBJECTIVES OF THE INDUCTION COURSE

---

1. To ensure that students deal successfully with the intellectual and social transition which is a concomitant of entry into the sixth form.
2. To create the conditions in which students are likely to use the first year in the sixth form productively.
3. To ensure that decisions about subject choice are made in a manner which fosters a sense of commitment to the discipline.
4. To prepare pupils for independent study and to sharpen the relevant study skills.
5. To alert pupils to the causes of failure in higher education and help them to avoid it.
6. By intelligent anticipation to inoculate students against sources of stress which can lead to underfunctioning.
7. To help them develop their sense of responsibility towards the school, showing them ways in which this can be achieved commensurate with their age and state of young adulthood.

To allow for real discussion and participation by the pupils, at least three days should be devoted to the course, and any attempt to restrict it to an information-giving process foredooms it to failure. If the course helps to produce positive attitudes to sixth-form study and prevents inertia and dissatisfaction, then it is an excellent investment of time.

Opportunities should be provided for small-group discussions and activities, and also for individual interviews between teachers and pupils which allow a working relationship to be established. The organization of the course demands careful thought in order to keep a flow of stimulating activities. One way of achieving this is by using the second-year sixth to conduct small-group discussions and devise some of the activities. Their involvement adds to the significance of the course for the newcomers, and proves that the relationship between teacher and taught is really one of active collaboration. At the same time the second-year sixth reinforce their sense of competence and maturity, and consolidate their study skills.

A worthwhile adjunct to the course is a study-skills booklet which also covers learning styles and ways of developing viable coping strategies. A joint working party of tutors and students could profitably do this for the induction course.

The induction course will, among others, probably include the following topics, which have been restricted to headings and a few brief notes.

CONTENT OF THE INDUCTION COURSE

---

1. *Choice of A-level subjects*
   Even at this stage, pupils may be choosing subjects unaware of the demands of the particular discipline. If staff suspect that this is so the student should discuss it with the subject specialist. One way of acquainting a pupil with the nature of the subject is to let him talk it over with a member of the second-year sixth taking the subject who has been adequately briefed.
   A simple self-assessment sheet can be devised which enables pupils to assess their academic and motivational strengths and weaknesses as a basis for the discussion with the member of the second-year sixth.
   The costs of either doing a subject or evading it may still be an essential topic: in cases where career plans have crystallised, the student may have to face the fact that he will have to take a subject that he dislikes or else modify his career plans.

2. *Study skills*

The induction course will direct the students' attention to the possibility that they have relied upon mechanistic devices which, if continued, can impede the type of thinking required for good performance at A level. Hence the induction course will encourage students to examine their study skills to see if they need modification. Elimination of uneconomic and faulty methods of study is as important as the acquisition of new skills.

Intensive effort should be focused on helping the new entrants to cope productively with independent study periods. The aim of the induction course is to present a challenge which is constructive in nature and isolates the main themes; thereby increasing the likelihood of the student making an energetic and successful start in his sixth-form studies.

3. *The reasons for failure in the sixth-form*

It is important that the points also indicate the methods of coping with them. The link with the reasons for failure in higher education should be underlined, helping the student to see the relation of his current learning to eventual success or failure.

4. *Responsibility to the school*

Although many sixth-form students view the prefect role with coolness, if not with active distaste, they are, on the whole, still ready to accept responsibilities that they consider appropriate to their age and status as senior members of the school. Many schools find their sixth-form students ready to assume responsibility for such activities as:

helping remedial pupils;
taking charge of certain out-of-school activities and clubs
supporting individual pupils in need of help
helping in pastoral activities with younger age groups
participating in guidance programmes for the fifth year concerned with study skills, examination anxieties and preparation for examinations.

The way the sixth form make their contribution to the life of the school may be less important than the fact that the opportunity is present, because this allows the sixth-form to be integrated into the life of the school, without preventing younger pupils from achieving positions of responsibility and leadership. Indeed, the strategy indicated allows the sixth-form to foster these qualities in pupils.

It is unrealistic to ignore the requirements of the sixth-form student who is not as academically successful as some of his fellows. Positive discrimination, to meet the needs of a sub-group, is not the same as treating them as inferior, for to ignore their needs is to guarantee minimal development. It is, however, important not to undervalue the new type of student.

Some of these sixth-form students are, in popular language, late developers—something that is costly to those who experience it. Such students can be clumsily assertive, a state due to their attempt to compensate for inadequacy felt in the past and not discarded, together with a readiness to assume that their academic age-mates and teachers look down on them.

Many are in a state of tension which springs from internal conflict. Their self-respect is low, causing them not only to doubt themselves, but to suspect the motives of others. They become unduly sensitive to signals of devaluation which they must refute, often perceiving such signals where they do not exist. A student who reacts in this way is, unconsciously, reacting to a discrepancy between his actual and ideal selves. The former is a source of threat because he is still a relatively inadequate learner, and yet his ideal is academic. It is likely that failure will be his lot, because his learning strategies are inappropriate.

In groups of such students, certain themes stand out which can be dealt with through group counselling and guidance. First, there seems to be an over-valuation of the minimal educational qualifications needed to obtain the employment they desire. This indicates a degree of personal immaturity that needs kind but firm guidance. Let me make it clear that most less academic students have realistic goals and appreciate their sixth-form experience as a means of reaching these goals. The problem arises when the student sees membership of the sixth-form as an end in intself, rather than as a means to a future goal. Such pupils can be helped through programmes of group counselling which have a strong vocational element coupled with an equally strong behavioural one. The vocational element will help them realistically assess their aptitudes, relating these to the world of work, at the same time emphasising job satisfaction which matches their personality. The behavioural element is based on approaches such as those of Krumboltz and Thoresen (1969), which attempt to tailor the situation to fit individual's needs. The tutor responsible for these groups will work out programmes providing the participants with better study skills, extending their social competence and powers of communication, and increasing their sense of control over events.

A programme for personal development in the sixth-form

Pupils, and for that matter their teachers too, often regard general-studies periods with mild dislike as something which has to be endured. Many students see these periods as contributing little of either present or future value for them. But the survey by King *et al.* stressed this age group's declared need for personal development, and this can be done through general-studies courses if they are reshaped.

Such courses offer the teacher a way of exploring issues that concern anyone who wishes to understand himself and the world around him. Far from being divorced from the other work of the sixth-form, the sessions enable the teacher to show what the factual content of his subject contributes to other areas of life.

Sixth-form tutors will obviously wish to work out the precise objectives of such a programme for themselves. A starting point for discussion and experiment is given below.

POSSIBLE OBJECTIVES FOR THE PROGRAMME

1. To encourage students to make more realistic assessments of their behaviour and to judge others less impulsively.
2. To make it possible for students to examine how they manage their tensions and to assess the viability of their methods of problem-solving.
3. To aid the development of autonomy, by helping the student recognize how he calls out other people's responses towards him, coupled with awareness of his motivation when he either attacks or supports other people.
4. To reinforce the habits of offering support to others and of co-operating in the solution of problems.

One outcome of such a programme may be an increase in co-operation and support amongst the students, without eliminating competition, which can co-exist with it. It seems to me that individuals perform best in a social climate of acceptance and support in which the whole group is striving to achieve, but in which the "winner take all" idea has been dismissed as puerile.

1. *Factors which influence the quality of learning*
   (a) The danger of closing one's mind by making immediate decisions about the nature of a problem. This could be contrasted with learning to form a tentative hypothesis, and then to search for confirmatory and contradictory evidence.
   (b) Examination of our beliefs about causality and the way this influences our approach to problems. This could lead to an examination of our ideas about the nature of truth—do we see it as absolute and immutable or as conditional, propositional and relative?
   (c) Examination of our reaction to stress and challenge in learning situations. Do we actively search out solutions, realizing that a number of answers and strategies exist, or do we tend react by avoidance or taking the course which involves least effort?
   (d) Consideration of what motivates us to work. Is this based upon external rewards or upon living up to an ideal which we have developed for ourselves?

2. *The importance of the self-concept*
   (a) The importance of our self-pictures in shaping our behaviour. The kind of self which we try to present to others.
   (b) Coping with the discrepancy between our ideal self and the self that we see ourselves to be.
   (c) Constructively dealing with the feeling that others are imposing on us an alien self-image through their expectations and sanctions.
   (d) Recognition of the link between our concept of ourselves and choosing a career likely to embody a satisfying lifestyle.
   (e) Understanding the link between a low level of self-respect and unsatisfactory relationships with other people.
   (f) Moving from a negative position to being clear about our strengths and making a commitment to some purpose in life.

3. *Interpersonal perception and the judgement of others*
   (a) Personal needs and their influence upon our judgements.
   (b) The process of attribution by which we interpret the motives of others. Examination of this process which is essentially one of inference.
   (c) Assumed or real similarities and differences between ourselves and others.
   (d) The factors which cause like or dislike of others. What lies behind the reaction?
   (e) The link between our picture of ourselves and the judgements we make about other people.

4. *Authority and leadership*
   (a) The nature of leadership. Is it a personality quality or does it relate to particular situations?
   (b) The relationship between leader and followers. Is there an exchange process at work? What power is held by the followers?
   (c) What types of leadership exist?
   (d) Examination of the nature of authority. What gives those in authority legitimate power?
   (e) Under what conditions have we the right to repudiate authority?

5. *Attitudes—their nature and function*
   (a) Why do we hold attitudes? What function do attitudes serve?
   (b) How do we acquire important attitudes?
   (c) The constructive or defensive nature and uses of attitudes.
   (d) Changing our attitudes. Group influences which prevent or facilitate change.
   (e) Prejudice.
   (f) Attitudes, labelling processes and the allocation of reputations to groups of people.

6. *Social anxiety*
   (a) Discussion of social anxieties associated with interaction with:
       strangers;
       those with whom we are close.
   (b) The source of social anxiety. Is it mainly derived from:
       the bodily self;
       the inner self.

(c) Evaluation of the situations in which social anxiety is most frequent:
unfamiliar situations;
situations in which we are in the limelight;
situations in which we feel we are being evaluated;
situations where people of our own age group are important;
situations where older people occupy the main roles.

7. *The concept of self-fulfilment*
   (a) Our model of the nature of man:
   man as a reactive being dependent upon external rewards and punishments;
   man as a being determined by forces beyond his control;
   man as a being in control of his own destiny.
   (b) The degree to which each of us is able to construct his or her own social reality. The importance of our predictions. Making self-fulfilling prophecies which shape what happens to us.
   (c) The problem of determination contrasted with development. The conditions which lead to development.
   (d) The ambiguities and lack of intellectual rigour in some popular conceptions of self-fulfilment.
   (e) The relationship between self-fulfilment and the needs of others.
   (f) Self-produced factors which stunt our personal development.

8. *Behaviour in groups*
   (a) Examination of the expectations we habitually bring to group situations. Their impact on our group behaviour.
   (b) The processes of making a role within the group: allocating roles to others, including that of a scapegoat; taking a role—what lies behind the roles we take?
   (c) Defining the various sources of power within a group.
   (d) Bargaining and negotiation in various groups including the tutorial. This looks at the allocation of identities and reputations; the nature of personal attraction; and the mechanisms of pairing up against others or forming coalitions.
   (e) Decision-making within groups compared with individual decision-making. How the information used in decision-making is presented within the group; the acceptance or diffusion of responsibility for the decision; and finally, the

relation of the foregoing to the level of risk in group decisions.

(f) Groups and the imposition of an identity. Is there a danger of a norm of mediocrity being unconsciously imposed in some groups?

9. *Decision-making in the sixth-form*

(a) Examination of the kind of decisions which have to be made in the sixth form. The values which underlie our decisions. Expediency, long-term consequences, and our sense of obligation, both to ourselves and others, as factors in our decision-making.

(b) The nature of moral judgement in the mature person. The importance of internalized standards: exploring the difference between infantile and adult forms of internalized control. Conditioning versus rationality. The factors influencing us: the need for affiliation and approval; matching our behaviour with our ideal self; prudentiality; the consequences to others.

(c) Career choice. Investigation of the life style attached to a career which would satisfy the individual. The link between the self-concept and the occupational self in a particular career. Investment of time and working out the routes available to us in reaching our goals.

10. *Behaviour linked with active achievement*

(a) Beliefs about luck versus persistence and the analysis and development of the necessary skills.

(b) The ability to set clear short-term targets and organize one's work.

(c) Analysis and understanding of one's learning style and taking measures to make it more productive.

(d) The development of key skills.

A final stage of this programme will be to prepare for higher education, paying attention to the simple problems of budgeting, accommodation, relationships with tutors and the life style of a student: often not anticipated by those entering higher education and therefore a source of strain. This stage should also include discussion of the desirability of a gap between school and higher education. Many students who have experienced such a gap see it as helpful. Such discussions will, of course, merely present the issue to students as a matter for personal decision.

135

REFERENCES

Atkinson, J. and Feather, N. (1966) *A Theory of Achievement Motivation*, New York: Wiley.

Bailey, R. (1972) *Factors Influencing Choice of Subjects at Advanced Level and Factors which Influence Choice of Course at University*, Unpublished D.S.C. Dissertation, University College of Swansea.

Bales, R. (1970) *Personality and Interpersonal Behaviour*, New York: Holt, Rinehart and Winston.

Birney, R., Burdick, H. and Teevan, R. (1969) *Fear of Failure Motivation*, New York: Wiley.

Buckton, A. (1971) *Problems of Sixth Formers and their Implications for a Counsellor*, Unpublished D.S.C. Dissertation, University College of Swansea.

Elkind, D. (1970) *Children and Adolescents*, New York: Oxford University Press.

Erikson, E. (1968) *Identity, Youth and Crisis*, London: Faber & Faber.

Fogelman, K. (1972) *Leaving the Sixth Form*, Slough: N.F.E.R.

James, W. and Rotter, J. (1958) Partial and 100% reinforcement under chance and skill conditions, *Journal of Experimental Psychology*, Vol. 55, pp. 397–403.

Keniston, K. (1972) In: Cottle, T. (Ed.) *The Prospect of Youth*, Boston: Little, Brown and Company.

King, E., Moor, C. and Mundy, J. (1974) *Post-Compulsory Education: A New Analysis of Western Europe*, London: Sage.

King, E., Moor, C. and Mundy, J. (1975) *Post-Compulsory Education II: The Way Ahead*, London: Sage.

Kohlberg, L. (1969) In: Goslin, D. (Ed.) *Handbook of Socialization Theory and Practice*, Chicago: Rand McNally.

Krumboltz, J. and Thoresen, C. (1969) *Behavioural Counseling*, New York: Holt, Rinehart and Winston.

Newberry, S. (1974) *The Difficulties of Adjustment for Girls in the First Year of the Sixth Form*. Unpublished D.S.C. Dissertation, University College of Swansea.

Newsome, A., Thorne, B. and Wyld, K. (1973) *Student Counselling in Practice*, London: University of London Press.

O'Brien, C. (1972) *The Suspecting Glance*, London: Faber & Faber.

Rotter, J. (1966) *Generalized Expectancies for Internal versus External*

Control of Reinforcement, Psychological Monographs, Vol. 80, No. 1, Whole No. 609.

Swift, B. (1973) Job Orientations and the Transition from School to Work. *British Journal of Guidance and Counselling*, Vol. 1, pp. 62–78.

Taylor, P., Reid, W. and Holley, B. (1974) *The English Sixth Form*, London: Routledge & Kegan Paul.

Wankowski, J. (1973) *Temperament, Motivation and Academic Achievement*, Birmingham: University of Birmingham Educational Survey.

Weiner, B. (1974) *Achievement Motivation and Attribution Theory*, Morristown, New Jersey: General Learning Press.

Wheeler, H. (1974) *The Career Aspirations of Able Girls*, Unpublished D.S.C. Dissertation, University College of Swansea.

White, R. (1959) Motivation reconsidered: The concept of competence, *Psychological Review*, Vol. 66, pp. 297–333.

CHAPTER FIVE: KEY POINTS

THE TASKS OF THE PASTORAL SYSTEM

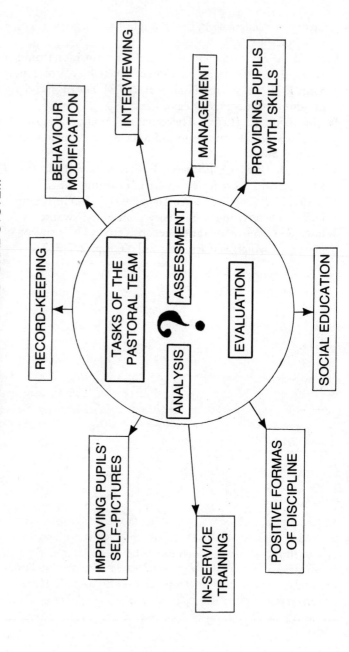

THE BASICS OF PASTORAL CARE AND GUIDANCE

Summary

THE CENTRAL ARGUMENT

One salient element of this complex chapter is that evaluation is to be welcomed by the pastoral team rather than avoided. It is argued that the pastoral team should take measures to assess the success or failure of activities an integral part of the system. The need to understand the conflicting definitions of the learning situation emanating from pupils and teachers, is underlined heavily. The relationship of these latent processes to the development of the identity as a learner and as a pupil is also given prominence.

TECHNIQUES

Techniques are given careful attention, although with reference to the writer's earlier work to avoid replication. Especial attention is paid to the adaptation of methods of behavioural modification to the secondary school. Realism and economy in the employment of such methods come to the forefront of the discussion. There is heavy endorsement of the importance of all members of the pastoral team's acquiring the skill of rapid and accurate assessment of situations, in which due respect is paid to the context of an incident. Much behaviour cannot be comprehended accurately if the context is not taken into account.

The need for every age and ability group to receive appropriate forms of social education is stressed, as is the involvement of the pastoral team in this provision. Social education is not the prerogative of the less able or disadvantaged. There is an examination of the tendency for social education to become a ritual and meaningless activity, a palliative which operates to drain off tensions or an attempt to compensate for the defects of the family or neighbourhood. Suggestions are made for the development of a skills-based approach to social education. This moves from self-exploration and the positive presentation of oneself in daily life to involvement with the community. This simple concentric approach should be applied to each age level and assume increasingly complex forms in the upper part of the school.

RECORD CARDS

Disquiet is voiced about some record cards currently in use. These seem to incorporate static, trait conceptions of personality which deny the facts of adolescent development and change. Record cards which reinforce or even create self-fulfilling prophecies handicap the pastoral endeavour. If they fail to give due weight to the situational and temporary elements in behaviour, they are misleading. Suggestions are made for the development of record cards which isolate key situations for learning and the maintenance of order.

The pastoral concept

During the next decade education in general, and the comprehensive school in particular, is likely to undergo prolonged and critical scrutiny, concerned with how effectively the institution achieves its basic tasks and deploys its resources. We should welcome the experience, for it can result in the elimination of inefficiency and an increased level of professionalism.

How will pastoral care be affected? A pastoral effort which does not seek actively to provide pupils with the skills they need for success will, in practice, reinforce the position and failure of those pupils currently described as disadvantaged. Good intentions, unaccompanied by clear objectives and well-thought-out methods of guidance, are unlikely to change the behaviour of difficult or disruptive pupils or to solve such problems as truancy. We must learn to use methods which lead to positive transactions between teacher and taught and which encourage a climate in which under-functioning is less likely. It is essential to make a realistic assessment of the pupil's needs and the reasons for his behaviour, develop a long-term programme of guidance which anticipates situations, and foster a team effort which is carefully co-ordinated and controlled. How can this be done?

The major weakness in the pastoral system often stems from the fact that form tutors have not had the training which allows them to detect and deal with the first signs of stress and difficulty. Obviously, there cannot be accountability when form tutors do not know what they are expected to do, and it is unreasonable to expect the inexperienced teacher to be able to give adequate pastoral help to his form. In schools where the form teachers are not performing their pastoral roles efficiently, I have found that there is often a defect in management relating to the year head or head of house, who do not have clear responsibilities for the regular training of their form tutors or for organizing the development of materials for pastoral periods. Training is most effective when provided by those in constant contact with the tutors who actually do the work, and who themselves are involved with the pupils.

Obviously efficacious action will not occur when the form tutor misinterprets the recommendations of the year or house head because he has not fully comprehended them. It may be the starting point for further problems of communication between the two: the form tutor resisting suggestions, anticipating that they will fail; the year head feeling threatened by lack of results, and reacting by questioning the tutor's interest in his work and concern for pupils.

The senior management of the school must accept their responsibility for creating the conditions where mutual understanding is inadequate. The heads of years or house must be given every chance of correcting tutors' misconceptions and providing them with the skills they need for work with the form groups.

The wise form tutor will rely as little as possible upon formal interviews, reserving them for the occasions where the implicit subordination and ceremonial have some purpose, or for the pupil who has asked if he can talk about something that is worrying him. It

141

is the ten minutes discussion, repeated at intervals during the year according to the pupil's need and mood, that is most useful in modifying behaviour. Moreover, the informal situation is less likely to contain cues which arouse socially desirable responses, when the pupil gives the answers that he thinks we want to hear. Holt (1964) amusingly shows how pupils learn the teacher's communication style and the use they then make of this to produce counterfeit rather than real learning. Exactly the same processes, bringing similar outcomes, are activated by clumsy interventions by the teacher in pastoral interaction. A form tutor who cannot face honestly the fact that he avidly questions pupils, has only himself to blame if at the end he is forced to realize that he still does not understand the problem. It is easy to forget that it is acutely uncomfortable for the pupil to be probed, and the tutor should not be surprised if pupils later seem reluctant to approach him with problems. It may be helpful to underline the fact that the assessment process in pastoral care is a two-way one: we are the object of a critical gaze as searching as that which we fasten on the pupil; and he passes his evaluation on to his friends. In the past, I have found it important to point out to teachers in their first year the need to take special care with the first pupil who asks them for help.

Good pastoral work like good academic work is based upon an open style of thinking which allows one to formulate tentative hypotheses before proceeding to validate them as the evidence emerges. The tutor who seeks a quick solution and therefore thinks in terms of "the problem" rather than the relationship between a particular version of a problem and the individual in question, is liable to be working with something he has invented rather than the real-life pupil. Closed minds create futility, and our actions tell the observer more about us than those whom we claim we are helping.

Excellent descriptions of the work of the form tutor are given by Marland (1974) and Blackburn (1975); and for basic techniques the reader may consult Hamblin (1974). Here the objective is to examine the factors which facilitate or prevent attainment of our goals and to introduce additional ways of working which are especially appropriate for the form tutor.

The principles of the early detection of pupils at risk, and of anticipating difficulties rather than letting them reach a stage of crisis, would be endorsed by most of us as major components of the general aims of the pastoral system. But how do we achieve this state of affairs? Tutors should be trained to observe pupils' behaviour patterns and then interpret their significance. But this is not so easy in practice. It is a commonplace that different types of behaviour have the same roots: hence low self-esteem will manifest itself in one pupil by avoidance and shyness, in another by arrogance and bravado. Therefore if we search for the causes of behaviour, the likelihood of error is seen to be high. How, then, can the form tutor assess the significance of behaviour?

It may be more profitable to focus our attention on the outcomes and pay-offs of behaviour, rather than searching for causes, for this is a chancy process which probably reflects our implicit ideas about personality, rather than what is actually motivating the pupil. This has led me to present a framework for the functional analysis of behaviour based on the fundamentals of behaviour modification. Obviously the age and ability of pupils will determine the application of this approach. Older and more intelligent individuals will benefit from exploring the reasons for their behaviour, although understanding does not automatically guarantee modification. The world contains many people who have understood why they do things of which they disapprove, yet continue to do them, suffering guilt and anxiety as a result.

Anything from the past still operating in a person's life will display itself in his current behaviour, especially when he is under stress, interacting in a group, or confronted by an unfamiliar situation. He brings sets of expectations which he proceeds to confirm and employs habitual methods of coping, whether or not these are relevant. The tutor, therefore, must be trained to observe behaviour carefully and record observations systematically. His observations will necessarily be limited, and will need to be integrated with information from his colleagues, although this should be about behaviour in defined situations and not statements of presumed motives. Why, for instance, is a pupil a nuisance with one teacher and not with others, or why does he perform well in certain situations and badly elsewhere?

The pastoral system is concerned with positive forms of discipline which aid the pupil's development of autonomy. There can be no caring without control; but concern may involve a tough-minded approach in a pupil's best interests. We will encourage sensible decision-making and initiative in every age group as a means of helping pupils reach autonomy, but to allow grossly egocentric behaviour to continue is different, for it harms other pupils and possibly prevents those pupils from reaching an autonomous state of rational functioning.

The pastoral team have a duty to intervene in such cases. There are pupils who refuse to see that their behaviour is a source of difficulty for themselves and for others. They deny that they have a problem. If a pupil feels the need for change, then it is likely we will be successful, but our responsibility to those who have no appreciation of the need for it cannot be evaded. Some pupils cannot, through immaturity, perceive the links between their own attitudes and behaviour and the reactions of adults and peers about which they complain. We have to make this clear to them, not punitively, yet firmly. Other pupils are aware of the problems which seem to dog their attempts at learning or building good relationships. They dislike this, but not knowing how to begin to find a solution, persist in the non-productive behaviour, often blaming others for their misfortunes. Tutors faced with such a pupil need, as a first step, to present themselves as a source of potential reward rather than blame, although praise must be realistic. Only after analysing the behaviour should they attempt to intervene actively by working out strategies for change with the pupil. Realism demands that the tutor has a systematic plan which begins by presenting small tasks at which the pupil is likely to be successful, and which moves on to more difficult ones as the pupil is ready. To do this the involvement of subject teachers is critical. The approach should be part of a carefully co-ordinated plan consistently applied at all levels.

Time is necessary for this conception of the pastoral system to have an impact on educational attainment, largely because tutors and heads of year or house have to acquire skills. We are failing to equip pupils with the means of dealing with negative influences: rarely are they taught how to deal with "dares" and negative labelling as "yellow" or "chicken". Let the reader ask himself what he has done to help a marginal truant cope with an invitation to truant from a bigger or older boy.

Anticipation is a vital skill for the form tutor. It takes many forms, but essentially it requires the tutor to develop a style of thought which automatically directs his attention to the social context in which the changes he is helping to induce will take place. We must always look beyond the pupil's immediate behaviour to assess the reactions of those likely to be affected by it, a "ripple effect" in fact. The concept of interaction means that behaviour is reciprocal. Thus if a person changes, those with whom he interacts have to adapt to

144

that change. The most important reactions come from his friends: they may respond in a supportive manner; they may be hostile to the development, attempting to coerce him back to his earlier behaviour by labelling him as a "creep"; even more subtly, they may show that they doubt the reality of the change, thereby undermining his confidence and strengthening any doubts he holds about his capacity to succeed.

The tutor's appreciation of the importance of anticipation is expressed through talking to the pupil about the likelihood that he will meet these reactions wihtout condemning his friends or giving the impression that his new behaviour will inevitably alienate him from them. He will need simple and practical ideas for coping with the situation: I use simple diagrams and decision-making exercises to provide the pupil with the necessary skills. The "ripple effect" can of course, be good as well as bad. If other pupils see one or two of their number beginning to attain success, this may encourage them. Indeed, when I worked with difficult classes in dockland, I deliberately worked with the opinion leaders first, to stimulate the desire for achievement in the classmates for whom they acted as models to be emulated. I adopted the appreciative position advocated by Matza, communicating my respect for them and rewarding their strengths in the classroom setting. To have done otherwise would have activated the "us against them" ethos which was particularly strong in their sub-culture. None of this meant that I abandoned my standards of excellence; only that I had to express these values in a way adapted to their basic orientation to authority. Perhaps this shows how the "ripple effect" can be positive when we select the opinion leaders of the class as targets for positive help.

It would be cowardly to evade the fact that anticipation of barriers to change in pupils includes the assessment of colleagues' reactions. It is frustrating when a pupil who is honestly trying to improve seems to meet a barrage of negative signals from a particular teacher. The most that we can do is to encourage the pupil to continue his efforts and suggest ways in which he can convince that teacher of his sincerity. Structural measures are necessary if these situations are to be dealt with. The pastoral care conference may help when it gives the teacher concerned the chance to hear favourable reports of the pupil from his colleagues, although even then he may resolutely refuse to modify his attitude. The long-term solution comes from the introduction of an in-service training programme, where the folly of this behaviour is made apparent to such teachers, although one may question their ability to relate it to their own classroom interaction with pupils. The professional problem posed by such teachers who ought not to be in the profession is one to which we seem to have no answer at present.

The underlying processes within the classroom

Formulation of clear objectives for the pastoral system is a necessary step in enabling it to contribute actively to the raising of educational and behavioural standards, but specification of objectives will not guarantee that the desired result is reached. If it is to be a means of overcoming the effects of deprivation and of compensating for cultural disadvantage; if it is to be an effective agent of socialization, in the fullest sense of the term, then the pastoral team must invest considerable effort in the task of understanding and harnessing the subterranean life of the classroom, and of the informal groupings amongst pupils which are as significant as those formally imposed upon them. One must realize that a masked conflict of interests exists, only manifested sporadically, which I have called psychological truancy, although we often seem unaware of the significance of the minimal effort which accompanies it.

Any reader who wishes to comprehend the nature of these underlying classroom processes should consult the excellent work by Bellack *et al.* (1966), Boocock (1972) and Hargreaves (1972 and 1975). One point that must be considered is the way we fail to face squarely the fact that the theme of *trust versus suspicion* runs throughout classroom life. Jackson (1968) has stressed that three basic messages are transmitted to pupils in the classroom: that they must learn to live in a crowd; that they must realize that they are under constant evaluation; and that they accept the power of the teacher. Yet these are not conditions which should necessarily produce the distrust, conflict and sense of alienation that concern us.

Clearly, the same demands can be expressed in ways which either convey respect for those to whom they are addressed or evoke resentment. The team can analyse this fairly straightforwardly, although effort is needed to implement changes, for pupil reaction will savour of the response, "What are they up to now?" It is possible to see a link between teaching methods and the underlying attitudes which lead to disaffiliation from classroom purposes and occasionally to disruptive behaviour; for the more passive the teacher's methods, the more discrepant they are from the form of learning meaningful to many who come from a poor verbal culture. They deny such pupils the conditions in which they can begin to use language as a tool for understanding the world and controlling themselves, and prevent them from developing mature styles of thinking. This central factor of inappropriate teaching method is one which seems to lead to the state of suspicion that is the hallmark of many classrooms is further reinforced by the feelings of some pupils that the work they undertake in the classroom is irrelevant to their future lives. The desire to "get a good job" is a basic desire for most pupils, which, as Enquiry One (1968) showed, is a perception of the purpose of education held by their parents.

As the group of tutors begins to explore the less obvious aspects of their pupils' response to the classroom, they may find that not only are the tasks met in the classroom of doubtful significance to the pupil, but, equally crucially, the rewards for learning have unsuspected associations. Hargreaves (1967) made the point that for pupils in certain classes the teacher's approval was the equivalent of a punishment, for it cost him the regard of his peers. It seems that we need to examine in some detail the costs of the role of the good pupil. Ostensible punishments such as caning and suspension may carry the more valuable rewards of confirmation of toughness, and as someone prepared to challenge the system. Rewards offered by those who define your position in a way which violates your own conception of autonomy are, in any case, scarcely likely to be acceptable.

Nothing that has been said should be taken as a plea for the lowering of teaching standards; indeed such an analysis calls attention to the need for better preparation, a wide range of activities and materials, and more efficient techniques of classroom management. The importance of order is treated by Nash (1974). He found that pupils believe that the teacher has an obligation to keep order. Sumner and Warburton (1972) undertook as part of their research the comparison of extreme groups, of industrious pupils and of those allergic to school. The latter's responses indicated that they see order and control as necessary for learning, although they are ready to exploit its absence. They believe that it is their teachers' responsibility to make them work and establish discipline. From the viewpoint of the educationist, such undue reliance upon external controls is regrettable and represents a failure on the school's part.

The pastoral team should focus on the meanings of the behaviour they observe, paying due regard to the subjective elements which shape both teachers' and pupils' actions. If this method of analysis is applied to specific incidents either frequent or serious in their consequences, then much can be done to modify the underlying processes which shape pupils' reactions in the classroom.

A piecemeal technique of this kind may, at first sight, be unattractive because it lacks precision, but as the year head and his tutors gain experience and the ability to share their perceptions, they can begin to construct a coherent picture of the dynamics within the classroom which impede learning, and so construct strategies for modifying them. At a mundane level, the structured investigation of incidents, using the framework set out below, is not without its merits, for it allows the energy often dissipated in blame-pinning to be used to increase our powers of prevention. Too frequently, the causes of an incident remain unmodified, so that when we relax vigilance we often find it repeated. The interested reader will find the scholarly work by Deutsch (1973), on conflict and its resolution, stimulating reading.

AN ELEMENTARY FRAMEWORK FOR THE
ANALYSIS OF SPECIFIC INCIDENTS

---

1. A careful assessment of the relevant characteristics of those involved, the pastoral team taking care to avoid premature categorization as aggressive or inadequate.
2. Evaluation of the participants' beliefs about the nature of the situation, followed by investigation of their justification for their behaviour, remembering that justification may differ with the audience.
3. Consideration of the relationships between the participants prior to the incident. A key factor will be their beliefs and expectations about each other. The subjective element in the beliefs of each actor about the person's view of him seems a central factor in understanding the significance of the incident.
4. The issue around which the incident seems to centre needs to be examined very carefully: does it, for example, involve a challenge to the teacher's authority or an attack on the pupil's self-respect? The reality of these things is immaterial, it is the belief that it was present that is important.

5. Any assessment of an incident which does not include the audience is likely to result in distortion of the analysis.
6. A comparison of the intended and actual outcomes of the incident for the participants and for other interested parties completes this elementary frame of analysis. The pastoral team will have to establish the gains and losses for each party, considering the effects on their reputations and the likely consequences for future relationships between them.

This schedule has the merit of simplicity; yet its consistent application by a number of tutors to key incidents in each year group, followed by detailed discussion of the implications of the findings, will contribute to the awareness of processes which facilitate or impede instructional activities.

A group of tutors operating in this way is applying to their daily tasks the basic tenets of the social psychology of interpersonal perception. They are realistically adapting to the fact that each person who interacts with another does so in terms of his perceptions or cognitions of that other, whether or not these correspond to reality. They will realize that the interactional system of the classroom generates new motives which can either go against our basic endeavour or reinforce it. We must not lose sight of the fact that motives are learned as well as innate.

A positive response to learning and new techniques is only likely when the barriers and hazards emanating from these essentially subjective elements of classroom transactions have been recognized, taken into account and then modified by the teacher. In a recent discussion of classroom observation Walker and Adelman (1972:1975) demonstrate that it is hard to make sense of verbal communications in the classroom without information about their specific context. Meanings are therefore context-bound, particularly in the case of those pupils from backgrounds which stunt their language skills, who often respond to the general setting and its associations, rather than the precise verbal content of the teacher's statements.

Such pupils see no need, nor have the skill, to code their messages to meet the other person's viewpoint. It is the teacher who has to learn to code his messages with sensitivity to their impact on his pupils, as a preliminary step in modifying their reactions to the learning situation, opening the way to more constructive relationships. The pastoral team can lead the way in this: for otherwise

149

their claim to be concerned with raising the standard of performance is a hollow one.

The self-concept

In a discussion of the teacher's role as a counsellor, Hamblin (1974) gives a model of the major aspects of the student's role which the effective school tries to enhance. These are:

the student's self-image, or the way he perceives and evaluates himself;

the student's level of aspiration, which involves a desire for excellence and a sense of personal power;

the student's social skills, including those of perception as well as action;

the student's academic achievement.

Everything in the school, from the organization of the curriculum to the rules about entry to classrooms, contains positive or negative messages about pupils' identities. A positive self-concept is the foundation for responsible behaviour, and therefore the pastoral team must always ask themselves what definitions of the pupil's selves emerge from the procedures and routines of the school. Marland (1974) helpfully draws our attention to Wall's (1948) description of the philosophical, social, sexual and vocational selves which begin to develop during adolescence as determinants of behaviour. The present writer would like to stress two things often neglected by the pastoral team: first, the importance of the body image as the source of many difficulties, some of which may be expressed by disruptive behaviour; and second, the importance of the concept of the self as a learner.

Many of our most difficult pupils come from sub-cultures where the physique is important, its importance being mainly expressed in terms of toughness and of stereotyped ideas of masculinity. For fuller information the reader should consult Conger (1973) or Wenar (1971). But the form tutor should understand that hormonal and bodily changes of the pre-pubertal growth spurt and of early adolescence can increase self-doubts and emotionality, leading to exaggerated responses to environmental stress.

The late-maturing boy or girl may present problems in school, both sexes showing signs of tension and maladjustment. The age range for the commencement of physical puberty is wider than we think. The origins of the problems which do occur lie not so much in the pupil's physical condition as in the psychological and social concomitants, especially the reactions of parents and the pupil's age group. The mother of the late-maturing pupil may become over-anxious or unduly protective. Boys who reach puberty later than most of their peers tend to have developed restless and clumsily assertive behaviour or undue dependence upon adults, either of which can earn them the dislike of both teachers and peers. My work with such pupils suggests that underneath are feelings of inadequacy, negative self-images, fears of rejection, or of being dominated which brings them into conflict with both parents and teachers. On occasions they find themselves at odds with the law as a result of their impetuous coping strategies.

The lot of both sexes in relation to the body-image in adolescence can be an unhappy one. Boys tend to dislike being too short; the tall girl feels that her height makes her unpleasantly conspicuous in a group. Fears and problems centred around sexuality are still strong in the present-day adolescent, and anxieties about the practice of masturbation are far from eliminated, such guilt not solely being the prerogative of boys. Individual help is needed, for many pupils cannot discuss these matters in a group, and for this they must trust the person in whom they confide and believe in his or her capacity for understanding.

The pastoral team needs to take the pupil's reaction to his or her bodily development into account in assessing the reasons for prob-lematical behaviour. We notice the obese boy or girl who may feel ashamed of the condition, but we may not be so aware of others who may perceive their bodies almost entirely negatively, focusing on their unbecoming features alone and exaggerating their importance. Such unhappiness, often quite acute, remains undealt with, and only when there is a crisis does it filter into our perception. It is disturbing that we have not learned to deal with the problems posed for some girls by their physical development. The hormonal changes which precede the first menstruation can lead to irritability and fatigue; yet we merely react to the behaviour by exhortation or blame, without giving thought to its origins. The tension experienced by some girls during the immediate premenstrual period may be compounded by the anxiety associated with taking an examination and we have no solution for the resulting unfairness.

The importance of the pupil's concept of himself as a learner and the potency of his predictions in shaping his behaviour have already been stressed. The form tutor should take this into account in assessing the pupil's needs.

The desirability of facilitating the development of self-awareness and providing the means of self-assessment is beginning to percolate into our schools, especially through current approaches to careers education. Hopson (1973) provides the teacher with a very useful guide to methods. Consider the dilemma of the boy whose traditional sexual self sharply separates what he considers man's from woman's work. Then, for reasons of aptitude or economic necessity, he finds himself moving towards a career in catering or hotels which in some ways he considers feminine or servile. Equally, the girl with a desire to take up a career in engineering or surveying may find that her friends and parents hold occupational stereotypes which arouse tension between her choice of career and the concept of femininity which is also important to her. These illustrations show the influence of the self-concept in making a satisfying choice of career. I would, however, argue that we need to revise our concept of social education, and involve the whole pastoral team in making a determined and methodical attempt to extend the social and perceptual skills of pupils. Hence the focus of effort is on the third element in Hamblin's (1974) description of the output of the secondary school: the teaching of interpersonal competencies.

Social education

Social education has acquired respectability since the Newsom Report (1963) advocated courses which paid attention to the social aims of education and prepared pupils for life. But the observer cannot help but be uneasy at the way this has been interpreted by some schools. If social education is confined to a limited section of the school population—the less-able statutory-age leavers—then surely there is a curious conception at work, both of the nature of social education and of the pupils who are to benefit from it. In this case social education would reinforce divisiveness within the school, unless it is a long-term and carefully planned part of the school's pastoral activities. Clear objectives are therefore essential, because they allow us to see the directions which such courses are taking and assess their connection with the other aims of the school. Equally, these objectives should be shared with the pupils, allowing them to assess the value and relevance of the enterprise.

At its best, the comprehensive school represents an attempt to create a learning environment in which each pupil can develop his potentialities to the full. Evaluation of what is happening is crucial at a time when social education is developing rapidly. We need to ask whether programmes of social education constructed on an *ad hoc* basis are possibly counter-productive because:

(a) they lack real intellectual content and fail to extend both the thinking and social skills of the pupil;

(b) no systematic analysis of the skills that pupils are intended to acquire was undertaken before the content of the programme was formulated, therefore measures for their development could not be systematically incorporated;

(c) the links between the development of the individual's social and communicative skills, group interaction and his understanding of the community have not been apprehended.

Evaluation of the manner in which social education is carried out in schools leaves one with the strong impression that at the moment there are three basic modes of functioning: the ritual, the palliative and the compensatory. The first two may well be a product of the attempt to devise more relevant courses for pupils in their final year when the leaving age was raised to sixteen. The ritual situation is essentially one of reaction to the thinking of such documents, as the Schools Council Working Papers Nos. 11 and 17 (1967; 1968), or is initiated without real conviction as a response to the suggestions of advisers or inspectors. The purposes of social education are conceived as extremely limited, and the main emphasis is on some form of community service.

In the palliative situation social education programmes are devices to manage tensions during the final year. This evades the uncomfortable task of assessing why so many pupils become disenchanted with schools. Teachers often claim that such social education schemes, which again stress community work, improve relationships with their pupils and build up self-respect in the latter. Yet is it not disconcerting that good relationships can only be established in activities which are only marginally related to the main task of the school?

The compensatory view of education is the most useful of the three, largely because it has clearer and more positive objectives: the modification of negative attitudes and distorted perceptions which create a negative view of school and impede progress; the extension of the repertoires of behaviour available to pupils, thus helping them deal with challenge and stress more constructively; and finally, the inhibition and replacement of responses which bring them into unnecessary trouble. Carefully planned and methodically implemented, this form of social education, far from confirming the position of the disadvantaged, gives them the means for success in school as well as the autonomy for which they crave.

Social education, therefore, should be a co-ordinated activity which commences in the first year and continues until the pupil leaves school, its content and form dictated by the pupil's age and the demands made upon him by school and neighbourhood. The overall objectives of such a programme might well be:

(a) the stimulation of the development of personal values and helping pupils clarify them;

(b) the provision of the skills necessary for achievement, including study skills and the ability to plan ahead;

(c) the development of belief in the need for inner controls and the opportunities to exercise them;

(d) the promotion of a wide range of skills necessary for social competence, ranging from standpoint-taking to the management of stress;

(e) the learning of decision-making skills.

The year head and his form tutors would be responsible for devising the activities, but there must be co-ordination to ensure that each year's work leads on to the next. Within each year it may be useful to take a concentric approach which begins with the individual, moves to the group and then relates what has been discovered to the wider aspects of the community. The sudden growth in a pupil's social relationships during his first year at the comprehensive school, coupled with their growing complexity, could form the basic theme for the individual and group aspects; and the relevance of what has been learned for successful membership of organizations such as the youth club and the changing responsibilities of the adolescent within the family could be stressed. This method reflects the belief expressed by Adorno *et al.* (1950), in their study of the authoritarian personality, that it is only the man who can understand himself who can begin to understand the world around him.

The final term of the first year and the first two terms of the second year are points at which many pupils begin to develop negative attitudes towards themselves as learners, and towards the school and teachers. Here the programme will sharply focus on interaction within the school, the development of study skills and the need to be able to plan and work for long-term goals.

Social education is not moralizing, and the team must use activities based upon situations of immediate concern to the pupils. Problem-solving situations form the core of the programme, employing role-play, decision-making exercises, simulations and games. These methods require careful preparation, good classroom management and clear presentation of the objectives, but the teacher's essential task is to make the underlying principles explicit, helping pupils discover other situations in and outside the school where they can be employed. Transfer of training does not occur by chance, it has to be stimulated. Concern with interpersonal behaviour and the acquisition of skills does not mean that there cannot be a concrete end product, such as a personal portfolio of work, or a project or a year exhibition, for pupils need evidence that they are learning. The same standards of excellence applied to the more traditional subjects will be relevant to the social programme.

Hamblin (1974) outlines a programme which uses the above principles, involving activities centred around such topics, at the individual level, as:

(a) learning to give a favourable impression of myself;

(b) how I judge other people and how they judge me;

(c) when I feel I am being picked on;

(d) changing my behaviour.

These topics are presented as situations which need solving, and the principles are extracted by the teacher from pupils as they reveal the solutions they have reached. This scheme makes pupils aware of the following processes in a way discussion alone could not:

(a) the way they call out responses from others and are responsible for their behaviour;

(b) the habitual way they cope with making mistakes or losing face;

(c) the costs and consequences of their actions;

(d) the labelling processes in which they themselves indulge and the way they activate this in others;

(e) the level of risk in decisions;

(f) the bargaining strategies they use with peers, parents, and sometimes with their teachers;

(g) the need to understand the viewpoints of other people and the mistakes they can make in this;

(h) coping with the tensions of learning and social interaction;

(i) understanding the way they model themselves on others.

The skills of planning, of setting short-term goals and of breaking a task into methodical steps rather than tackling it haphazardly are all germane to this view of social education. Each can be put into a problematical situation which captures the pupils' interest. Many adolescents lack the skills to cope with conflict and the escalation of confrontation, finding themselves in untenable situations. Such themes as the following are useful in group work:

(a) how do we get· what we want from a group?

(b) the kind of people I like in a group;

(c) responsibilities within a group;

(d) how do we co-operate with other groups?

(e) getting things done within a group.

This list, merely an indication of the type of topic around which activities are centred, involves an appreciation of:

(a) coalitions and other divisions in group situations;

(b) leader–follower relationships;

(c) co-operation and conflict with other groups;

(d) scapegoating and other processes which involve the allocaton of roles and reputations within a group;

(e) maintaining one's own identity within the group;

(f) information-processing and making decisions in a group setting;

(g) the impact of group membership on individual standards and achievement.

The general programme can include exploration of:

(a) destruction of property—one's own and that of others;

(b) testing the limits and the rules of an organization;

(c) being falsely accused;

(d) nervousness about answering questions or doing tests;

(e) personal appearance;

(f) handling money;

(g) failure in homework;

(h) staying away from school;

(i) the body image;

(j) leadership in emergencies;

(k) family situations;

(l) authority relationships;

(m) unfairness.

The methods used in such an activity-based programme may be unfamiliar to some teachers, and therefore a few examples are given below. It is hoped that these elementary examples will encourage the enthusiastic teacher to develop other approaches for himself.

1. *Purpose*
   (a) To draw pupils' attention to the effect of opposition and support on the way they reach a decision.
   (b) To look at the consequences of a decision.

2. *Organization*
   (a) The class spontaneously divides itself into groups of four.
   (b) The pupils should be in the fifth year.

3. *Steps*
   (a) Before the lesson prepare a brief tape-recording of two situations which pose a problem to be resolved. The recording can be made by a pupil of that age group and presented in the first person. Two possible situations are:
   (i) The conflict between the desire to go sailing and to stay indoors and work for examinations four weeks away. The pupil belongs to a sailing club and has made a first-rate contribution in inter-club competitions. Unfortunately, he has fallen behind with his revision because sailing has occupied so much of his time in the past few months. What should he do?
   (ii) The conflict experienced by a boy or girl earning £2.50 a week from his part-time job. His parents only give him 35p a week pocket money *because he has the job*, but all his friends get at least £1.00 a week. What should he do? Should he give up the job, persuade them to give him more, or accept the situation? He feels that this parents are punishing him because he has the job, although they really feel that having too much money is not good for him.
   (b) In each group one pupil takes on the role of this pupil, whilst the others try to prevent him finding a solution or making a decision. The role-acting pupil is required rationally to refute the arguments of those who attempt to oppose him. Fifteen minutes should be allowed for this.
   (c) The second taped situation is then played.
   (d) The pupil who played the role of decision-maker in the first situation has to try to work out a solution, but this time his friends support him as he talks it out. They will pay particular attention to the consequences of his proposed solutions.

158

(e) General discussion then follows.

It should be structured by the teacher to include:

(i) evaluation of the difficulties in making up one's mind when others support or oppose—many pupils often find it easier to come to a decision under opposition, and the probable consequences of decisions made in these circumstances should be explored;

(ii) similar situations in their own lives should be examined, and the influence of friends in making decisions.

(iii) the possibility that the decisions made in one or other of the conditions may be more risky can be explored.

WHAT HAPPENS WHEN A FRIEND INVITES YOU TO TRUANT WITH HIM

1. *Purpose*

(a) To allow discussion and to provide experience of solving constructively a problem often met by a pupil.

(b) To give pupils experience of sharing ideas and evaluating them.

2. *Organization*

(a) The class is divided into small working groups of four pupils.

(b) This activity is intended for second-year pupils.

3. *Steps*

(a) The following statement is duplicated and given to each member, or recorded on tape:

Bill, who travels with Peter on the bus to school, tries to persuade Peter to come with him to the park for the day. Bill has made up his mind to do this, but he wants company. Peter refuses, saying that he wishes to go to school as he enjoys it. His friend then calls him "chicken" and "yellow", and when Peter does not seem to respond to this he says that Peter "is letting him down and showing that he isn't a real friend after all". Peter values Bill's friendship, but is determined to get on in school and not get into trouble. Bill is failing in most of his school work and often stays away, although he has never asked Peter to join him before.

Peter has to decide what to do. He intends to go to school, but he would like to keep Bill's friendship. Can you find a way out for Peter that will give him both things he wants? Perhaps there is also a way of persuading Bill not to truant.

(b) The groups discuss this situation for 10–12 minutes.

(c) The teacher then initiates a brain-storming session. He explains that he wants as many ideas as possible from the class about solutions. Stress that they must not criticise any idea as it is produced. The teacher writes all the ideas up on the board. Allow 5 minutes for this.

(d) The small groups examine the ideas, choosing those that they think are sensible. The discussion lasts about ten minutes.

(e) Groups write down their solutions.

(f) Class discussion of the consequences of various solutions for *both* boys then takes place with a final summary by the teacher.

Transfer of training from these activities to other areas of the pupils' lives must occur if this method of social education is to justify the time and effort. The onus is on the teacher to facilitate the transfer of skills through the way he structures the final discussion and a high degree of skill and classroom management is required of him.

The connection between the underlying processes which shape life in classrooms and the interactional view of social education which has been put forward will be clear to the reader. If the methods advocated are developed thoughtfully and applied consistently, then form tutors will be able to make a real contribution to the effectiveness of the school as a socializing agency. Active affiliation to the school is encouraged because the pupil's sense of power is built up as he acquires the skills of self-management.

Social education is only one tool, albeit an essential one, in our quest for a vital pastoral system. If it is combined with strategies of action which utilize the principles of behavioural theory in ethical and civilized ways, then we may well achieve our end. There is adequate evidence from such writers as Krumboltz and Thoresen (1969), and Thoresen and Mahoney (1974), that behavioural theory provides the means for developing not only self-control, but a satisfying classroom life in which pupil and teacher alike can be more truly themselves without the constraints of habitual patterns of response which bring little or no reward to either.

In this chapter, the emphasis has been on pastoral care as a systematic effort aimed, first, at developing a sense of purpose and direction which springs from the pupil's self-respect, and, second, at providing him with the skills essential for the realization of his objectives in life. In the next few pages it will be argued that the application of the principles of behaviour modification—the qualifications implied by the word "principles" should be noted carefully—will provide the form tutor with tools to facilitate pupils' development and acquisition of competence.

If prejudice closes our minds to this possibility, we ignore the fact that much of our work as teachers is concerned with either inducing certain behaviour which we consider valuable, or, more or less successfully, struggling to eliminate others. Whether we admit it or not, we are engaged already in an attempt to modify behaviour. Reward and punishment play an important part in discipline and classroom interaction, and it should reduce resistance to behavioural theory to see that these two processes are at its centre.

The methods advocated here increase, rather than reduce, the pupil's power to take responsibility for his own behaviour, and his awareness of the way he contributes to what happens to him. Therefore the form tutor and the pupil engage in a partnership, working together to understand the situation, and then working out strategies for changing the pupil's behaviour. Realistic recognition is given to the fact that the pupil is largely responsible for creating his own environmental contingencies, stressing self-determination rather than ignoring it.

The task of the form tutor who uses this kind of behaviour modification is to help the pupil examine his behaviour problems, learning difficulties or failures in relationships, in a way which indicates the specific steps he can take to resolve them. Training in problem-solving forms the core of this type of behavioural guidance. Far from manipulating the adolescent to produce automatic responses, one is actively helping him to understand his contribution to the events which bother him; encouraging him to plan and then implement new ways of behaving which bring him previously unavailable satisfactions.

Three main applications of behaviour modification exist: individual work on problems, where the form tutor or head of year or house puts himself at the pupil's disposal; group work to examine common sources of difficulty in the pastoral periods; and finally, the use of friends as a source of support for one another, as surely friends are potentially more effective than we can ever hope to be. Truancy is a problem for which we are currently seeking a solution. Experiments by Beaumont (1976) and Tumelty (1976) demonstrated that persistent truancy could be overcome by behavioural approaches in which peers played a crucial role. Friends or classmates in one experiment were given minimal training in support; they then provided this in the classroom and playground whilst the erstwhile truants struggled for success in their classwork and their relationships with other pupils. Beaumont's work also illustrates how pupils with similar tendencies can be prevented from reinforcing each other's negative behaviour or strengthening their hostile perceptions of the school and the teachers' intentions.

There can be two forms of behavioural work: individual or special group work with pupils with a severe problem. This is backed by a programme of general group work related to the developmental tasks of adolescence. Peer supports can be mobilized effectively in both categories. The emphasis upon behaviour creates a sense of purpose and allows the formulation of clear objectives for each session; the sharing of ideas and resources can be systematically encouraged so that pupils learn the habit of co-operation; and friends can be trained to help each other attain their self-set targets, encouraging the essential transfer to other situations.

To apply the technique of behaviour modification to our daily pastoral work, we must train ourselves to observe what a pupil *actually* does, rather than making assumptions about it. To do this something like the framework on page 163 could be used.

This elementary framework allows us to assess:

the types of behaviour that the pupil needs to acquire;

those which he will have to reduce in frequency or intensity, if not totally eliminate;

the ways his present types of behaviour can be used more effectively.

There are many pupils who, under the surface, wish to change their behaviour or improve their attainment, and it is only when we show them pragmatically what they can do that they begin to act upon their inner wishes.

A FRAMEWORK FOR THE OBSERVATION OF A PUPIL

1. Ask: in which situations does he tend to behave in the way which produces problems for himself and for others? ⟶ 2. Ask: in which situations does he not behave in his way.

3. COMPARISON OF THESE TWO TYPES OF SITUATION MAY REVEAL THE FACTORS THAT TRIGGER OFF HIS DIFFICULT BEHAVIOUR

4. Ask: is there a pay-off for these two types of behaviour? Does he get his own way or gain the plaudits of his friends? ⟶ 5. Ask: what forces seem to maintain his behaviour?

6. ASSESSMENT OF THESE FACTORS WILL ALLOW ONE TO APPROACH THE PUPIL IN A PRACTICAL WAY

Not only should we learn to observe the pupils, but we may occasionally encourage them to analyse what they themselves are doing, rather than reacting automatically. They may note the number of times they engage in a particular behaviour, or some pupils could keep a diary about their behaviour, feelings and reactions to events and people. This shows that pupils are expected to become actively involved in the effort to change, not merely responsive to the tutor's injunctions and suggestions. Initial results may be sporadic, but as tutors develop the skills and concern is shown, behavioural problems will decrease.

A behavioural method which uses diagrams will tend to yield better results than one which uses verbal reinforcements alone. They isolate steps to learning goals and, perhaps for the first time, the target is made clear to some pupils. To modify successfully his behaviour a pupil must know, first, what he has to do to be successful in that particular area of learning; and second, the signs that he has been successful. The importance of clear objectives, both long term and intermediate, cannot be overstressed.

Diagrams can be used to spell out the alternatives available to the pupil; the costs of different kinds of behaviour in a situation; and the probability of a coping strategy producing the desired results. Tasks should be approached systematically in a way likely to bring success, because they have been arranged in a hierarchy of difficulty.

The examples of diagrams on pages 165 to 170 are varied. They indicate the general approach, but cannot convey how the pastoral worker and the pupil co-operated. The reader may speculate about the particular problems of the pupils with whom the diagrams were involved: in most cases their production is a joint effort of pupil and tutor, rarely, if at all, are they produced by the teacher as the equivalent of a visual aid in a lesson.

We have dealt with the consequences of behaviour, but it is also profitable to pay attention to its antecedents. Pupils who understand what triggers off certain sequences of behaviour ending in punishment or a sense of shame and guilt have made the first step towards the inhibition of such unthinking reactions. To achieve this it is essential to examine a particular incident in depth, preferably a recent one. The procedure might go like this. A fourteen-year-old boy complains that his teachers are picking on him. I listen with courtesy and respect, and then ask, "What do you think *you* could do to stop them picking on you?" Perhaps a glazed expression comes into his eyes at this novel response. I then explained that it is not solely a one-way situation, as the pupil is suggesting. The example is then examined in depth and a strategy worked out to prevent the production of the habitual set of responses. Sometimes, it takes very little stimulation for a pupil to begin on the task by saying, "I've got it—you mean if I didn't do . . .". In more deep-seated situations, of course, behaviour modification will be more difficult.

Diagram 1

COSTS AND CONSEQUENCES

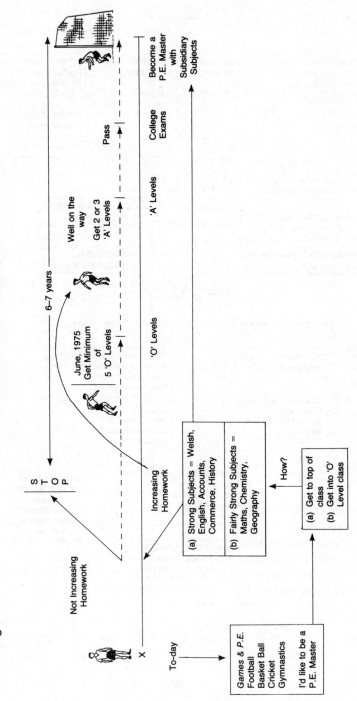

Diagram 2

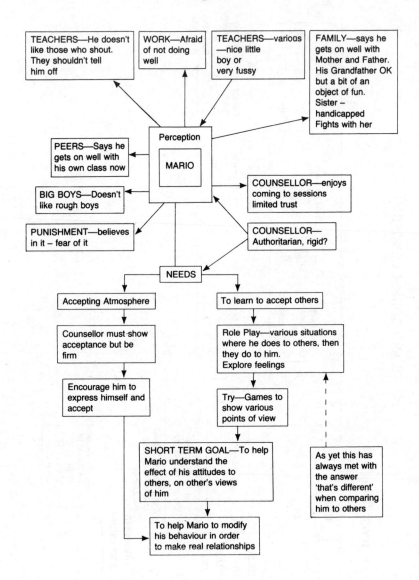

TEACHERS—He doesn't like those who shout. They shouldn't tell him off

WORK—Afraid of not doing well

TEACHERS—various —nice little boy or very fussy

FAMILY—says he gets on well with Mother and Father. His Grandfather OK but a bit of an object of fun. Sister – handicapped Fights with her

Perception

MARIO

PEERS—Says he gets on well with his own class now

BIG BOYS—Doesn't like rough boys

PUNISHMENT—believes in it – fear of it

COUNSELLOR—enjoys coming to sessions limited trust

COUNSELLOR— Authoritarian, rigid?

NEEDS

Accepting Atmosphere

To learn to accept others

Counsellor must show acceptance but be firm

Role Play—various situations where he does to others, then they do to him. Explore feelings

Encourage him to express himself and accept

Try—Games to show various points of view

SHORT TERM GOAL—To help Mario understand the effect of his attitudes to others, on other's views of him

As yet this has always met with the answer 'that's different' when comparing him to others

To help Mario to modify his behaviour in order to make real relationships

Diagram 3

How John feels towards the subjects he takes

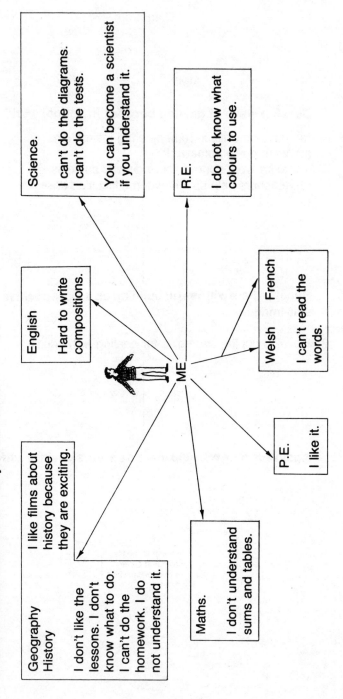

Science.

I can't do the diagrams.
I can't do the tests.

You can become a scientist
if you understand it.

R.E.

I do not know what
colours to use.

English

Hard to write
compositions.

French

I can't read the
words.

Welsh

P.E.

I like it.

ME

Geography
History

I like films about
history because
they are exciting.

I don't like the
lessons. I don't
know what to do.
I can't do the
homework. I do
not understand it.

Maths.

I don't understand
sums and tables.

Diagram 4

AIMS   John.

1. **Develop ways of gaining success in school work**

   (a) develop skills in remembering instructions
   (b) write down homework
   (c) extra work done in more difficult subjects
   (d) teachers help sought when difficulties arise

Success here will help in building up a more positive self-image

2. Develop coping strategies for dealing with adults

Again success will help towards a more positive self-image

Diagram 5

TOWARDS A POSITIVE SELF-IMAGE

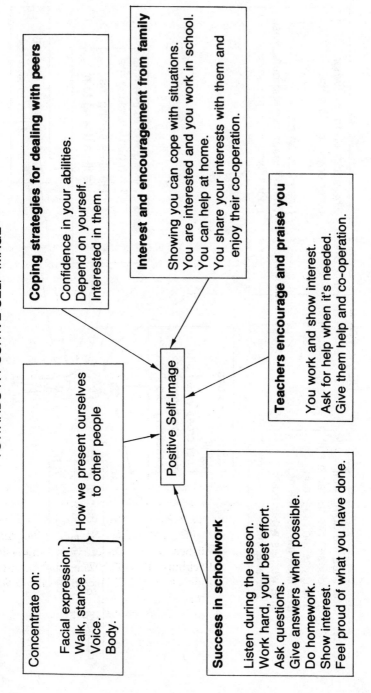

Coping strategies for dealing with peers

Confidence in your abilities.
Depend on yourself.
Interested in them.

Interest and encouragement from family

Showing you can cope with situations.
You are interested and you work in school.
You can help at home.
You share your interests with them and
   enjoy their co-operation.

Concentrate on:

Facial expression. } How we present ourselves
Walk, stance.   to other people
Voice.
Body.

Positive Self-Image

Teachers encourage and praise you

You work and show interest.
Ask for help when it's needed.
Give them help and co-operation.

Success in schoolwork

Listen during the lesson.
Work hard, your best effort.
Ask questions.
Give answers when possible.
Do homework.
Show interest.
Feel proud of what you have done.

Diagram 6

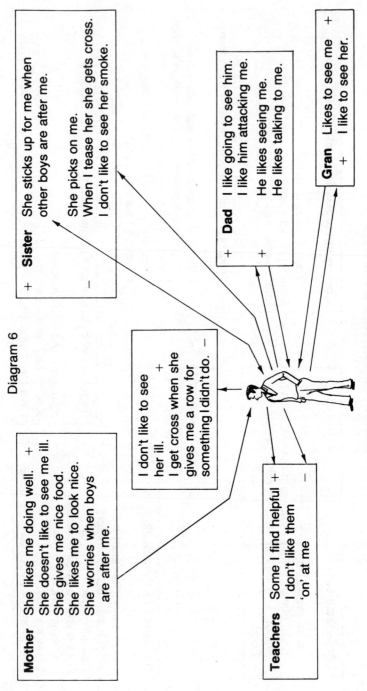

Sister

+ She sticks up for me when other boys are after me.

  She picks on me.
  When I tease her she gets cross.
− I don't like to see her smoke.

Dad I like going to see him.
+ I like him attacking me.
  He likes seeing me.
+ He likes talking to me.

Gran Likes to see me
+ I like to see her.
+

Mother She likes me doing well. +
  She doesn't like to see me ill.
  She gives me nice food.
  She likes me to look nice.
  She worries when boys
  are after me.

I don't like to see
her ill.
+
I get cross when she
gives me a row for
something I didn't do. −

Teachers Some I find helpful +
  I don't like them
  'on' at me −

John's Life Space Diagram

Kelly's (1955) fixed-role therapy is a safe and very practical means of helping pupils. The tutor writes a brief description of someone with similar problems to those of the pupil, asking him to assess how sensible the proposed measures are. The usual response is, "Are you talking about me?" and an honest answer is given. The pupil then either rewrites the description to suit himself or accepts what has been produced by the tutor. The pupil then tries out these kinds of behaviour, it being emphasised that he or she is not committed to them. This reduces the consequences of failure and allows for adaptation. After a few days, other elements are added to the description so that a graduated attack is made on the problem. Thereby introducing into Kelly's useful technique one of the key principles of behaviour modification. One must appreciate the full significance of the element of "make-believe" in preventing anxiety because of the threat of failure.

All this sounds very time-consuming. But it need not be so if the tutor uses the tape-recorder. He can record a brief sketch and then allow the pupil to listen to it on his own. Then together with the tutor, the pupil records his own modified plan of action. This helps pupils stand back from their immediate feelings and look at themselves relatively objectively. The subsequent steps and modifications are similarly recorded and evaluated by the pupil with minimal support from the tutor. In some cases, I have used a friend of the pupil to support and make suggestions. In others, I have let the pupil listen to the whole sequence of recordings, as a means first of assessing his achievement, and second of drawing out the principles he has used so that he can apply them to other areas of behaviour.

Many readers may be surprised that little mention has so far been made of the concept of reinforcement. In my opinion, its pastoral use is to help the teacher to anticipate breakdown points and achieve success. The teacher who fails to discover that he is unintentionally encouraging deviant behaviour by paying more attention to it than to the positive behavior he claims to encourage is wasting time. Most pupils value our approval and positive attention, looking for compensations elsewhere only when they feel them unobtainable. This is not a case of passively pleasing the teacher, but one where basic human needs for acceptance and affiliation are being met.

Punishment cannot be eliminated, but it should be minimal and effective. It must not present the pupil with an adult model of aggression or leave him with a feeling of injustice and grievance. But it is not easy to make our punishments constructive. The pastoral team needs to evaluate the punishment system, asking what pupils actually learn from it and how it should be reshaped to allow it to contribute to order and discipline. There is a possibility that behaviour has a different significance for the pupil than we assume. The teacher who ejects a pupil ignominiously from a lesson he dislikes may, in fact, be giving him a reward.

Many punishments merely identify and attempt to inhibit undesired behaviour. To be effective, it should incorporate a careful delineation of the desired behaviour and the way the pupil can achieve it, together with a positive expression of belief that the pupil will drop the immature behaviour as unworthy. Punishment should be given as soon as possible after the offence and, where appropriate, take the form of the withdrawal of some privilege which the pupil is anxious to regain. It should also be one which is clearly related in the offender's mind to the context and the victim of the misdemeanour. This may be difficult to achieve, for at present the responsibility for punishment is often laid on the head of year or house.

The early identification of pupils who are becoming the focus of disciplinary efforts is an aspect of positive discipline. Such pupils learn avoidance behaviour, and also gain the prestige which comes from admiration of their toughness by some of their peers. Behaviour-modification principles imply that the pastoral team should ask what is being learned under such conditions and which kinds of behaviour are receiving reinforcement. Pupils may be learning to lie, cheat, work in a subterranean way to disrupt a class and to truant. As professionals, we have a responsibility to interrupt this pattern, taking positive and firm measures, including involvement of the home, especially the father, as the mother often conceals misbehaviour from him. The pastoral team has to devise a consistent policy of handling the individual which ensures that his mechanisms cannot operate. Surveillance must be efficient, and persistence of effort is essential, for difficulties of this type do not appear suddenly and it is probable that the pupil has acquired skill at avoidance over some years. It is unrealistic to think that the situation can be modified in a few weeks, and prolonged effort of a planned type will be necessary.

Researchers have sometimes been confounded by the fact that pupils who ought, by objective standards, to feel deprived, resolutely refuse to adopt this stance. Similarly, many pupils who come from grossly disturbed homes or whose parents are indifferent, if not actually hostile, to education, function well in school, although the literature would lead us to expect the reverse.

172

This leads us to recognize two things. First, it may be more profitable to study the characteristics of the successful pupil from such backgrounds, learning from them what can be done to help those unable to overcome environmental limitations. Second, over-emphasis of home conditions hides the fact that pupils are more than their backgrounds. If concern with home background diverts our attention from the basic eductional task, then it is time we began to question the relevance of this concern.

Without meaning anything derogatory, our job is to help the pupils for whom we are responsible to rise above the limitations of the home to live fuller and richer lives than those of their parents. This is what education seems to be about. However, it is also essential to stress that I have no desire to divorce home and school. The point at issue is how *much* and *what* knowledge about family background, is it desirable to collect. Too much knowledge is as incapacitating as too little, especially if we are unclear what is salient and what is not. Sometimes we should question this tendency in the pastoral system to collect material about the families of those whom we teach when more important information about performance in the classroom is available and yet is ignored.

Records and the Pastoral System

Continuity of concern, the essence of pastoral care, requires the storage of information, and consequently a recording system designed to help a teacher teach his pupils more effectively. Hamblin (1974) has raised basic questions about the form that record cards should take, and they will not be repeated here. At present many school record cards offer little practical help to the teacher who wishes to make realistic adaptations of his teaching methods to a pupil. Worse, many contain sections on the assessment of personality that are of doubtful validity. Adolescence is a period of rapid change, yet these entries seem to invite judgements which freeze a dynamic process, possibly encouraging unhelpful labelling of the pupil. Error is very likely, because we make unverified assumptions from observations of behaviour about the existence of character defects. Profound judgements are therefore made on minimal evidence: not only minimal, but often open to alternative interpretations. Therefore it seems sensible for the pastoral team to devise a system of recording which avoids these potential distortions, and provides the teacher with information that can be used constructively in the classroom.

What information is likely to make a healthy learning environment and is also ethically proper to record? The record card or portfolio should be concerned primarily with behaviour. But rather than focussing our perceptions on the home, and perhaps imputing conditions which are highly speculative, it seems more productive to assess the pupil's behaviour in school. A record card or portfolio would be concerned with the feature given in the facing table.

A record card aimed at encouraging development would carefully analyse the pupil's strengths and weaknesses in terms that have meaning for its users. It is useful to indicate the pupil's reactions to different types of lesson, revealing that mathematics and physical education seem to provoke certain responses, whilst other lessons do not. If we knew that those responses consisted of forgetting to bring essential equipment or trying to make the teacher eject him from the class, then we could begin to deal with them.

The fact that a pupil lacks the finer skills of co-ordination necessary for certain tasks in metalwork or craft, or the skill to break a task down into steps, therefore tackling it haphazardly, would lead to corrective measures by the competent teacher. Apprehension about apparatus in the gym may be masked by unwillingness to change or aggression, diverting our attention from the real cause. In the large comprehensive school, too often marked by a rapid turnover of staff, such information has to be discovered anew by each incoming member if there is no record. The result is often growing apathy and diminishing performance on the pupil's part, and sometimes antagonism between pupil and teacher.

Practical help comes from records which contain an analysis of the pupil's reactions to stress or frustration. Does he tend to react by fight, or by psychological, if not physical, flight? The picture of the way a boy or girl manages tensions will allow the teacher to avoid confrontations, which in no sense means that he is abdicating control. This type of record contains information about the incentives to which the pupil responds, and the strengths on which the teacher can build: the positive is as important as the negative in this practical form of record-keeping.

What then is the difference between this record card, essentially home-made, and the usual type? Rather than merely stating that a pupil is unreliable, we try to locate situations in which he displays unreliability and the reverse. Difficulties in study skills play an

174

THE CONTENT OF A BEHAVIOURAL RECORD CARD OR PORTFOLIO

CLASSROOM BEHAVIOUR

General Habitual patterns of behaviour.
Breakdown points.
Control measures to which pupil responds
positively.
Avoidance patterns of behaviour.
Incentives and rewards meaningful to the pupil.
Reaction to praise or blame.

Practical Co-ordination and skills in various situations.
Special practical abilities.
Positive or negative behaviour in situations where
he is allowed to take the initiative.
Behaviour in situations where there is an element
of danger, e.g. workshop or swimming bath.
Co-ordination in physical education, using
apparatus or games.
Ability to plan the steps in a practical task.

Academic Strengths and weaknesses.
Special sources of difficulty.
Preferred modality or style of learning.

OUTSIDE THE CLASSROOM

Friends Type.
Skills at making friends.
Behaviour associated with good relationships
with peers.
Behaviour which is the source of difficulty.

Breaks and Signs of disruptive behaviour.
dinner-time

PHYSICAL

Bodily development.
Speech.
Gestures and movement.
Vision.
Hearing.

important part, for it pays more attention to the processes by which pupils learn than to the content of what is learned. Yet any difficulties in the basic subjects are carefully recorded. Dubious judgements about temperament can be avoided, but the new teacher will learn that it makes little sense to say that a pupil is confident or not, for observation reveals that he is confident in some situations and not in others. Once we begin to examine the differences between the two types of situations, the crucial act of assessment is under way, and we can take meaningful steps to help him.

There are limits to what should be recorded. We may need to register things which have previously escaped our notice, but they may be too personal to be recorded. One of the responsibilities of the year or house head as co-ordinator will be the regular inspection of records to ensure that they contain nothing distasteful, unhelpful or out of date. This method of recording allows one to shed material from the pupil's past, rather than preserving it, almost as if we meant it to be evidence against him, so shackling him to his past.

It may seem that such records impose undue burdens upon the teacher and form tutor. Yet in practice, if well thought out and a format devised which requires minimal writing, they should be no more time-consuming than present forms of recording. Obviously, a new system should be introduced gradually, experimenting with alternative forms. Clear objectives and training in the economical writing of reports are essential if the records are not to be as loaded with illicit judgements and irrelevancies as the traditional card.

REFERENCES

Adorno, T., Frenkel-Brunswik, E., Levinson, D., and Sanford, R. (1950) *The Authoritarian Personality*, New York: Harper.

Bellack, A., Kliebard, H., Hyman, R., and Smith, F. (1966) *The Language of the Classroom*, New York: Teachers College Press.

Beaumont, G. (1976) *A Comparison of the Effect of Behavioural Counselling and Teacher Support on the Attendance of Truants*. Unpublished D.S.C. Dissertation, University College of Swansea.

Blackburn, K. (1975) *The Tutor*, London: Heinemann.

Boocock, S. (1972) *An Introduction to the Sociology of Learning*, Boston: Houghton Mifflin.

Conger, J. (1973) *Adolescence and Youth*, New York: Harper & Row.

Deutsch, M. (1973) *The Resolution of Conflict*, New Haven: Yale University Press.

Enquiry One (1968) *Young School Leavers*, London: H.M.S.O.

Hamblin, D. (1974) *The Teacher and Counselling*, Oxford: Blackwell.

Hargreaves, D. (1967) *Social Relations in a Secondary School*, London: Routledge & Kegan Paul.

Hargreaves, D. (1972) *Interpersonal Relations and Education*, London: Routledge & Kegan Paul.

Hargreaves, D., Hester, S., and Mellor, F. (1975) *Deviance in Classrooms*, London: Routledge & Kegan Paul.

Holt, J. (1964) *How Children Fail*, New York: Pitman.

Hopson, B. and Hough, P. (1973) *Exercises in Personal and Career Development*, Cambridge: C.R.A.C.

Jackson, P. (1968) *Life in Classrooms*, New York: Holt, Rinehart and Winston.

Kelly, G. (1955) *The Psychology of Personal Constructs*, New York: Norton.

Krumboltz, J. and Thoresen, C. (1969) *Behavioural Counseling: Cases and Techniques*, New York: Holt, Rinehart and Winston.

Marland, M. (1974) *Pastoral Care*, London: Heinemann.

Matza, D. (1969) *Becoming Deviant*, Englewood Cliffs, New Jersey: Prentice-Hall.

Nash, R. (1973) *Classrooms Observed*, London: Routledge & Kegan Paul.

Newsom Report (1963) *Half Our Future*, London: H.M.S.O.

Schools Council Working Paper No. 11 (1967) *Society and the Young School Leaver*, London: H.M.S.O.

Schools Council Working Paper No. 17 (1968) *Community Service and the Curriculum*, London: H.M.S.O.

Sumner, R. and Warburton, F. (1972) *Achievement in Secondary School*, Slough: N.F.E.R.

Thoresen, C. and Mahoney, M. (1974) *Behavioural Self-Control*, New York: Holt, Rinehart and Winston.

Tumelty, M. (1976) *A Study of the Effectiveness of the Peer Counselling of Truants*, Unpublished D.S.C. Dissertation, University College of Swansea.

Walker, R. and Adelman, C. (1972) *Towards a Sociography of the Classroom*, Research Report, London: S.S.R.C.

―― & ―― (1975) *A Guide to Classroom Observation*, London: Methuen.

Wall, W. (1948) *The Adolescent Child*, London: Methuen.

Wenar, C. (1971) *Personality Development*, Boston: Houghton Mifflin.

177

CHAPTER SIX: KEY POINTS

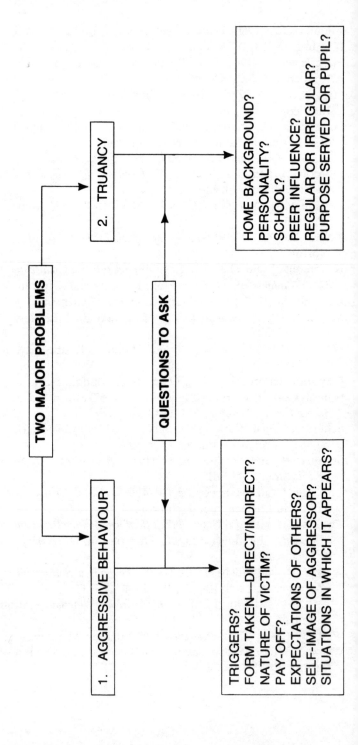

TWO MAJOR PROBLEMS

1. AGGRESSIVE BEHAVIOUR

2. TRUANCY

QUESTIONS TO ASK

TRIGGERS?
FORM TAKEN—DIRECT/INDIRECT?
NATURE OF VICTIM?
PAY-OFF?
EXPECTATIONS OF OTHERS?
SELF-IMAGE OF AGGRESSOR?
SITUATIONS IN WHICH IT APPEARS?

HOME BACKGROUND?
PERSONALITY?
SCHOOL?
PEER INFLUENCE?
REGULAR OR IRREGULAR?
PURPOSE SERVED FOR PUPIL?

MAJOR PROBLEMS: AGGRESSIVE BEHAVIOUR AND TRUANCY

Summary

THE CENTRAL ARGUMENT

The basic contention is that the answer to the problems discussed in this chapter will be found within the school once the pastoral team is organized effectively. Although some guidance and help from outside will always be necessary, the school where the senior management ensure that teachers take a truly professional approach, can institute measures which sharply reduce the severity of these problems.

AGGRESSIVE BEHAVIOUR

Certain attitudes and methods of approach to pupils can either reduce aggressive tendencies or strengthen them. In many cases of bullying or aggression the victim and the aggressor are almost identical in personality. The most serious problem for the pastoral team may be the pupil who attracts bullying. The importance of understanding the contribution of the self-picture of the aggressive pupil is stressed as a preliminary to intelligent remedial action; and a taxonomy of those likely to resort to aggressive behaviour is presented.

There follows a simple framework for the analysis of aggressive behaviour and the construction of remedial measures. This stresses that most of the aggressive behaviour met in the secondary school is instrumental rather than angry. Hence one must always look for the pay-off. Early detection and intervention coupled with firm control are advocated, although the teacher must not provide the pupil with yet another powerful aggressive model. Suggestions are made for pastoral activities which provide the aggressive pupil with essential skills and supports. This chapter then points to the difficulty of dealing with the growing frequency of indirect and passive forms of aggression which lead to friction in the classroom and contribute to under-functioning.

TRUANCY

The complexity of the phenomenon is discussed, and the need to link identification of the type of absence to the action taken. The discussion centres around three main factors:

the family and general background of the truant;
the personality of the truant;
the school from which he absents himself.

Truancy is basically seen as a tendency to avoid challenge and difficulty, although other factors are given due weight, including the need to provide success for certain groups of pupils. A two-pronged attack on the problem, which involves the pastoral team in detailed planning and consistent action, is presented. This looks at structural measures on the one hand, and at individual problems on the other.

SPECIAL UNITS FOR PUPILS WITH
BEHAVIOURAL DIFFICULTIES

Plans based on the writer's experiences are presented for the development of units which have a more positive function than that of a depository for the most difficult pupils within the school. The tendency for such units to assume a custodial role or become a sanctuary is deprecated, and a strategy recommended to ensure that deficits in pupils' skills are recognized and measures taken to rectify them. Plans are given for the pupil's induction, constant evaluation of the original diagnosis of his needs, and his re-integration into the mainstream of the school. The aim is to ensure a constant flow of pupils in and out of the unit, so that it makes a real contribution to the solution of problems of maladjustment and other difficulties within the school.

Aggressive behaviour in schools

Exaggeration of the violence and aggressive behaviour in schools is common in the popular press. Yet there is some evidence that we are currently meeting a disturbing number of incidents of aggression, if not actual violence, towards teachers, whilst bullying and incidents of violence among pupils may well have increased sharply, especially among girls. The problem needs carefully-thought-out, professional intervention, involving firmness and without provocation, avoiding sentimentality, whether directed towards the victims of aggression or shaped as a denial of the possibility that pupils could do such things. A pastoral system which detects the pupil's first tendency to seek a violent or aggressive solution to problems, and follows by firm and consistent action, is essential if bullying and aggression are to be eliminated.

There are, however, attitudes held by groups of staff which seem to encourage aggression amongst pupils. Their reaction seems to be custodial, clearly communicating negative expectations to those whom they teach. Much is encapsulated in the frequent remark, "They mustn't get away with it or the rot will spread." In practice, such teachers arouse in pupils resentment which could be avoided, and encourage the tendency to divide the world into the strong and the weak. Therefore such teachers are actually creating frustrations which are released in the lessons of those teachers whom the pupils see as weak, or implicitly collude with these pupils by highlighting the difference between their style of teaching and the more liberal style of their colleagues.

Many teachers have faced recent changes in secondary education positively, but some seem to look back to a past golden age and perceive only the negative in the current organization of education, communicating their dissatisfaction and cynicism to both colleagues and pupils. A preliminary step in reducing aggression could be a survey of staff attitudes which either exacerbate or reduce these tendencies in pupils. We need not lower the demands we make on pupils in order to eliminate disruptive behaviour, but watch for the manner of expression and the accompanying signals of respect or ottherwise.

Consideration of this problem means that we have to look critically at many things that we take for granted. Labelling is often taken as the equivalent of an explanation of behaviour. Unfortunately, the allocation of a reputation is often accompanied by reactions on the part of those who label, or who accept its validity without evidence, which call out aggressive responses from the pupil. This is then taken as confirmation that this label is correct but it is an open question whether the chicken or the egg came first.

Bullying must not be tolerated within a school, but this should not blind us to the possibility that the victim may be partially responsible for what happens. Sentimentality leads us to concentrate on the aggressor; yet the real menace may be the pupil who attracts bullying. Such a pupil calls out responses from others who are themselves insecure or maladjusted, with the result that the staff's energy is used up in dealing with individual incidents. When I have dealt with a case of bullying, I have considered the bully and the bullied simultaneously, working out why that particular boy or girl was the recipient of aggression rather than others as small or shy as the one attacked.

Drapkin and Viano (1974) suggest that the victim may play an active part in his victimization. We need to avoid righteous indignation, for, as Toch (1972) points out, in many cases the victim could quite easily have been the assailant had the circumstances been slightly different. Those of us who have to deal with violent incidents often find it difficult to distinguish between victim and assailant with regard to their social background, character and personality. We must train ourselves to ask why a particular individual became the victim: asking what there is about him which invites this type of attack? Often the victim is locked into a provocative relationship with the aggressor, or he may possess habits of speech or physical movement that earn him derision. He may find the attention he gets from adults a more than adequate compensation for bullying or he may derive a concealed enjoyment from witnessing the condemnation of others. When such elements seem very pronounced, the child-guidance service should be consulted.

Aggression and anger are not the same thing. Much aggressive behaviour rarely reaches the level where it is visible to the staff because it is of the cool, calculating type, designed to produce a reward for the individual. We can fail to note what the aggressive individual gains if he is allowed to continue unchecked. Many so-called unsocialized pupils are actually well socialized for the world as a jungle, and have learned that they can get their own way through skilful exploitation and the threat of aggression, and only show anger when this mechanism is interrupted and their desires are thwarted. We are concerned with reality and must learn to see what we have avoided seeing and contain and control firmly, without falling into the trap of presenting a model of aggression ourselves to the pupils.

Let us ask in which situations is a pupil aggressive and in which is this tendency dormant. It is especially important to ask how he shows his aggression. Later we will see that passive and indirect forms are more difficult to handle than more overt ones. A pupil may cleverly use his tongue to arouse a vulnerable pupil, and then guides him into a situation where he explodes. The instigator assumes a front of respectability, watching the other act out the scene for him with inner delight, but apparent outrage. Such plausible individuals are skilled at emotional blackmail and can leave us almost doubting the validity of what we have observed.

The next step is to search for the pay-off, which may be a con-cealed one. Sometimes a pupil may behave so as to be ejected from a lesson as a punishment, which to him only meant escaping from a situation where he risked being exposed as stupid or incapable of coping. An additional reward may be the reactions of his friends. There are also times when it is worth looking at similarities between victims. If the well-dressed boy or girl, the effeminate or the more able boy is always being attacked, this *may* indicate something sig-nificant. It is only by analysing the situation carefully that we can make an intelligent, humane and firm approach to the aggressive pupil.

Some aggressive pupils see themselves as champions of their friends against enemies whose defeat will help them acquire prestige. The "us against them" view is evident in these pupils, with the enemy as authority, so we must examine our teaching methods to check that they do not unwittingly confirm these fantasies. Many pupils begin to enjoy their reputations and find compensations within them. Early intervention and the establishment of positive relationships are the only viable solution, for once established, many forces combine to keep the pupil in this negative role.

Self-respect is often the issue at the heart of aggressive and disruptive behaviour. Sarcasm may be more destructive than corporal punishment, although I hold no brief for the latter. Frequent resort to corporal punishment can reinforce aggression. When an adolescent feels attacked, he is likely to respond aggressively and angrily. Behind some incidents of aggression we shall probably find a real or imagined threat to self-esteem. Such threats can lie in various areas: social competence, status among friends, masculinity or feminity, recognition as a near-adult. Whatever the basic cause and precise form of the aggressive response, it is important to perceive the anger which tells us something helpful about that boy or girl and their areas of vulnerability.

These two broad areas of aggressive behaviour, the first utilitarian, as a means of gaining desired rewards; the other an angry response to what the individual interprets as an attack on his self-image, cannot be treated in the same way. The former must be detected as early as possible, and the pupil must learn that intimidation will not work. The egocentrism of the adolescent and the upsurge of emotionality associated with bodily changes and hormonal imbalances can sometimes cause omnipotent fantasies. That is normal, but acting them out in real life is not. Firm containment and control are essential, and referral for further help may be necessary in certain cases.

This dichotomy of these types of aggressive behaviour should make us think clearly about the consequences of methods such as role-play, and about the dangers of relying upon the catharsis theory of aggression. This unthinking approach is encapsulated in the remark, "Let them get it out of their systems". Far from "getting it out", some experiences of role-play may be "stamping it in". If role-play is a powerful tool, and many therapists, including Moreno (1951), would agree, then we should be extremely cautious about stimulating adolescents through their playing of violent roles. Elms (1969) has remarked that "Role-playing is one of the great natural persuaders"; if so, surely it should be handled with integrity and thought be given to the personality of the individual asked to play a role and the nature of that role. Role play can be helpful when it is designed to teach positive behaviour, but we must bear in mind the ever-present danger of reinforcing the wrong things.

Such cautions do not stop us from trying to deal with the problem. We should be able to provide pupils with ways of coping with those who use manipulative aggression, through decision-making exercises and other activities. Intimidation by pupils against other pupils has especially gained in strength, especially in minor bullying and limited protection rackets. But the extent of the problem in the whole school is rarely, if ever, known. This disturbing situation is facilitated by divisions amongst the staff which result in inconsistent discipline and contradictory behaviour by different form tutors when bullying is reported.

Angry aggression or responding to some real or imagined attack on self-respect needs to be treated differently. The individual is particularly vulnerable, and the impingement of others on this sensitive area provokes strong reactions, making them feel that the best form of defence is attack. Personal guidance orientated towards building up the pupil's self-respect seems the best way of dealing with these incidents. The discussion of reactions to provocation should be secondary to the building of inner strengths, because responsible behaviour is unlikely to be a permanent feature of the daily life of those who have a low level of self-respect.

Who is likely to resort to aggressive behaviour?

The first group of pupils is composed of those who lack verbal and social skills, being inarticulate and bad at co-operation. These pupils are often not very bright, and may be somewhat clumsy. They lack the verbal skills to use humour as a means of reducing tension, and often receive cavalier treatment from staff and pupils until they suddenly explode. This discharge of feeling often leaves them confused and anxious, and the whole process recommences. Unfortunately their limited ways of managing tensions leads them to be labelled as unpredictable or odd.

Next there is a small group who feel that only their own needs are of social relevance, and perceive other people as objects or tools to serve them. They react with acute aggression when this does not occur. Perhaps such pupils account for only 0.005 per cent of the secondary-school population, but they can absorb an undue amount of staff time. They promise to reform today with every sign of sincerity, but tomorrow finds them behaving exactly as before. Their appreciation of right and wrong is an intellectual experience unbacked by real feelings. These pupils *may* be those whom Bowlby (1946) first described as affectionless. In any case, our experience shows us that something is wrong and we should refer them for psychiatric diagnosis and possible treatment.

185

Unfortunately, treatment for the adolescent psychopath is almost non-existent, so it is important that they be detected at entry to the secondary school. When there is behavioural evidence, this should be given, clearly and objectively to those to whom the pupil is referred. The clinic may need the type of statement which quotes the date and time of each incident, describing what happened and the pupil's reactions. The mechanisms of such pupils are well developed and highly convincing, and time may prevent full exploration of the problem. Early detection and referral is crucial, for it is almost impossible to find residential placement for a pupil who has reached the age of fourteen.

Insecurity is often strong in those who choose violent and aggressive solutions for their problems. The inconvenience and hurt they cause often obscures this. Their aggression is often a defence against inner insecurity, because to some degree it keeps control of events in their hands. They can initiate, rather than passively wait for things to be done to them. It has often struck me that some of these pupils are basically authoritarian personalities whose lives are dominated by a sense of threat and who cannot tolerate ambiguity and uncertainty. The instant meaning they impose on a situation makes them feel compelled to attack.

The next group can be seen from two viewpoints. First, they come from a sub-culture in which violence is justified. They lack prudential morality, acting impulsively, without counting the costs of their actions to themselves or others. The second standpoint deals with the importance of access to the skills needed for the successful carrying out of delinquent acts. Bandura and Walters (1959:1963) and Bandura (1969) show that a major factor is the exposure to models of aggression. These models must be rewarded visibly for their behaviour and must be both powerful and attractive. Many of our aggressive pupils come from families where parents and elder brothers or sisters are seen to gain their ends through aggressive behaviour. The siblings provide attractive sources of imitation.

The extreme types briefly portrayed should alert us to the complexity of the problem of aggression, especially when reference to a real individual shows that he displays elements from two or more of these types. Perhaps the most useful thing which emerges is that aggression tends to come from those who feel vulnerable, powerless and dissatisfied. It is also the weapon of those defective in other methods of expressing feelings and inadquate in interpersonal relationships. We have also seen the possibility of a link between sporadic aggression and a threat the the pupil's self-respect. These points will be the basis for developing measures for dealing with aggression within the school.

Types of aggressive behaviour

The reader who wishes to follow these theories of aggression in more depth is recommended to read Buss (1961) and Singer (1971) for interesting and reasonably wide-ranging accounts, whilst Berkowitz (1962) and Knutson (1973) explore in more detail certain aspects of the topic. On page 188 is a simple list of some of the major theories which deal with the problem and the suggestions that are being made.

Perhaps these obvious forms of aggressive behaviour are not the most important that the pastoral team has to deal with. Indeed, other forms may have an even more detrimental effect on the functioning of the school. Buss (1971) distinguished between active and passive forms of aggression, suggesting that each can be given either direct or indirect expression. He also discriminates between verbal and physical forms of aggression. Probably the most frequent type of aggressive and disruptive behaviour that the pastoral team has to deal with falls into the indirect and passive categories, such as the practical joke, the spreading of rumours or passive resistance.

These forms of aggressive behaviour are problematic because they offer little direct challenge that can be faced. It has already been mentioned that the most serious form of truancy is psychological truancy where pupils deny the legitimacy of the educational process, working only if they are compelled, and even then investing only such energy as is necessary for minimal satisfaction of the teacher. This situation demands all our goodwill and every scrap of teaching skill, for somehow we must overcome the state of inertia.

The pupil who communicates monosyllabically in the classroom and tutorial, although making sure that we see him behaving differently in other situations, is communicating certain negative things about us and the values we represent; yet it is hard to deal with this quite subtle mode of aggression without becoming ridiculous. If we show irritation to pupils who passively obstruct, they claim that they have done nothing. Although this is exactly the situation of which we complain, these pupils maintain a front of conformity. There are many variants of these techniques which are essentially aggressive in

187

intention, for not only do they render the pupil partially immune from our influence, but these pupils are well aware of our impotence.

Verbal aggression is very difficult to deal with in the large comprehensive school. The pupil who spreads malicious gossip about

THEORIES OF AGGRESSION

1. **The catharsis explanation** that the expression of aggression operates to purge the individual of inner tensions.

2. **The frustration hypothesis** that aggression is primarily a response to the thwarting of the individual's attempt to reach important goals.

3. **The instigation and inhibition theory** which stresses the relative strengths of the instigation to aggression in both the environment and the individual, and the constraints on the overt expression of aggression from either the environment or the individual's conscience and self-concept.

4. **The self-concept theorists** emphasize the adolescent's perception of himself as tough or as someone who would not use violent methods, but also pay attention to the way he promotes or defends his self-image and to challenges to his self-respect.

5. **The social-modelling approach** focuses on the fact that the adolescent tends to identify with powerful models who get rewards from aggressive and violent behaviour.

6. **Social-learning theory** draws attention to the fact that aggression can be learned as a habitual mode of interaction. It emphasizes the rewards of aggressive behaviour, although an important component of the theory is the expectation of attack which develops in the individual. Thus he maintains a readiness to respond with aggression.

7. **Arousal theories** stress the importance of visual and other stimulation from the mass media or crowd situations in lowering the threshold of violent or aggressive behaviour.

another and then watches the results from a safe distance can cause enormous trouble before he is located. He is also dangerous, because he can distort the form tutor's role into that of detective. Equally difficult is the practical joker who assumes a bland expression which one knows to be a form of insolence, although his words are polite as he suggests how unreasonable it is that anyone should think him serious. If a group is involved, then he expresses incredulity at the idea that they should take his fun seriously, implying that any right-minded person ought to accept that he was joking.

Verbal aggression can assume forms as distasteful as the grossest physical attack. It is partially based on pupil's needs to be accepted by their fellows and their dislike of appearing different from the norm. A group may make harsh and derogatory comments about another girl in her presence, forming a closed circle from which she is excluded. She is totally ignored, together with her remarks, and so communication is one way. This turns her into a non-person, arousing a profound sense of powerlessness. Perhaps this indicates the gravity of indirect and verbal aggression, and the need to help pupils cope with this and, more usefully, to regard it with distaste as unworthy of mature persons.

Campaigns are mounted against pupils. These can grow very quickly and become part of the form or year interaction which is difficult to modify. To punish pupils who are conducting a campaign against an individual, is to run the risk of increasing their hostility towards that individual. But the pupil who is attacked feels very isolated, because a complaint increases the repercussions.

The pastoral team must develop sensitivity to signs of indirect and passive aggression if they are to intervene early and anticipate potentially serious situations. The situation should certainly be discussed in the guidance programme, especially towards the end of the first year and during the second year when negative attitudes of various kinds develop. The school will have made it clear at entry that bullying will not be tolerated, but we should be aware that pupils see bullying in purely physical terms, although they understand very well the potency of these other forms. Diagrams, cartoons and humour are necessary to take away the idea that such behaviour is adult and enable pupils to see it in perspective. Once the infantile quality of such mechanisms is appreciated, the majority of pupils discard them, although a moralistic or over-intense approach is likely to boomerang by giving this behaviour the attraction of something forbidden.

The physically aggressive pupils can be helped in a number of ways. Pastoral conferences can devise a consistent policy of controlling these pupils, embodying a plan for building up their strengths and securing their success in school. Under the guidance of the chairman, usually the head of year or house, or the counsellor, the reasons for disruptive and aggressive behaviour become clearer and members of staff begin to appreciate the pupil's needs. Systematic follow-ups are necessary, and future conferences to assess and revise strategies. The early detection of pupils who are vulnerable to bullying or show signs of resorting to physical force to gain their way is most likely in a pastoral system where the tutor has a clear job specification and the year or house head has both the training and the opportunity to carry out his managerial functions. A well-organized pastoral system can build up an effective routine and set of procedures for dealing with problems.

If a certain school faces particular problems, it is essential to provide special help for pupils who are at risk because they either attract bullying, or are impulsive and aggressive. Within a school there can be found one or more teachers with a knack of handling such pupils, and they should help to solve the problem. The formation of small pastoral groups of about ten to twelve pupils which maintain a special relationship with their tutor over several years yields results with minimal effort on the school's part. Such pastoral groups need to be allocated time and to have a carefully devised programme of activities, including study skills. They provide the security needed by pupils at risk. Sixth-form pupils often provide valuable help with the groups, especially at lunchtime. Perhaps it is not improper to suggest that the school should reward the teachers who undertake this work as generously as possible. The group-guidance programme for aggressive pupils would probably include the following.

1. Extending their repertoire of behaviour by teaching them different ways of acting in situations which seem to be associated with their bullying or a source of breakdown. Simulations and exercises will be used for this purpose.

2. Role-play of a *constructive* type which helps them develop the capacity for empathy and taking other people's viewpoint.

3. Changing their view of the world through discussion and activity; although this must be centred around familiar situations and not tied to vague themes.

4. For both boys and girls, particularly for boys, modelling on a competent figure of the same sex.

5. Examination of how they cope with situations which produce feelings of insecurity, and how to react productively.

6. Teaching prudential morality.

It may be argued that the measures suggested are discriminatory, but it is a positive form of discrimination to remedy deficits of skill and ameliorate conditions which cause underfunctioning and trouble for these pupils. The behavioural approach described in Chapter 5 will be employed in the remedial programme, providing clear objectives and allowing pupils to experience success. We forget that pupils must not only succeed, but know that they have succeeded! The steps mentioned above will be backed by links with parents: the pupil should know that his parents will learn about his bullying and aggressive behaviour, for, after all, some parents play a role in creating victims.

Recent years have seen a plethora of comment on the growing aggressiveness of girls, but in my opinion it is the potency of the factors inhibiting the expression of direct physical violence which has been reduced, whilst violence itself has acquired a greater legitimacy. Thus the barriers against the expression of aggression have been partially removed. Rosser and Harris (1965) claim that females have been released from "compulsive domesticity" within the family, but is this so for all sectors of the population? Working-class girls have always had to resist male dominance aggressively within the family if they were to avoid becoming servants carrying out all the chores, whilst their brothers were exempted.

Discussion with girls displaying aggressive tendencies shows the changes which have occurred in a few years. Five years ago they would have claimed that they merely created the climate for violence at the disco, allowing their boy friends to act out the violence. Now they honestly report that they fight over their boy friends with other girls, alongside those boyfriends or against them if they feel this justified. Perhaps it suffices to say that much which was previously latent or invisible is now openly brought into the school. Girls of this type are keenly sensitive to any hint of patronage, suggestion of inferiority or uncertainty on the teacher's part. Many are aware that male teachers tend to manage them by establishing joking relationships with them and they increasingly voice resentment about this, although they find it more tolerable than the "nagging" they claim to receive from some female teachers. Many male teachers behave in a dangerously familiar way and then are completely disconcerted by the provocative advances of some girls. Studies of sexual behaviour in adolescent girls, such as those reported by Ehrmann (1964), have suggested that females in the lower levels of ability and education become more active sexually at an earlier age than their peers who are more able academically. Such findings largely come from the U.S.A., although they seem to be meaningful in this country, even when changes in the sexual attitudes of the middle-class adolescent during the last ten to twelve years are taken into account. In the last few years girls have tended both to take more aggressive initiatory roles in sexual relationships and to subject their partners to highly critical evaluation, and many boys feel demoralized in face of the stringent standards and comparisons of their girl friends. It is of little consequence whether these standards are backed by first-hand sexual experiences. The girls apply them and judge their partners by them.

This section is concerned with aggression and not sexuality, although the two seem to be linked. Part of the problem of aggression amongst adolescent girls may be due to the change in the female's role, but has this gone far enough to account for the phenomenon we are trying to explain? Earlier physical maturation now occurs, but we cannot assume that mental and emotional maturation necessarily accompany it. Girls can be pushed by both the physical facts and the expectation of earlier maturation into a premature and hence pseudo-adoption of maturity. In this, sexuality is salient, but, even more important, girls have adopted a tough and aggressive approach which parallels that of their boy friends. The last few years have seen the growth of unisex and the more overt manifestation of lesbian tendencies in some older girls. It is stupid to try and allocate a single cause for these changes, for some girls see aggressiveness as an essential condition for the rejection of their femininity, others as an integral part of their sex role. There are no easy answers to these questions.

It is foolish to exaggerate the problem of violence amongst girls, as to pretend that it does not exist. Belson (1975) has shown surprising evidence of willingness to indulge in acts of violence, although the most violent twelve per cent of the sample accounted for over eighty per cent of the violence. However, real sex differences still exist, and violence by girls probably amounts to only about one tenth of that by their male counterparts.

The greatest mistake would be to treat aggression by girls as different in kind to that by boys. It seems to have the same functions, and therefore the remedies and treatment will be the same. Unfortunately, many schools seem to meet girls' aggression with the ineffective device of suspension: ineffective, because the girl usually returns to school after a short period of suspension with her reputation for toughness and aggression enhanced, and may desire to maintain her reputation as a delinquent heroine.

In concluding the brief discussion of aggressive behaviour it seems wise to stress the importance of detecting, and then acting upon, the first small signs of it. If these go unchecked, they can develop into grave situations which absorb energy and time. Protection rackets begin in the first year with playground demand for crisps, sweets and the odd five pence. Pupils should know that these things will not be tolerated, and be confident that something will be done about justified complaints. We can be ambivalent about pupils who complain of bullying or teasing, seeing them as either inadequate or responsible for their situation. Both may be true, but our task is to help them extricate themselves from untenable positions, and gain the skills to avoid future incidents. Our own schooldays are potent determinants of our attitudes in these matters, all the more so because we do not recognize their influence. Our lack of awareness can put us in the position of implicit collusion with the bully and the machiavellian pupil.

Truancy and the pastoral team

It is difficult to assess fully the extent of truancy, mainly because the traditional method of recording absences hides its severity. Dawson (1974) remarks that "A ninety per cent attendance does not tell you whether a hundred children have been absent for half a day or ten children have truanted for a week". If the figures gave the percentage of children absent for a session or more, rather than the percentage of actual attendances based on the total possible attendances, then the urgency and severity of the problem would become evident.

In the search for solutions it is tempting to look outside the school, to truancy centres, special classes or so-called experts. But first we should ask, "What is there in school for some pupils when they do come?" If there are forces and procedures within the school which interact with others to lead to truancy, then it is only sensible to identify them and deal with them methodically. This is a hopeful point of view, even if it brings initial discomfort, for it suggests that remedies can be devised, and preventative measures taken as part of pastoral work.

Let us be realistic. It is highly improbable that we could eliminate truancy completely from the secondary school, but we could reduce it sharply. The first step is to help staff understand the complexity of the problem by identifying and assessing the nature of the different categories of truancy. We then have to develop ways of helping those who fall within the different broad groups, building in measures for assessing the needs of individuals who present special problems. Measures to combat truancy will have little impact if they are unco-ordinated, haphazard attempts by individual teachers. In tackling the problem we have to concentrate on three main areas. First, we must examine the personality of the truant, trying to detect if it is different from that of non-truants. If we do find differences, we have to decide whether they are relevant to the truancy, and not too easily assume causality. Second, we may need to consider the truant's family background and the impact of a socially deprived neighbourhood upon him. Third, we must examine the school situation from which the pupil absents himself.

Out of these three elements, our main remedial effort will be directed towards the truant's behaviour, especially his tendency to avoid challenge or indulge in avoidance behaviour, and towards conditions within the school directly or indirectly linked with his truancy. The indirect factors take us back to what I have described as the subterranean life of the classroom, requiring us to understand how pupils view the cirriculum and the meaning they give to class-room transactions.

Types of truancy

Let us briefly look at school phobia, phobia meaning a state of dread or an irrational fear. Phobic pupils often settle down quickly and work well once they are in school, and therefore it seems that the prospect of going to school is the intolerable factor rather than the actual experience. Kahn and Nursten (1969) portray the school phobic as tending to come from a materially good home, of average or superior intelligence, but both Chazan (1962) and Hersov (1960) report a wide range of intelligence in the phobics they studied.

Parental relationships play a large part in many reported cases of school phobia, although we must not assume that it is always the parents' fault. Some children are over-dependent or react to stress and unfamiliar situations or new demands in ways which leave their parents with little alternative than to over-protect. Parents can make a direct contribution to school refusal, for Cooper (1966) suggested that the school phobic is reacting to intolerable stresses, produced by such factors as unduly high parental expectations for academic success, unremitting demands for conformity and other severe distortions in the interaction between child and parent. In any case, there is much that we do not yet know about the cause of this condition.

There is little reason to doubt that school phobia is a clinical problem in which internal conflict and some form of anxiety play a large part. Its connection with the inability to cope with stress is illustrated by the way school phobia often appears at the onset of physical puberty, when emotion surges up and there is the sense of vulnerability increases. Yet Clyne (1966) found evidence of school phobia before puberty. When school phobia appears at the onset of puberty, it is probably the culmination of a long-standing state of affairs which has led the child to see the world in terms of overwhelming threat. In this situation, only the family—despite the fact that the tensions probably originate there—offers a safe retreat.

Detection before the acute phases of school phobia develop, is part of the pastoral task. We must watch for pupils who show signs of tension in tests and unfamiliar situations or when required to expose themselves to the limelight by reading in class or assembly. Not all will be school phobics, but they do need help, and some will develop into school refusers if not helped. The pupil who has to be sent home frequently during the first year of the secondary school because he has a headache or stomach pains is at risk. It is important to check on those who use the medical room regularly and quietly investigate their reaction to school. When pupils of this type also develop minor illness at the beginning of term or are late back after a half-term break, we have signals of the need for serious assessment.

Truancy proper takes two forms. The first is illegitimate absence without parental knowledge. Sometimes the mother may be in

195

collusion with the pupil, whilst the father may not know. Caution in telling the father is essential, for there may be good reasons for the mother's concealment, but in many cases it is important to ensure that he knows. Second, there is a growing group of truants whose parents know of their absence and disapprove of it, but who are unable to make the pupil attend school. Withholding by parents, as opposed to truancy by pupils, takes many forms. Some parents actively instigate the absence. Girls tend to be the victims of withholding, especially in one-parent families or if there is a sick or feckless mother at home. The word "victim" is used deliberately, for many of these pupils wish to attend school. But withholding is not confined to feckless and single-parent families. It is very strong in rural areas where children give seasonal help with planting and other farm tasks. Here it is hallowed by tradition and is very difficult to eliminate.

Masked truancy is something that the comprehensive school has suffered from, although it is coming under control. In the "clocking in" version the pupil appears for registration and then disappears. There are variants in which a pupil misses a selected lession regularly or randomly absents himself from the occasional period. In the former, the teacher may not realize the pupil is missing, in the latter, plausible excuses can be produced which are often difficult to check. When it is suspected that this type of absence is growing, the only answer seems to be a checking of the group at some convenient point during the lesson. When this is necessary, one becomes aware that certain teachers are in implicit collusion with truanting pupils. One of my students, when exploring truancy within a school was asked by a teacher: "Do you think I'm going out of my way to force them into school, so that they can disrupt the few who want to learn, and make my life hell into the bargain?"

There is little point in repeating information presented in Tyerman (1968), Turner (1974), and West and Farrington (1973). But it may be useful to suggest strategies for coping with truancy, bearing in mind that my general thesis is that the answers to the school's problems will come from within rather than without.

Strategies for coping with truancy

The two most common explanations for the increase of truancy are the pupils' background and the growth of large secondary schools.

Reynolds (1974) has questioned the view that the personality, family and social background of the truant are the key factors. Why do some pupils with low ability and attainment, who come from bad homes and whose personality is less than optimal, still attend school regularly? As Reynolds points out, to say that because pupils do not want to go to school, there is something wrong with them rather than with their schools, is unconvincing. From my point of view, we should ask quite bluntly, "What is there for certain pupils when they *do* come to school?"

For his intensive research, Reynolds studied nine secondary-modern schools between the academic years 1966/7 and 1972/3. Different levels of absence were found in these schools, which had similar intakes and social settings. Reynolds therefore argues that only a small proportion of the variation in truancy rates between schools can be explained by differences in the pupils. Other important factors are the attitudes of the staff and their methods of teaching and organization.

We cannot say with certainty which attitudes and methods have positive and negative effects. The same teaching methods may have different effects in another school or have to be presented differently. We should not advocate blindly the wholesale adoption of so-called progressive methods without relating them to the pupils' needs. For as Sumner and Warburton (1972) suggest, many pupils from disadvantaged backgrounds think that it is the teacher's responsibility to make them work. Enquiry One (1968) also showed that pupils who are statutory-age leavers, probably the group most likely to truant, place great value on traditional subjects which they see as related to getting a job. We must obviously keep an open mind.

Size is often blamed for difficulties, and a large school does, of course, require extra good co-ordination, communication and management. Galloway (1974), in a survey of comprehensive schools in Sheffield, showed that chronic absenteeism rose by nearly three hundred per cent over the primary-school level. This happened in the second year in the comprehensive school. But he suggests that size of school is not related to the percentage of chronic absences, and also that extreme variations exist between schools of similar size. Several comprehensive schools had a ratio of 3:1 chronic truants as compared with the primary school; others had a ratio of 15:1; and in ten schools the results were even more extreme. In the face of such evidence it is impossible to insist that there is a necessary relationship between size of school and level of truancy.

Studies into the truant's personality shows no single pattern. Truants tend to claim to be bored and to need constant stimulation and excitement: something often associated with delinquency, as Downes (1966) brings out. They have negative attitudes to authority in general and school rules in particular. Apathy is often characteristic of their view of the world, and school seems irrelevant to them. Many are strongly orientated towards their peer groups, and loyalty to group values often means that they are vulnerable to delinquent pressures. Much less frequently, the truant can be an isolate who is vulnerable to bullying. According to research, three factors associated with truancy are important:

(a) perception of school activities as unrewarding and irrelevant;

(b) a strong tendency to avoid demands;

(c) a drift towards an aimless pattern of life.

Case studies undertaken by my students suggest that many parents of truants have rejected the pupil by the time he or she has reached the age of fourteen, whilst relationships between father and truant are especially negative. Jones (1974) provides evidence that a number of truants come from homes where child–parent relationships are poor. Rebellion against the home is often brought into the school, and many of our disruptive and truanting pupils are at least as hostile towards their parents as they are towards us.

These facts underline the importance of early contact with the home and effective detection of the first attempt at illicit absence. It is only sensible to try to eliminate truancy when most parents still retain some interest in the children. Equally, we must recognize that home–school contact has different meanings at different ages. A study by Lindley (1976) revealed that even pupils from good homes become more resistant to contact between home and school as they grow older. After the first three years, more pupils expressed reservations about the propriety of such links, seeing them as an implicit attack on their autonomy. This is even truer for the smaller groups where parents and children are in active opposition.

The truant's family is often marked by disorganization and lack of foresight. It is possible for both parents to go to work and for the home to be well organized and the adolescent's physical and emotional needs met. In the homes of truants, however, the feckless and disorganized mother leaves home in the morning without preparing clean clothes and food for the children. Girls take the brunt of this, and many are ashamed of the state of their clothing, but seem unable to do anything about it without some support from the school. Many of these girls are taking on serious responsibilities at home when the mother is ill or absent. They then find themselves resenting signals of irresponsibility from some unthinking teachers. The home economics department has often proved a source of support. The girls can be taught to keep their clothes clean and allowed to wash them if facilities are lacking at home. The development of a "uniform bank" is also useful, although it is wise to make a small charge for it which takes away the taint of "charity" and brings the sense of "getting a bargain" to the surface.

Truancy can be sharply reduced if we base our approach on both caring and control and ensure a consistent team effort. The pastoral effort is most likely to be effective if it consists of a modern version of Morton's Fork. The first prong is a viable system of detecting those at risk and showing them that they cannot truant without detection. The second requires the team to look at the educational needs and success, or lack of it, of those pupils liable to truant. Both prongs are a necessary basis for tackling the problem.

The team should first examine the efficiency of detecting early signs of truancy. These will include the inspection of registers by the form tutor to detect patterns of absence, and follow-up by the head of year or house and the educational welfare officer. Later, other issues arise. The pupil who truants in the second year has frequently absented himself during the last term or two of the primary school, showing that he is at risk. When such pupils feel the impact of change, the tendency to absent themselves emerges. With entry to the secondary school the pupil again conforms to attendance requirements. Linked with this is the problem of punctuality. Slackness about this and the accepting of excuses can cause pupils to begin imperceptibly to modify their ideas about the need to attend school regularly. Measures to check unpunctuality are essential, although there is little point in making an anxious pupil afraid to come to school because he has missed the bus. Consistency of approach is essential, and this may mean that a pastoral conference has to be held to work out ways of helping a pupil. This should be preceded by an assessment of the pupil's needs by the year or house head.

With any determined attack on truancy, the reception back into school is critical. Often this consists of immediate harangue or a self-eroding punishment; and then we wonder why the pupil is absent next day. Arrangements must be built up for the form tutor to provide support for a truant who returns to school. If the tutor gives friendly support, help with missed work, examines the pupil's difficulties in relating to teachers and peers, and builds up study skills if necessary, then there seems greater likelihood of the pupil's stopping his truancy.

This approach will draw the staff's attention to the need to examine measures to help a pupil cope with the cumulative step-by-step subjects after absence, whether illegitimate or not. Difficulties arise because a pupil has missed a vital step in a mathematical process, and the ensuing failure can reinforce the tendency to absent himself. A school which cannot describe the steps taken to help pupils who have been absent catch up, is in danger of creating truancy.

One structural measure of great importance is the report system for persistent truants. The transfer of responsibility for his attendance to adults is an example of these pupils' tendency to rely on external supports rather than take active charge of themselves. Such a system has to be consistently carried out and thoroughly checked. Many pupils can change their avoidance behaviour only when they are compelled to attend lessons in this way, but the system has to be backed by more positive forms of help. Some pupils are relieved by this approach because they can then resist the pressures of older unemployed friends or fellow truants by saying that they have no alternative because of the check being made on them.

The final structural element is evolving a working policy with the educational welfare officer. Not all cases need his attention. Too much time spent on hardcore and chronic cases should be avoided if other pupils are receiving only minimal attention and learning to truant.

Success depends on a planned, phased and steadily maintained effort. Attention to peripheral measures may be crucial. If one has a truancy problem in the afternoons, then it is sensible to review lunch-hour arrangement, checking dinner queues and trying to develop useful activities which reduce the impulse to wander off. Many schools fail to make full use of their youth wings, which can provide constructive support.

For the second prong of the attack, the pastoral team will need to find out how a deviant or negative identity is being built up for certain pupils or groups of pupils within the school. Researchers stress that many truants are either frightened or resentful, rather than

200

inherently difficult. Many less able pupils cannot plan ahead and are therefore dependent upon immediate rewards. They need clearer short-term goals and a more structured learning process. They must get success, know how to get it and know that they have got it.

Truancy is marked by avoidance behaviour, yet one often finds that learning tasks are presented in a way which makes them appear irrelevant or impossible. The answer for many pupils lies in the reform of the disjointed curriculum which creates rigid boundaries between subjects and fragments relationships with teachers. Less-able pupils may need longer blocks of time and careful exposition of the links between subjects and their relevance to life. But this must be done with clear short-term targets, signals of success and a supportive structure. Team teaching gives them the opportunity to relate more consistently to a teacher.

Careers guidance, orginally conceived in limited terms, has given way to the wider concept of careers education. Work experience based on careful selection, preparation, supervision and follow-up can help to deal with truancy if implemented in the fourth year, rather than in the final year for the statutory age leavers. Pupils' experiences can then be used in a carefully designed programme aimed at easing the transition from school to work, by giving pupils the skills to deal with the psychological and social factors which cause breakdown at work. Many young people fail in work not because they cannot do the job, but because they cannot make the necessary adjustments to their role as young workers. Hayes (1970) and Moor (1976) discuss these factors clearly.

If truancy is avoidance behaviour, then truants probably lack coping skills. Sassi (1973) used group counselling, whilst Beaumont (1976) undertook an exciting programme of behavioural counselling to develop mutual supports and self-help amongst a group of truants. One central feature of this experiment was a study-skills tape which presented pupils with models of behaviour in key learning situations. The aim was to help them cope with frustration and to develop the skill of making a positive attack on learning problems. Investigation of what truants do when they absent themselves from school suggests that, on the whole, they do remarkably dull things such as sitting in the local cafe making a cup of coffee last most of the morning. Surely we can compete with this once we are determined to tackle the problem.

It is useful to identify the pupil with low motivation as soon as possible. A useful measure was devised by Entwistle (1968). The following simple scale has also proved helpful in promoting self-analysis and initiating an attack upon the problem of evasion and poor attitudes towards learning, in both individually and in groups.

Name ....

Age ....

What is the purpose of this activity?
Most of us want to do well in school, even when we feel that we are not doing well or say that we "don't care". We can hide our real feelings only too easily.

The sensible thing to do is to look at our feelings and try to get an idea of the reasons for not doing well. The two activities which follow overleaf will help you work out some answers for yourself.

Please put down what you really think—the answers will not be shown to anyone else. It does take a bit of courage to be honest with yourself, but it is worth it.

What to do
Overleaf you will find some statements often made by pupils of your age. If you think you would say this, tick the box in the column marked LIKE ME. If you would not say this, tick the box marked NOT LIKE ME.

IDENTIFY YOURSELF

IN THE CLASSROOM

	Like me	Not like me
1. I want to be top of my class		
2. I always sit at the back where the teacher won't notice me		
3. I enjoy doing tests		

	Like me	Not like me
4. I try hard to get things right		
5. Teachers always say I must work harder		
6. I never seem to have my books		
7. I like answering questions in class		
8. I look out of the window a lot		
9. I never seem to get my home-work done on time		
10. I ask the teacher for help if I don't understand		
11. I think most lessons are boring		
12. I often start thinking about other things during lessons		
13. I always try to get better marks in a test than I got before		
14. I try to make my friends talk to me in class		
15. I never seem to hear what the teacher is saying		
16. I take a pride in neat work		
17. I think it's easy to get away with things in class		

YOUR FRIENDS

	Like me	Not like me
1. My friends think it is all right to have a day or two off from school		
2. My friends think teachers are always picking on them		
3. My friends want to get on in school		
4. My friends want to leave school as soon as possible and start work		
5. My friends want to go to college		
6. My friends think homework is important		
7. My friends are at the top of the class		
8. My friends think games more important than lessons		
9. My friends like reading		
10. My friends wear the school uniform		
11. My friends want to do well in school		
12. My friends get poor marks for their work		

CHECK UP ON YOURSELF

What to do

Below are some difficulties many boys and girls meet. If you feel that any of them apply to you, put a tick on the line against that statement.

1. Losing my books   ———
2. Always late to school   ———
3. Never able to ask a question in class   ———
4. Forget what the teacher tells me to do   ———
5. Often told off for talking in class   ———
6. Can't keep my work neat and tidy   ———
7. Find it hard to take notes in class   ———
8. Seem to get 'picked on'   ———
9. Can't find time to do my homework   ———
10. Get worried about tests   ———
11. Always losing my property   ———
12. Get called names by other boys and girls   ———
13. People seem to expect me to get things wrong   ———
14. Don't seem to be able to read as well as the others   ———
15. Don't have many friends in school   ———
16. Find *some* lessons too hard for me   ———
17. Don't like PE   ———
18. Can't settle down in class   ———
19. Other boys or girls get me into trouble   ———
20. Never chosen to do things at school   ———
21. Often lose my money at school   ———
22. People think I'm a bit of a bully   ———
23. Find it hard to hear what the teacher is saying   ———
24. Can't see the blackboard very well   ———

Please write any difficulties that are NOT on this list in this space, and over the page if there is not enough room here for you.

If the school is to reduce its own contribution towards creating truancy, we must see that one factor which can push pupils towards it is the image that the school creates of itself, through teachers' attitudes and methods. Many pupils who truant see school as not only uninteresting but uninterested in them. One must create a positive picture of the school which will make them want to come. They come when they feel wanted and achieve success.

The organization of special units for pupils with behavioural difficulties

Suspension rates probably bear little direct relation to the number of pupils within a school with behavioural difficulties. Suspension may be a self-defeating policy which increases, rather than reduces, problems because the suspended pupil often returns to school after a few weeks with his reputation for toughness and delinquency enhanced. He or she then proceeds to act out this reputation. Suspension is a failure on the part of the school, unless the pupil is dangerous to other pupils and to himself.

A school attempting to solve its problems constructively will probably consider the development of a unit for disturbed and difficult pupils. Here certain basic questions must be asked. What organizational structure is required for an adequate and meaningful service? What methods of treatment are needed and are applicable in terms of the school's resources? Where can the school obtain advice and support in the planning and development of such a unit?

The unit should help pupils learn new ways of managing their social and emotional relationships. It should analyse the skills a pupil needs and work in a planned way towards clearly defined behavioural ends. It should use the educational skills of teachers as the basis of treatment. As Hamblin (1975) argues, it is more constructive to see maladjustment as a disordered and ineffective lifestyle rather than a form of sickness or pathology.

The sanctuary or the too prevalent "sin bin" approaches must be discarded resolutely in planning the unit. Both types of organization are negative, and would confirm the deviant identity of the pupil who enters it. Indeed, badly planned units not only crystallize negative identity but may give it new dimensions. If connotations of abnormality seem to permeate the treatment, this will stimulate adverse labelling and can lead to serious resistance to co-operation by both pupils and their parents. The result is that the unit merely becomes a threat which compels pupils to conform.

Cost-effectiveness applies as much to units for disruptive pupils as to any other area of allocation of resources. Hence placement in the unit should never be intended to be permanent, and the aim should be to give pupils intensive help for the shortest possible period, maintaining a steady flow of cases in and out. And the pupil should be encouraged to attend any classes or activities where he seems to be functioning adequately.

Once procedures and objectives of the unit have been thrashed out, it is essential that all staff members should understand exactly its functions and how to make use of it. Pupils must be carefully selected. To allow staff to herd every difficult child into the unit is a recipe for disaster. An initial evaluatory period of six months allows staff to develop skills and to assess the snags and seek remedies. How do we choose which pupils to include? The prognosis of the pupil's response to help seems of prime importance. Balance within the group has to be maintained, for one does not want a group of aggressive pupils who reinforce one another's behaviour.

Contact with parents is vital at the stage of selection. Parents must be convinced that it is not punitive and that it is meant to help their child succeed in school. Information given by parents during such an interview is often invaluable in devising the child's programme.

The pupils also must be interviewed. Several members of the unit team should interview a pupil, explaining its purposes in positive terms. The seriousness of the pupil's behaviour and the need to tackle it as efficiently and quickly as possible must be made clear. There is no point in disguising the gravity of his situation and the need for something to be done. Such messages, if honestly given are helpful rather than destructive.

One person working part-time in the special unit takes responsibility for the over-all surveillance of a small number of pupils, and relates therapeutically with that pupil and undertakes essential counselling and guidance. He will assess progress and ensure that the remedial programme is being followed. This teacher is also responsible for drawing up a programme of activities in conjunction with the school counsellor or another trained person, as well as with the other members of the unit team. The educational psychologist has special skills which can be used constructively in the diagnostic task which precedes the pupil's entry to the unit.

The simple procedures outlined above ensure a purposeful entry to the unit and continuity of concern and method. The teacher with special responsibility for the pupil will be very active during the period of re-establishment in the normal life of the school, and will often maintain the relationship for a year or so after the pupil leaves the unit, providing him with a lifeline if he runs into difficulties and helping him manage conflict and tensions economically.

The key idea behind having an individual programme for each pupil in the unit is, as Hamblin (1975) argues, to create an adaptive working and learning environment. The principles of behaviour modification provide a framework within which pupils can be encouraged to learn new ways of coping with problematical situations. Our aim is to make the pupil an active participant in modifying his life-style rather than a passive recipient of actions of which he does not see the point.

Many of the techniques discussed in this book and in Hamblin (1974) will be used, including the participation of friends as a source of support. We shall try to build up the pupil's ability to see other people's point of view and help him understand that he himself plays a major part in bringing out irritable responses in those of whom he complains. It should be evident that the special unit attempts to prepare pupils systematically for successful functioning in the normal classroom.

Many approaches to disruptive pupils attempt to cope with the difference in their learning style by programmes stressing physical activity and a sense of adventure. Pupils obviously benefit from these, but they must be assessed against the curriculum and the activities already available for the less academic pupil. Special activities of the outward-bound type may produce gains in some pupils, but we need to answer to key questions:

With which pupils do such programmes succeed or fail?

In what ways do they aid the pupil to adjust to school?

Re-establishment of the pupil into the everyday life of the school should be gradual. To be in the unit one week and totally divorced from it the next, is likely to lead to breakdown and a reversal of the changes in attitude and behaviour which have been achieved. The final stage in the unit should anticipate difficulties and prepare the pupil for dealing successfully with them. Systematic examination of likely breakdown points is undertaken through intensive counselling of the pupil by the teacher who has developed the key relationship with him.

Sometimes it is difficult to get one's colleagues to accept the wisdom of letting the pupil return to the ordinary classroom setting. But this can be overcome by consultation and planned reintegration of the pupil. If this is done in a carefully graduated way, by allowing him to cope with the classroom situation where he is likely to experience least difficulty, before proceeding to the next one, then the doubtful teacher can be shown that the pupil is making an effort. Failure to plan the reestablishment of the pupil into the system is as costly as the failure to evolve clear objectives for the unit.

REFERENCES

Bandura, A. (1969) *Principles of Behaviour Modification*, New York: Holt, Rinehart and Winston.

Bandura, A. and Walters, R. (1959) *Adolescent Aggression*, New York: Ronald Press.

——— & ——— (1963) *Social Learning and Personality Development*, New York: Holt, Rinehart and Winston.

Beaumont, G. (1976) *A Comparison of the Effect of Behavioural Counselling and Teacher Support on the Attendance of Truants*, Unpublished D.S.C. Dissertation, University College of Swansea.

Belson, W. (1975) *Juvenile Theft: The Causal Factors*, London: Harper and Row.

Berg, I. (1969) School Phobia—Its Classification and Relationship to Dependency, *Journal of Child Psychology and Psychiatry*, Vol. 10.

Berkowitz, L. (1962) *Aggression: A Social Psychological Analysis*, New York: McGraw-Hill.

Bowlby, J. (1946) *Forty-Four Juvenile Thieves: Their Characters and Home Life*, London: Baillere, Tindall and Cox.

Buss, A. (1961) *The Psychology of Aggression*, New York: Wiley.

——— (1971) Aggression Pays. *In* Singer, J. (Ed.) *The Control of Aggression and Violence*, New York: Academic Press.

Chazan, M. (1962) School Phobia, *British Journal of Educational Psychology*, 32, Part 3, November.

Clyne, M. (1966) *Absent*, London: Tavistock.

Cooper, M. (1966) School Refusal, *Educational Research*, Vol. 8, No. 2.

Dawson, A. (1974) R.S.L.A. Truants are Shaking the System. *Times Educational Supplement*, 25.5.74.

Downes, D. (1966) *The Delinquent Solution. A Study in Subcultural Theory*, London: Routledge and Kegan Paul.

Drapkin, I. and Viano, E. (1974) *Victimology*, Lexington, Mass: Lexington Books.

Ehrmann, W. (1964) Marital and Non-Marital Sexual Behaviour. *In* Christensen, H. (Ed.) *Handbook of Marriage and the Family*, Chicago: Rand McNally.

Enquiry One (1968) *Young School Leavers*, London: H.M.S.O.

Entwhistle, N. (1968) Academic Motivation and School Attainment, *British Journal of Educational Psychology*, 38.

Galloway, D. (1974) Big is Not to Blame, *Times Educational Supplement*, 18.1.74.

Hayes, J. (1970) *Occupational Perceptions and Occupational Information*, Unpublished Ph.D. Thesis, University of Leeds.

Hamblin, D. (1974) *The Teacher and Counsellmg*, Oxford: Blackwell.

—— (1975) The Counsellor and Strategies for the Treatment of Disturbed Children in the Secondary School, *British Journal of Guidance and Counselling*, Vol. 3, No. 2 July.

Hersov, L. (1960) Refusal to Go to School, *Journal of Child Psychology and Psychiatry*, Vol. 1.

Jones, D. (1974) The Truant, *Concern: Journal of the National Children's Bureau*, No. 14, Summer.

Kahn, J. and Nursten, J. (1968) *Unwillingly to School*, Oxford: Permagon.

Knutson, J. (Ed.) (1973) *The Control of Aggression*, Chicago: Aldine.

Lindley, L. (1976) *An Investigation of the Links Between Home and School*, Unpublished D.S.C. Dissertation, University College of Swansea.

Moor, C. (1976) *From School to Work*, London: Sage.

Moreno, J. (1951) *Sociometry, Experimental Method and the Science of Society*, New York: Beacon House.

Reynolds, D. (1974) Some do, some don't, *Times Educational Supplement*, 10.5.74.

Rosser, C. and Harris, C. (1965) *The Family and Social Change*, London: Routledge & Kegan Paul.

Sassi, L. (1973) *The Effects of Counselling on School Truants*, Unpublished D.S.C. Dissertation, University College of Swansea.

Singer, J. (Ed.) (1971) *The Control of Aggression and Violence*, New York: Academic Press.

Sumner, J. and Warburton, F. (1972) *Achievement in Secondary School*, Slough: N.F.E.R.

Toch, H. (1972) *Violent Men*, Harmondsworth: Penguin.

Turner, B. (Ed.) (1974) *Truancy*, London: Ward Lock.

Tyerman, M. (1968) *Truancy*, London: University of London Press.

West, D. and Farrington, D. (1973) *.Who Becomes Delinquent?* London: Heinemann.

CHAPTER SEVEN: KEY POINTS

BASIC DIMENSIONS OF FAMILY STRUCTURE

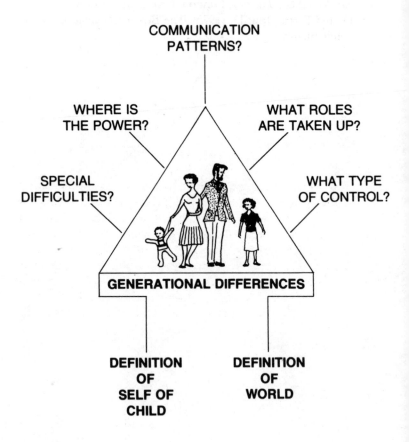

COMMUNICATION
PATTERNS?

WHERE IS
THE POWER?

WHAT ROLES
ARE TAKEN UP?

SPECIAL
DIFFICULTIES?

WHAT TYPE
OF CONTROL?

GENERATIONAL DIFFERENCES

**DEFINITION
OF
SELF OF
CHILD**

**DEFINITION
OF
WORLD**

THE FAMILY: FORCES AND PRESSURES

Summary

THE CENTRAL ARGUMENT

The pastoral team must accept that they cannot change the family. They will, however, find it helpful to appreciate the dynamics of the family and the complex interaction within it. These shape the behaviour of some pupils, often in a way which has negative consequences within the school setting. Such difficulties are not confined to those who come from impoverished or overtly delinquent homes, nor do the forms they take necessarily involve aggressive or disruptive behaviour. The pastoral team should understand that the most they can do in many cases is to help the pupil for whom they are responsible react to family circumstances in ways which have the least adverse consequences.

BASIC DIMENSIONS

The analysis undertaken in this chapter focuses on key elements which appear to influence strongly children within the family. These are:

the content of the maternal and paternal roles;

the way power is exercised and who holds it;

generational differences and the way these are expressed;
the style and content of the family communication system.

PATERNAL DEPRIVATION

Emphasis is given to the importance of paternal deprivation, especially in relation to the adolescent boy. The destructive effects of paternal rejection of the son and daughter are made clear, as is the importance of the male pastoral care-worker who can build stable, warm and containing relationships.

PROCESSES WITHIN THE FAMILY

The description of the processes operating within the family includes the way in which family interaction builds up a definition of the outside world, accepting that this can be positive as well as negative. The creation of a symbolic environment within the family receives considerable attention because this often has a profound impact on the child's conception of himself, especially his ability and temperament.

THE SINGLE-PARENT FAMILY

The dangers of the two-parent family where chronic conflict exists between the parents and where the children are used as weapons, are made clear. Equally, whilst the difficulties of the one-parent family are examined, the myth that it is necessarily an unfavourable environment in which to rear children is exploded. Next comes a treatment of the problems of the one-parent family under stress due to parental inadequacy or emotional disturbance.

BEREAVEMENT

The consequences of bereavement for the adolescent are examined. The discussion highlights the possibility that the damaging stresses which adolescents have to face do not stem from direct reaction to the loss, but from the surviving parent's distress and failure to work

214

through the mourning process. The impact of bereavement is also related to the two major developmental tasks of adolescence and the way in which development may be impaired. The pastoral worker is alerted to the importance of maintaining an unobtrusive surveillance of the pupil if periods of stress, such as examinations, have to be faced shortly after the bereavement, or if a transition, such as that from junior comprehensive to senior comprehensive school or from school into work, has to be made.

Why study the family?

Two extreme positions can be held by teachers about the desirability of directly working with parents and understanding the family's contribution to the pupil's problems at school. The first is based on the thesis that our basic task is instruction and that this can be conducted independently of parental contact, and also, by implication, that family forces do not affect the ability or desire to learn. This view reduces parents to the status of tiresome necessities who should not intervene in the life of the school unless requested. The other extreme standpoint stresses the importance of links between school and home and sees the home as the major factor in success or failure at school. Both viewpoints are unhelpful. The former ignores the Plowden Report (1967) and the Newsom Report (1963). Newsom argued that parents cannot delegate their responsibilities for guiding their children; that many problems could be helped if teachers knew more about pupils' home circumstances; and that parents should be given greater knowledge of what goes on in school. The latter viewpoint denies that the school can exercise a socializing influence independent of the home. One cannot conclude that the family is necessarily more important than the school in shaping a child's response to learning.

We must, however, accept the fact that we cannot change the family. But we help the pupil to react less destructively to pressures from home. We can teach constructive approaches to learning, and can often make a real impact on the problem of deprivation by tackling it in a pragmatic way.

A home which builds up a negative, perhaps almost paranoid, perception of those in authority, or one which creates a climate in which challenge is evaded through excuses, will have a profound effect on the way the pupil functions at school. No inevitable relationship exists between such forces in the home and on performance and behaviour at school. Personality and the constraints and structure of the school will act as mediating forces. Therefore different pupils with roughly similar influences at home express their attitudes through widely varying behaviour. One might be overtly aggressive, whilst another would seem to conform, refusing to involve himself in the learning process but not provoking confrontation.

At times we may find ourselves talking about social class as if it had a uniform impact upon children. But within the family some aspects of social class membership are stressed whilst others are reduced. Swift (1966) showed that fathers blocked from promotion themselves, but whose position in industry as foremen and supervisors gave them a vista of what was possible, stressed the importance of achievement and raised the level of their children's performance in the eleven–plus examination. This is one example of how some families filter out the values of the working class to which objectively they belong, emphasising middle-class values and behaviour. Problems also occur when the parents' perceptions are unrealistic or when they are accurate yet unaccompanied by the necessary skills.

More light on the importance of the family is given by Glueck and Glueck (1962) and Walker (1968). In areas where delinquency is rampant, there is as much difference between families in the same street, as when one district is compared to another. A number of studies, including that of West (1969), show that in poor neighbourhoods interaction within the family can stimulate delinquency but that attraction toward the family is linked with resistance to petty crime.

Identity primarily comes from within the family, and self-definitions can be hard to reject. Cooper (1971) argues fiercely that the family is a destructive institution which imposes unwanted roles and destructive identities upon individuals. Laing and Esterson (1964) demonstrate the way interaction within the family compounds and possibly creates schizophrenia. Although such matters are beyond the province of this book, we can agree that there are few loves as intense as family loves and few hates as permanent as family hates. Therefore as teachers we must be aware of the dynamics of the family and how they affect functioning within the secondary school.

The family has two basic and irreducible functions. These are the primary socialization of the children and the stabilization of the personalities of the adult members, which means that the parents use the family to meet their emotional needs. It would be illuminating to explore in depth the implications of the fact that while the modern nuclear family is ostensibly child-centred, the children are essential for the adults' emotional satisfaction. The latter point may not be positive, unless we can confidently state what needs are being satisfied and assure ourselves that there are no detrimental effects on the children.

As our major socializing agency, the family both prepares the child for entry into larger social groups and, once he takes up roles in these groups, interprets what is happening to him. In my opinion, we do not help parents understand how much this interpretation contributes to the pupil's progress in school. The family instils the basic norms, especially those concerned with achievement and how to obtain it, including how pupils react to failure. Role behaviour is learned within it, especially sex-role behaviour.

The pastoral worker concerned about the pupil's family background needs to see that there are four interacting dimensions along which family roles can be analysed, namely the instrumental versus the expressive, power versus dependence, generation, and sex. I will try to show briefly how these four dimensions affect family life.

Despite some movement towards sexual equality, the adult feminine role is is still primarily conceived in terms of activities within the family, that of the male as anchored in the occupational world. The fact that the mother's financial contribution to the family budget is now almost as essential as the father's has done little to modify this bias. The paternal role is conceived in terms of action, disciplinary functions and achievement. Closely linked with this is the dimension of power versus dependence. The father ostensibly holds the power, although studies such as those of Young and Willmott (1957) and Willmott and Young (1960) show the mother as the central figure in a web of kinship.

Sex-role behaviour is salient in understanding the importance of the family in contributing to adjustment in school. The misery caused by such labels as ponce, poof, queer and creep is very real. Factors within the family create conflict about appropriate sex-role behaviour, and perhaps tensions about how sexuality is expressed. There is overwhelming evidence that the socialization of girls emphasises obedience and under-emphasises the need for achievement. This difference also appears in school discipline.

It is only since the work of Andry (1960) that the literature in Britain has shown an increasing interest in the father's contribution to his children's growth of competence. Clinically, it has long been recognized that the combination of a weak, ineffective father and a cold, unyielding mother is potentially dangerous, yet for years we seemed to consider only the mother's contribution to the child's well-being.

When analysing the phenomenon we should consider the life-style of certain occupational groups, such as a long-distance lorry-driver who arrives home for the weekend exhausted after driving under hazardous conditions. If he is met by a recital of woes, complaints about his offspring, and a list of chores to be tackled, there is little wonder that such fathers tend to opt out of family life. Similar patterns of behaviour can be detected in the life of the busy executive who arrives home in a state of intellectual and emotional emptiness. The enervation of middle age is not confined to manual workers!

The boy or girl whose parents are elderly tends to be especially vulnerable to stress. They often feel ashamed of their parents' age and avoid bringing their friends home even when the parents would welcome this. They are also often acutely aware of the discrepancy in values between themselves and their parents.

Biller (1971) has summarized the research relating to the father's influence on the healthy development of the children. He shows that a warm relationship with a father secure in his masculinity is the crucial element in the boy's adoption of masculine behaviour. Earlier research has shown that even when the father's absence is socially acceptable, as in the case of the services or the merchant navy, boys tended to be more poorly adjusted than their peers in families of similar background where the father was present.

Boys whose father was absent for long periods were inclined to be passive in their play and interaction with other boys but with strong fantasies of aggressively masculine behaviour. Or they adopted a facade of exaggerated masculinity which hid inner uncertainty. A boy who lacks the opportunity to observe closely the interaction of adult male and female may not learn the basic requirements of relating to females whose role is not that of mother. At the same time, the father's absence makes the boy's basic sex-role identification more likely to be strongly loaded towards femininity. With girls, the father's warm response to her femininity is essential for her self-respect, but the girl's basic identifications are with her mother. The negative effects of father's absence tend to be less marked with them than with boys. In the single-parent family a re-allocation of roles often occurs. In one sense the elder children are still a son or daughter, but in another they are taking on the role of parent because of the duties they perform with the younger children. In families where generational differences are sharply stressed, tensions will emerge during adolescence. Such families often contain parents whose attitudes are inflexible and who cannot adjust to changes in the child. This is often made worse by difficulties in communication, when a father begins to question his daughter about her activities. He believes that he is showing his concern, but she has interpreted his message as one of distrust and becomes antagonistic. A good programme of personal guidance will explore such difficulties honestly.

During adolescence generational difficulties are often very strong between the mother and daughter. Rivalry can develop between them, and mothers who have prided themselves on their good looks can project their growing dissatisfaction with themselves onto their daughters. They may become hypercritical and damage their daughters' self-respect. The mother who denies her age in her relationships with her daughter fails to see that she is building rather than demolishing barriers to communication, embarrassing her daughter in her attempts to deny real distinctions of generation.

These four dimensions within the family help us to assess the distortions and imbalances which seem to be related to a pupil's problems in school. Within the family the child acquires the basic capacity for empathy, but the family can give negative or confused identities which stunt their capacity if these four fundamental dimensions are marked by pathology. When constructive, the pupil can build a positive identity which allows him to respond to the needs of others, but if identity is confused or negative, one is unlikely to recognize the needs of others, let alone meet them. As Hamblin (1973) puts it, "I cannot put myself into another man's shoes if I am unsure of the I which is me". We need to understand how intra-familial processes create deviant or negative identities and then try to provide remedial experiences at school. The first approach concentrates on a particular situation. It may be one of crisis—either unanticipated or due to a long-standing set of tensions—or it may be because discipline within the family has become counter-productive because it is inappropriate to the pupil's age or physique. If it is the latter, then we will be concerned only when disciplinary methods at home inhibit functioning at school, showing that we are not concerned primarily with the home situation. We have a responsibility to act when we reasonably suspect cruelty or gross privation at home, but in such circumstances we initiate the action and then withdraw.

The situation in question can be caused by undue parental permissiveness, the impact of the size of the family, its expansion or contraction due to birth or death, or gross poverty and poor living conditions. In other words, we may become aware of something happening within the family to which a pupil is especially sensitive. His reaction creates difficulties for him at school. Awareness and discussion of such situations can prevent the transfer of hostilities into the school setting. Displacement of aggression seems especially relevant to the adolescent and his family.

Hamblin (1974) has argued for both caution and clear objectives in home visiting. If a visit is essential, then shrewd observation of the vulnerability of the sitting-room furnishings, the physical facilities for homework and the amount of play-space for the children, may be more important than the words spoken. An over-house-proud mother might well be associated with the problems which led to the visit.

The second approach is one where we attempt to understand the family as a unity of interacting persons, each of whom tends to shape his or her role according to the expectations of others. A mutual process of accommodation and of role-definition is at work within every family. Out of this emerges the self-picture of each individual. The expectations and evaluations of behaviour emerge from a scarcely discernible conception of the ideal role of father, mother, son, daughter, brother and sister. Not only does one member of the family modify the behaviour of the others, but this modification is itself a product of the way each of them defines and gives meaning to the actions of the other.

The family creates a symbolic environment for its members in which each develops his own definition of the family and its significance. This differs for each member, but we are more concerned with the shared definitions which relate to interaction and activities outside the family. If school and learning are perceived in negative terms, we have to take this into account. A view is built up in each family of authority, other people and the nature of the world, of cause and effect and the nature of achievement.

This view of the family reflects the insistence of many educationists that the child lives in a symbolic as well as a physical environment. When we analyse the family in this way, we are accepting that an adolescent acts on the basis of the meaning which he attributes to individuals. It is impossible to grasp the significance of family interaction if we restrict ourselves to an examination of separate roles, for as the role-holders interact, the situation changes. The members of a family are constantly defining and interpreting their relationships. If the family seems to be salient to the problem, the pastoral-care worker has to be alert to identify key interpretations which shape the actions which follow.

The family communication system contains messages which affect pupils' behaviour in school. Many are unrecognized, but if the view of the world which emerges from family interaction is threatening, the message, "defence is the best form of attack" may be the result. We cannot change the family but we can avoid confirming the paranoid viewpoint by clumsy and derogatory disciplinary measures. We also need to prevent confrontations through intelligent anticipation of the pupil's interpretations of our behaviour.

In some families the power structure is stressed and the parents brook no reasoning, let alone argument. In this case the child is forced to work in devious ways to gain his ends. It is little wonder that intelligent children emerge from such family structures with well-developed machiavellian tendencies.

We should not be surprised when we encounter very odd identities attached to the pupil about whom we are concerned. Some families feel strongly that "Nothing has gone right for us since we had him", and during adolescence, this feeling is intensified. Extremely difficult, and yet not uncommon, is the situation where family tensions make a scapegoat of one child. He or she becomes the recipient of all the feelings of failure, guilt and inadequacy of other members of the family.

Helping such a pupil is no easy task. Family unity is achieved through the scapegoat mechanism, and the child may gain attention, albeit of a negative type, and may be exempted from the responsibilities and chores expected of other members of the family. The mother, especially if the scapegoat is male, often has a close affectional bond with him, but if the child tries to move away from his role, then the mother reacts in a way which forces him back into it.

If the form tutor suspects that a pupil is being used as a scapegoat, he should discuss this with the head of year or house, because it is imperative that the school psychological services are consulted when scapegoating is severe. We can, of course, offer him additional support within school, provided that we realize that such pupils are often highly manipulative in their relationships outside the home. It is sensible to concentrate on giving the pupil the means of success and making satisfying friendships within the school. The dynamics of the scapegoat role are well described by Bailey (1973).

The family under stress

The broken family does not *cause* delinquency and disruptive behaviour. In fact, the two-parent family which is sterile emotionally is more likely to produce neurotic behaviour and anxiety than the cohesive and secure single-parent family. Distorted interaction within the family, if prolonged and severe, is more dangerous than either divorce or the absence of one of the spouses. Glueck and Glueck (1950) have provided some evidence that the inability of one spouse to carry out his or her role constructively, leading to unhappiness, is more closely related to juvenile delinquency than is divorce. The intensity and duration of the period of dissension and uncertainty which preceded the divorce, the child's vulnerability, and the ability of the parent who assumes total responsibility for the children to take on the duties of the absent one may be more important than the fact of divorce.

Let there be no mistake in this argument. Higher rates of delinquency seem to be present in homes broken by divorce and separation than in those where bereavement led to a single-parent family. But one must not automatically assume that a single-parent home is a poor one. The pattern of factors involved is complex, including, as West (1969) suggests, psycho-motor performance and also the degree of extraversion or introversion, if Eysenck's (1971) findings are applied to the analysis of the results of family breakdown.

The pastoral team should try to analyse a family which is undergoing stress. First find out if the stress is chronic and endemic, or sudden and therefore unanticipated. It is important to assess where the threat actually lies. It may be within the family, possibly the product of suicide, illegitimate birth, physical or mental illness. It may be outside the family—unemployment or neighbours' reactions to a family difficulty. If it is primarily within the family, then we can help those concerned to tackle it. If outside the family, we may have to confine our efforts to helping them react in a less costly manner.

Perhaps attention has been too intensively directed at the working-class family. The very real problems of the middle-class family, particularly those who feel themselves in a marginal position in the class structure, may have been neglected. Bott (1957) showed the importance of the network of kin as a source of support. This applies equally to both social classes, although the form of support is different. The working-class family often has a greater ability to cope with prolonged stress and to overcome crises, even if this means passively resigning to the inevitable. The middle-class family, with its long-term commitments, tendency to plan ahead on the assumption of security and inexperience of grave crises, suffer in other ways. Unemployment of the father may constitute a grave shock for which the family is emotionally unprepared. This may disturb the pupil, and produce in the middle-class family a sense of shame.

The family on the margin between the middle and working classes, anxious to stress its middle-class identifications, often seems especially susceptible to shame and guilt, because of their striving for respectability. In such families the adolescent is often the focus for shame and guilt. His school performance, social achievement and career choice are subjected to intense scrutiny. The teacher should try to detect these forces at work in the adolescent, whose defences often cause him to keep teachers at a distance through conforming and pleasing responses.

This kind of family is likely to precipitate delinquent or disturbed behaviour in the adolescent. Its prescriptions, admonitions and examples seem only to offer a negative identity. When the adolescents fail in school or somehow show that they are the very people their parents warned them against, the family finds itself in a position involving not only a sense of shame and inferiority, but conflict. The parents could get help from the probation officer, the school counsellor or the social services, but they cannot accept these supports without violating their aspirations. Neighbours may feel that the road is being brought into disrepute, and therefore they try to isolate the family and the boy or girl in trouble. Inner pressures boil up in marginal parents at signs that they are being critically assessed by those whose acceptance they desire. When the child's behaviour is the cause of this, the reaction is often severe, and they may put further pressures on the boy or girl which provoke rebellion or some desperate act of self-harm. A talk with an understanding head of year or deputy head will do much to help such a parent put things into perspective.

Within such a family disciplinary measures often stress deprivation and threat rather than positive incentives. The authoritarian family is liable to accentuate the emotional stresses and disturbances which are often part of adolescence. Night terrors, irrational fears about the dark and strangers, gross embarrassment about bodily functioning and development, and a harsh self-punitive approach can occur in early adolescence. The avoidance of deprivation merges with fear of failure as a motive for working and, coupled with their prudishness, they are liable to lose the sympathy of both peers and adults.

Very often such children resent our help. The initiative which should be the hallmark of adolescence has been destroyed by parental erosion of personality boundaries. For them contact with the teacher outside clearly prescribed situations means the risk of exposure and the loss of face. When working with such pupils we must, at first, be prepared to endure difficulty in getting an honest response, and it is only as they learn to trust that things begin to change. Such pupils reflect the attitudes and values of their parents, which are essentially defensive.

Let us always ask who takes the brunt of the stress within the family. It may be absorbed by one parent who copes well for a time but then begins to over-react. Many middle-class fathers are deeply shocked by redundancy, and crumple under it. Other parents are unable to cope with the emotional and practical repercussions of a handicapped child or the increasing invalidism of a partner. In such circumstances the stress may be falling on the other children. I find that many underfunctioning pupils in the fifth or sixth forms are, unknown to their teachers, providing support for inadequate parents at the cost of their own progress in school.

The one-parent family

The bereaved parent still has more social support than the divorced one, and this is particularly true of the mother. The one-parent family which is the result of death other than by suicide or sudden accident has had time to make the essential adaptations, and can usually cope with the transition into a one-parent family.

The divorced mother, however, is often a victim of prejudice even today. Their vulnerability makes them suspect that men are evaluating them as possible bed-partners. Where the marriage involved violence or distasteful forms of sexuality, the mother may be fearful of men and distrust both herself and them. These attitudes impinge on the children. Goodness can be presented as a feminine quality, whilst badness is linked with the male role. The introverted sensitive boy may, in this family, learn very odd attitudes to masculinity and himself. Where the head of family is a father alone, too great an intrusion by him into the girl's life will tend to masculinize her. Such processes have to be taken into account.

Pupils from one-parent families are more common in our schools than we suspect, for the Finer Report (1974) stated that one in ten of all families were one-parent families. The majority are headed by a mother alone, and, as Wynn (1964) states, the consequences of fatherlessness are primarily poverty. It would be useful for one member of the pastoral team to be responsible for keeping abreast of the changes in the system of social benefits. A talk with someone who understands the system often enables the parent to cope more effectively, thus relieving the pupil of stress which may be interfering with his adjustment at school.

Unless the mother is a professional, the fatherless family will probably experience hardship. We as teachers must do what we can to meet the needs of pupils whose healthy development is being impaired by their home circumstances. One recommendation of the Finer Report was that provision for older children should be made by the social services in co-operation with the local education authority. This would include the full use of the youth service—a resource we have not yet used to the full.

Stress in the adolescent from a one-parent family depends on the ability of the remaining parent to take on the duties and role of the other. The mother has to redistribute some of the father's duties among the elder children, and then combine the disciplinary and planning aspects of the paternal role with her maternal one. Some can do this and some cannot.

One-parent families, if cohesive and stable, are as emotionally sound places for rearing children as two-parent families. But if the mother is feckless and disorganized, she tends to behave in a cyclical way, letting chaos and disorganization develop, and then resorting to panic measures. Her clumsy over-reaction may precipitate the crisis she fears. If her anxieties have focused on her daughter who stays out late and is engrossed in a relationship with a boy friend, she may react by imposing savage restrictions on the girl. The dominant mother who uses emotional blackmail may push her son into drinking and exaggerated demonstrations of his masculinity. Perhaps it is better that the son or daughter reacts violently rather than becoming inhibited and retreating from the world. The latter reaction is likely in single-parent families occasioned by divorce which has left a sense of stigma. Then both mother and children often retreat into the closed family, maintaining vigilant defences against the outside world.

The following aspects of the one-parent family may impinge upon the child's performance in school:

finances;
control;
mother's adjustment and stability;
mother's inadequacy and disorganization.

It may not be so obvious that we have to take the grandmother into consideration. Many mothers have to rely upon their own mothers after divorce, especially if they have young children. This can be a source of tension. The children may be fond of their grandmother, yet bitterly resent her remarks about the father they may still love. Pulls for affection arise. The mother may feel that she is losing her children's love, especially when the grandparents compare favourably with the frequently tired and irrascible mother, adding to the emotional burdens of the daughter they are trying to help.

There exist key points at which the cohesion of the family is in danger. Ironically, the likelihood that the one-parent family may become a two-parent one is such a point. Children may have extremely strong reactions when the mother makes it clear that she is seriously thinking of remarriage. If the relationship with father is strong, they may feel that the mother is being disloyal to the dead or separated partner. Sometimes they fear that they will not be wanted, a viewpoint often associated with the potential spouse's having children younger than the adolescent. Many adolescents have built up satisfying roles for themselves in the family and then suddenly they face the prospect of losing their autonomy and power.

When boys realize that the pleasant friend is taking up a more permanent position in the family, they may be troublesome, but can usually accept their mother's desire for happiness and security. Provided that the potential stepfather has taken the trouble to build up a good relationship with the boy, eventual resolution of any difficulties will occur. Surprisingly, the girl often presents more cause for concern. A girl who takes a dislike to her mother's potential spouse is often ruthless in her attempts to disrupt the relationship. Firmness and concern are essential ingredients for resolving the situation. The pastoral team can help by giving the girl the opportunity to work through her complex feelings of love and hate for her mother and natural father. Strange ideas and long-concealed feelings will emerge, and only when these come into the open does the disturbed behaviour die away.

Fathers often have access to the children after divorce and separation. This can cause many subtle conflicts. A father may act in an irresponsible indulgent way and so create difficulties for the mother, who is made to appear dull, and drab. Mothers feel bitter when they listen to glowing accounts of the outings, and jealousy is sometimes not far away when the children make favourable remarks about the dress and charm of their father's new partner.

Fathers who take such stances with their children often suddenly lose interest in them. This unreliability has a profound impact on the young adolescent who has not recognized the changed nature of the relationship after the breakdown of the marriage. At one level the child may wonder what he has done to cause the father to reject him, whilst at another they may blame their mother. In any case, any mother who has had to cope with the frustration of children let down by their father finds it hard to forget or forgive him.

How can the pastoral team help?

As teachers we must never usurp the functions of parents. The helpful teacher is one who provides the pupil with the means of accepting the situation, making the best of it and finding compensations in other areas of life.

The school might build up a confidential list of pupils whom they believe to be at risk because of home circumstances. A symbol on the record card can indicate that information is held by a senior member of the pastoral team and should be taken into account before any serious step is taken. One obvious step is to train all form tutors to recognize the reasons for signs of stress, whilst the discipline policy should reduce rather than increase it. The eldest child in a family which has suffered disruption may need special attention. Schachter (1959), in his study of affiliative behaviour, suggested that the first-born will have a higher level of anxiety and hence a greater need to reduce anxiety and to affiliate with a group when under stress. Ring *et al.* (1965) argued from their findings that first-born children are not so much concerned with the reduction of anxiety as with self-evaluation, which makes them more responsive to the influence of others. Another reason for looking carefully at the first-born is that he or she will be more aware of the implications of the divorce and will have probably been more responsive to the emotional complications which preceded the breakdown. Such children may have been going through the early stages of puberty during the period of maximum stress of the family breakdown, and have been scarred by the experience.

Form tutors and teachers have to learn that the reaction to family breakdown is varied. In every case the pastoral worker should tackle the pupil's feelings rather than the superficial behaviour which these feelings produce. In contacts with the lone parent, especially the mother, we have to avoid implicit criticism and patronage, and it is crucial to avoid involvement in the allocation of blame. When necessary we must not hesitate to initiate action which links the parents with the social services and other relevant sources of help, especially the school psychological service.

With the pupil, our effort should be directed mainly towards preventing the growth of a deviant identity or a "chip on the shoulder". Reinforcement of successes rather than concentration on difficulties is the watchword. We must keep a vigilant eye on such pupils if they have to surmount a major hazard such as O-level examinations within a year of the family breakdown. The period of a year is not totally arbitrary, but it does seem that by then adaptation has usually occurred.

Bereavement

This brief discussion of bereavement will ask the pastoral team to look at it from a rather different viewpoint than usual. Instead of considering the adolescent's reaction to his personal loss, the critical factor may well be the way the surviving parent works through the process of mourning. Some adolescents have to give massive support to parents who react to the experience with pathological behaviour. Of course one must have compassion for such parents, but let us not lose sight of the fact that we are concerned with the child.

We must learn to analyse the situation by asking questions which reveal the complexity of the situation, such as:

who was it that died?
how did they die?
at what developmental stage was the pupil when the bereavement occurred?
what kind of relationship existed between the adolescent and the deceased?

From these questions it is clear that the main effects of bereavement which we have to take into acount are indirect. It is the responses of others that can have the greatest significance, rather than those of the adolescent with whom we are concerned. Despite this insistence, let me make it clear that I am not denying that real grief exists at the death of a parent or a brother or sister.

A number of writers, including Gorer (1965), have argued that in our society death is the ultimate obscenity which we cannot face. We attempt to disguise it in ways that lack the significance of the old mourning rituals, which stressed the separation of the dead from the living and placed them with the ancestors. Indeed the most sinister situation for the adolescent is where the dead person is kept alive as a force directing family interaction and a sanction against which rational arguments become almost impossible. Some boys and girls are faced with the daily burden of living up to the expectations of the dead father as interpreted by the neurotic mother. The emotional blackmail, tears and insidious invasion of the child's inner privacy cannot be shrugged off, and can produce guilt and uncertainty in the son or daughter.

We must rid ourselves of the delusion that bereavement is solely composed of regret and grief. Anger and hostility are never far away. Even while the priest declaims that the death is God's will and should be accepted, those who face him are already engaged in attributing blame. They blame God, the hospital, the doctors or nurses, the drugs, one another, and—potentially most damaging—themselves.

229

Mourning can be a process from which one emerges richer and more integrated. Bowlby (1961) describes the stages of mourning deeply and sensitively. Lindemann (1944) suggests that grief has three phases: emancipation from bondage to the deceased; readjustment to an environment from which the dead person is missing; and finally, forming new relationships which may eventually replace the lost one. This summary of the sequence of stages ignores the complexity of the process, but draws our attention to the crucial readjustments that have to be made.

Grief and the response to the deprivation brought by bereavement lie at the heart of the mourning process. At times we pay most attention to grief, but it is the sense of deprivation and consequent insecurity that may have the long-term consequences that create problems for the adolescent. The loss of a partner usually means the loss of part of oneself, for our sense of self not only lies within us, but is invested in our partner and extended to our environment. Some old folk face the loss of a partner with equanimity in comparison with their reaction to the loss of a well-loved house and surroundings. This does something to illustrate the difference between grief and deprivation. Often the wife who has lived almost vicariously through her husband, priding herself on having been a good wife doing all that she should, experiences deprivation most poignantly. For her, life has lost its purpose. If the sense of deprivation is strong and the adjustment to it is faulty, the adolescent within that family may have heavy burdens laid upon him.

Grief, of course, brings a sense of forlornness and helplessness. If we realize that we often do stupid things when we visit our own friends after a death in the family, we can begin to appreciate what the boy or girl has to face. We may, in effect, tell our friends to forget about it, although putting it less bluntly as, "try not to dwell on it too much". Indeed we often ignore that the greatest need of the person closest to the dead one is to talk about him. Yet if we have been fond of him ourselves, we can block their attempts to do this, protecting ourselves from discomfort. Realization of this enables us to understand the dilemma of the sensitive boy or girl who may have the added complications of adolescence to face.

Mourners can become irritable and restless after the funeral. They show deep anger towards those who are near them and whom they love. Boys and girls earnestly trying to help are bewildered and hurt by this. Here the form tutor or head of year can support such pupils and let them reveal their emotions without feeling guilty because they seem to be saying bad things about the parent they love. The mother also can become guilty about her behaviour, and if she tries to control it by psychological and physical withdrawal it can make things worse. If one suspects that the situation is progressively deteriorating, advice should be sought from the school psychological service.

Where the communication system within the family has been faulty, or where the authoritarian version of respectability has operated, the family's ability to meet stress realistically may be low. Almost inevitably, if there have been suppressed animosities and sexual difficulties between the parents, then pathological ways of dealing with grief are likely to come to the surface. If the pastoral team knows about such conditions and then bereavement occurs, it should keep a watchful eye for signs of stress. Parkes (1972) and Bowlby (1969) draw our attention to the form and function of distortions of mourning, and we should be aware of them. Sometimes, six months later, grief is as severe as in the first few weeks. This is a chronic situation which has to be dealt with by a specialist. There are some husbands or wives who seem unaffected by the loss, and the casual observer might think them callous. But some months later, the concealed grief suddenly bursts through. Another small group of people can only express their grief indirectly through hypochondriacal illness, which sometimes replicates the symptoms of the deceased, without organic cause. Each of these distortions is dangerous and a source of threat to the adolescent. We have a duty to support the pupil and see that the school psychological service is alerted.

The pastoral team must eschew sentimentality and yet be truly sensitive, for in no other area are we so likely to cause harm through good intentions unbacked by careful thought. Let the reader analyse his own feelings about whether one should tell someone that he is dying. It becomes even more alarming if the question is that of telling an adolescent that he or she is about to die. Ask yourself who is being protected by the decision not to tell?

The first question that has to be examined is, "Who is it that has died?" If the parent and the adolescent are of the same sex, there is often a relationship which includes rivalry as well as affection and friendship. If the relationship before death has been hostile, the initial reaction can be one of relief, but often with a tinge of guilt. If a father has been violent toward mother and children, and then the mother dies, the children's anxieties may provoke the very violence that they fear. Do not assume that the social services will know of the situation and take action, for this is not necessarily so. Special arrangements now exist in each area for dealing with actual and suspected violence, and every member of the pastoral team should be aware of them. Even in the absence of physical violence, there is no guarantee that the children are not suffering. Psychological warfare also exists in the family. If it is the father who dies, questions of money and control may become central for the pupil. Enough has been said to allow the reader to continue the exposition for himself.

When a sibling dies, the situation may possibly be more damaging psychologically than if the parent dies. The very closeness produces special anxiety at the death of a brother or sister. After such a bereavement, many pupils ask, "Will it be my turn next". If the one who died was of the same sex and older, the question is very liable to be in their minds. It seems, too, to be associated with the acquisition of identity, for this involves recognition of the finite nature of life. During the period when the question, "who am I?" is the adolescent's preoccupation in his moments of thoughtful withdrawal from daily life, he also begins to play with the concept of death. If there is undue anxiety, the onset of sexual impulses may activate fears of death in the dark and being buried alive. All this can accentuate the hidden anxiety of a child whose brother or sister dies.

Group counselling often brings to the surface themes of sibling rivalry and hostility. When concerned with one's own maturity, the immaturity of a brother or sister may be an intolerable nuisance, and families are often riven by comparisons. If the dead younger brother or sister was brighter and the elder child was often compared unfavourably with that sibling, the death brings complex feelings into play. If the dead sibling was older and held up as a model, there may well be initial feelings of relief. But sometimes the expectations centred on that child are brought to bear on the younger, less bright child. He then feels that his own personality has to be discarded for that of the deceased sibling.

If bereavement occurs in the early stage of adolescence, the impact may be on the sex-typed role behaviour of the pupil. If the child is made to feel insecure through the death of the parent of the same sex, the reaction may be that of prematurely crystallizing their identity. Young people have to achieve independence and this means separation from parents, but if the boy or girl has been at loggerheads with the parent of the same sex, there are two extreme responses. The first consists of wholesale adoption of the values and attitudes of the dead parent. The other extreme is to become the very opposite of what the parent would have desired. Later the futility of this becomes apparent, but it may be difficult to change, especially if the surviving parent has approved of the identity which has been assumed.

The girl entering puberty can react sharply to the death of her mother. A girl having difficult periods and who realizes that her mother has died of cancer of the womb is likely to have qualms about accepting her sexual role. Later, the girl seems specially at risk if her mother dies when she is making a first intimate relationship. If she dislikes her father, she may rush into an early marriage or more informal relationship in order to escape from home. Thus bereavement leads to the development of a relationship which might otherwise have withered. Equally, if she is loyal to her father and younger siblings she may feel compelled to look after them. Her boy friend may begin by understanding, but gradually becomes discontented, until a relationship which could have flourished is destroyed. The girl then feels ambivalent, if not downright resentful, about the demands her family make upon her.

We must always ask about the circumstances of the death. Sudden death is even more disruptive than death after illness, and the resulting disorganization sometimes puts enormous strain on the eldest child. Suicide brings a sense of shame even when it is concealed from the outsider. Many mothers seem to cope well for the first few weeks after the husband's suicide and then begin to act in ways which disturb the children. Adolescents from a family where there is some instability in the surviving partner, often raise questions about the meaning of the suicide for them. Naïve ideas about the inheritability of such tendencies come to the surface and great sensitivity is needed if the unspoken questions are to be brought into the open.

What practical steps can we take? First, let us consider but not intrude upon the pupil, though we can give them an opportunity to talk to us. Next we must be aware that the bereaved family is physically at risk during the first six months. The increased vulnerability to illness of the surviving spouse provokes anxiety in the adolescent. The children themselves seem to contract illness and lack resistance to infection. If examinations come within this period, a little extra help with study skills, methods of revision and question-answering is more useful than other forms of support. We can so easily be sympathetic at the moment of bereavement, but forget it six months later when the critical examination has to be taken.

The adolescent may also need some form of acceptable help to cope with the first holiday. We know that the peak periods for attempted suicides occur during weekends and public holidays, and one period of extreme vulnerability is Christmas. For many people it is associated with expectations never quite met or with the receiving of unwanted gifts. The writer is tempted to see Christmas as a time when people gather together under the guise of goodwill to reaffirm family hostilities and sharpen long-standing feuds!

If this has some seeds of truth, what about the adolescent who has to take the brunt of the mother's feelings during the first Christmas after bereavement? Some mothers emphasise that there will be less than before: something the children expect and accept. What they cannot take are incessant reminders of the fact. As the time approaches, the mother who is not coping becomes more overtly depressed and imposes a heavy emotional burden on son or daughter. In such circumstances a lifeline is necessary: a simple card with unsentimental good wishes to maintain the link with the outside world; the telephone number with the remark, "Well, let me hear from you, if you feel you'll have time"; the effort to ensure some contact with people of the same age. A depressed mother can be very successful in compelling the children to look inwards into the family rather than outwards where things can be seen in perspective.

Where a sibling has died, it is not uncommon for the mother to become harshly critical of the other children, nagging at them unremittingly for a time. It is difficult to intervene directly, but we can help the child understand what is happening, for he may well be bewildered and resentful. Even more difficult, at least initially, is the situation where the mother over-protects the other children, provoking in them rebellion and anger with which she cannot cope.

We should give unobtrusive support when the pupil meets stress within a year of bereavement. Especially we should appreciate the psychological significance of the first anniversary of the death. Having made a note of it, if signs of stress appear in the child, a quiet word may be helpful. Often the mother shows restlessness or irritability as the time approaches and may not recognize why. If the first anniversary is dealt with successfully, it indicates that the dead are where they should be—with the dead. It is always good to hear the bereaved say, "It's just over a year since he died".

Sometimes the parent is unable to talk about the dead partner to the children. If the child mentions the dead father or sibling, the mother turns away with tightened lips and disappears upstairs. The child, of course, learns not to say anything to her, but the desire to talk about the dead person often grows in intensity. We can do something about this, although if we broach the matter with the mother we must be prepared to meet unresolved grief and anger. On occasions I have found that the mother will indicate her changing attitude by giving her son or daughter some piece of property that belonged to the father. Alternatively, the pupil may discuss with us his feelings about the dead person, but feel guilty because it appears disloyal to the mother. Such feelings and complications cannot be avoided.

If the parent cannot cope, we may have to help the pupil discover how he can both support the father or mother and protect himself from undue demands. After all, he still has his own life. One helpful thing to do is to put the parent into touch with voluntary associations of those in a similar predicament. The pastoral team should maintain an up-to-date list of such organizations and their local representatives. If parents can discuss their situation with others undergoing similar experiences, it reinforces positive attempts to use the situation constructively.

Finally, the supreme test is to ask, "How would I feel if this were my child?" and "How would I feel if I were this child?" We then avoid crude reactions of "cheering up" and are unlikely to ask clumsy questions. A truly compassionate teacher can anticipate stress, and without implying that they are different from others, that extra bit of support can be given without ever mentioning the bereavement.

REFERENCES

Andry, R. (1960) *Delinquency and Parental Pathology*, London: Methuen.

Bailey, R. (1973) The Scapegoat—or The One That Got Away. *British Journal of Guidance and Counselling*, Vol. 1. No. 2, July.

Biller, H. (1971) *Father, Child and Sex Role*. Lexington: Heath Lexington.

Bott, E. (1957) *Family and Social Network*. London: Tavistock.

Bowlby, J. (1946) *Forty-Four Juvenile Theives: Their Characters and Home Lives*, London: Bailliere, Tindall and Cox.

—— (1961) *The Adolf Meyer Lecture: Childhood Mourning and its implications for Psychiatry*, American Journal of Psychiatry. Vol. 188, pp. 481–97.

—— (1961) *Processes of Mourning*, International Journal of Psycho-Analysis, Vol. 44, p. 317.

Cooper, D. (1971) *The Death of the Family*, London: Allen Lane.

Eysenck, H. (1971) (Ed.) *Readings in Extraversion–Introversion: Fields of Application*, Vol. 2. London: Staples.

Finer Report (1974) *Report of Committee on One-Parent Families*, London: H.M.S.O.

Glueck, S. and Glueck, E. *Unraveling Juvenile Delinquency*, Cambridge: Harvard University Press.

—— & —— (1962) *Family Environment and Delinquency*, London: Routledge & Kegan Paul.

Gorer, G. (1965) *Death, Grief and Mourning in Contemporary Britain*, London: Cresset.

Hamblin, D. (1973) *Communcation Within the Home*, Occasional Papers, Division of Clinical and Educational Psychologists, British Psychological Society, No. 3, pp. 115–124.

—— (1974) *The Teacher and Counselling*, Oxford: Blackwell.

Laing, R. and Esterson, A. (1964) *Sanity, Madness and the Family*, Vol. 1: Families of Schizophrenics, London: Tavistock.

Laslett, P. (1965) *The World We Have Lost*, London: Methuen.

Lindemann, E. (1944) Symptomatology and Management of Acute Grief, *American Journal of Psychiatry*, Vol. 101, pp. 141–148.

Newsom Report (1963) *Half Our Future: Report of the Central Advisory Council for Education*, London: H.M.S.O.

Parkes, C. (1972) *Bereavement*, London: Tavistock.

Ring, K., Lipinski, C. and Braginsky, D. (1965) Relationship of Birth Order to Self Evaluation, Anxiety Reduction and Susceptibility to Emotional Contagion, *Psychological Monographs*, Vol. 79, No. 10. Whole No. 603.

Schachter, S. (1959) *The Psychology of Affiliation*, Stanford, California: Stanford University Press.

Swift, D. (1966) Social Class and Achievement Motivation, *Educational Research*, Vol. 8, No. 2, pp. 83–95.

Walker, N. (1968) *Crime and Punishment in Britain*, Edinburgh: Edinburgh University Press.

West, D. (1969) *Present Conduct and Future Delinquency*, London: Heinemann.

Willmott, P. and Young, M. (1960) *Family and Class in a London Suburb*, London: Routledge & Kegan Paul.

Wynn, M. (1964) *Fatherless Families*, London: Michael Joseph.

Young, M. and Willmott, P. (1957) *Family and Kinship in East London*, Routledge & Kegan Paul.

CHAPTER EIGHT: KEY POINTS

DIFFICULT PROBLEMS

PASTORAL TEAM MUST HAVE INTELLIGENT AND INFORMED ATTITUDES & NOT ATTEMPT TREATMENT

ANOREXIA NERVOSA

CONSIDER:
1. POPULAR MYTHS
2. FAMILY RELATIONS
3. BODY IMAGE
4. MIRROR IMAGE OF OBESITY

ASSESS:
SUPPORTS THAT SCHOOL CAN GIVE

SEXUAL DEVIANCY

CONSIDER:
1. LACK OF FIRM KNOWLEDGE
2. LINKS WITH IDENTITY DIFFICULTIES OF ADOLESCENCE
3. PREJUDICE AND THE "NOTHING BUT DEVIANT" APPROACH
4. MORAL JUDGEMENTS

ASSESS:
PUPILS' NEED FOR HELP

SELF-INFLICTED INJURY

CONSIDER
1. ANTECEDENTS
2. PURPOSE
3. CONTEXT

ASSESS:
VULNERABILITY OF CERTAIN PUPILS

CHAPTER EIGHT

PROBLEMS OF PASTORAL CARE: SELF-INFLICTED INJURY, THE BODY IMAGE, AND SEXUALITY

Summary

THE GENERAL ARGUMENT

A number of problems which did not previously come to the attention of the teacher now do so. Three of these are explored although the exposition is far from complete. The objective is to give sufficient knowledge to allow teachers to offer pupils support and enlightened acceptance, rather than blind sympathy. This, of course, does not imply that they should deal in depth with conditions beyond their competence, and which require specialist treatment.

SELF-INFLICTED INJURY

It is possible to underestimate the forces which can propel the vulnerable adolescent towards self-inflicted injury. Unfortunately, current research suggests that the patterns of behaviour, attitudes and personal history associated with attempted self-harm are also found in other conditions. Therefore it is far from easy to detect those who may respond to stress with attempted suicide.

Those who attempt it need help in areas relevant to their social and

239

intellectual functioning in school. The pastoral team should find out about attempted suicide and the ways they can help the individual, avoiding any imputations of deviancy or the creation of a dramatic situation which focuses the limelight on that pupil. The seriousness of suicide attempts by male adolescents is indicated by the fact that although they form a much smaller proportion of attempted suicides, they heavily outnumber girls in completed suicides.

ANOREXIA NERVOSA

This is a complex condition involving family relationships as much as the personality of the anorexic. Despite the far greater susceptibility of females to this illness, it is not restricted to them. There has been a tendency in the past to over-rely upon physiological explanations, which are now subject to critical scrutiny. The layman often over-simplifies the problem suggesting that the female anorexic is rejecting her femininity and retreating from sexual demands. In some cases this is true, but as a statement about the aetiology of the condition, it has only partial validity. Similarly, it is fallacious to claim that the anorexic is uninterested in food: in fact, she is fascinated by it, centring her life around its emotional significance.

The contribution of the mother-daughter relationship to the onset and severity of anorexia is brought to the forefront. The connections between self-starvation and the need to achieve autonomy and emotional separation from the mother have been recognised in recent years. Another aspect of current debate is the possibility of distortion in the anorexic's body image.

SEXUAL DEVIANCY

The *mores* of our society and the influences of the mass media can make some adolescents doubt their sexual identity. Caution is required here, for the pastoral worker may hold unrecognised prejudices based on old, but powerful, ideas about what is natural and what is unnatural. We may also confuse what is unfamiliar, distasteful or even repulsive to us with what is morally wrong.

The argument in this chapter is against loose permissiveness, because this could confirm prematurely a sexual identity still open to change. The difficulty in dealing with this topic is not lessened through having to face squarely the fact that we do not know why one individual is heterosexual, another bisexual and a third homosexual.

Pupils who believe that they are sexually deviant are often afraid of their parents' reactions, especially the mother's reaction in the male's case. They need help and support with the difficulties of adjustment. Although the pastoral team will obviously direct them when necessary to other sources of help, understanding firmly entrenched in respect for the individual is essential. We can then help the individual reduce his deviancy, real or imagined, to proportions which do not handicap his functioning as a person.

Self-inflicted injury

Incidents in which pupils deliberately injure themselves seem to be growing in frequency; and as Bagley (1975) remarks, while the suicide figures for the population as a whole seem to be decreasing, those for the younger age groups are rising. Rutter *et al.* (1976) argue that adolescence is often a time of turmoil, inner anguish being expressed through feelings of misery, revealed to those whom the adolescent trusts, and through self-depreciation. Many young people try to put a good face to the world but the stress so increases that it leads them to some form of self-injury.

If we see the purpose of secondary education as solely that of formal instruction, so be it, but if we feel education to be more than this, it is imperative that we gain the essential knowledge to understand our pupils. At the moment there is ignorance, distaste and indifference in many schools, contradicting claims of being "child-centred".

Teachers often interact with their pupils in ways which reduce their self-respect. They spend more time castigating pupils about behaviour of which they disapprove, than encouraging them when they behave in ways that the teacher finds acceptable. This imbalance has most impact on the anxious boy or girl whose inner doubt is reinforced by the teacher's behaviour. High standards are essential, but demands should be put forward positively, so as to build up optimism. Winterbottom (1958) showed that the mothers of sons with high levels of need for achievement set high demands for their sons, but they did this in a way which clearly expressed their belief that those sons would succeed. Negative predictions predominate in some classrooms, the destructive element being the suggestion that the pupil will never be good enough to succeed. Barrett (1976) shows that many fifth-form pupils feel that the classroom endorses their uselessness. Little wonder that they react with despair, hostility or most damagingly, a superficial conformity which renders us almost helpless. The cycle is then complete.

The school does not cause self-injury, rather it exacerbates or does nothing to help. Otto (1965) found a record of poor school adjustment in the suicides he studied, but school factors were comparatively insignificant as the cause of actual attempts. However the school can be a contributory factor, for Barrett and other workers have found that thoughts of suicide and self-injury increase as the level of self-esteem falls. We are at fault in failing to detect the signals which indicate the pupil's distress. Jacobnizer (1965) indicates that covert and overt warnings usually precede actual self-injury. Indeed, it is often directly linked to the failure to perceive such signals.

Durkheim (1952) describes four major types of suicide: anomic, altruistic, egoistic and fatalistic. We can ignore altruistic suicide and look for attempts at self-harm which show signs of the other three. Anomic suicide comes when there is a weakness in the bonds which tie the individual to society. Egoistic suicide is similar, but the emphasis is less on lack of integration into society as on excessive individualism. Fatalistic suicide is a reaction to unbearable restrictions. Durkheim was, however, writing as a sociologist, but his explanations have fairly obvious psychological parallels. Weak attachment to age mates, sudden changes in personal circumstances, and inflation of the ego which leads to wild over-estimating of the individual's social influence will be often found in those who injure themselves.

When we discuss an instance of so-called suicide, we may be talking about an attempted suicide which failed, or intended self-injury without death being the object. What does it mean to that boy or girl? It could be an appeal for help or for love. There may well be an aggressive element in it; for a child may harm himself in order to create guilt in others, by blaming them for what they are supposed to have done to him. We cannot assume that the adolescent who takes an overdose necessarily means to commit suicide: many try to ensure that they will be found in time, or warn a friend. But any attempt is a sign of disturbance sufficiently grave to need skilled attention.

242

McCulloch and Phillip (1972) tell us that in their Edinburgh study one teenager in every two hundred and fifty deliberately injured or poisoned herself or himself each year. Suicide or attempted suicide in the twenties and thirties was usually preceded by attempts in adolescence. Thus attempted suicide in adolescence incorporates doubt about the individual's future stability unless he or she receives help.

Barbiturates are mainly responsible for the deaths caused by drugs, although aspirin is most commonly used in suicide attempts amongst adolescents. Fortunately, they usually take too many, vomiting before the drug has time to be assimilated. When found, an immediate medical examination is necessary, because the body sometimes behaves in strange ways under excitement and tension. Parents should be warned to remove medicines from the house. Young people taking barbiturates usually use drugs prescribed for others in the family, so that an immediate search of the home is vital. The availability of means plays a far higher part in many suicides than most people suspect, for Kessel *et al.* (1963) and Kessel and McCulloch (1966) suggest that many suicidal acts are impulsive. Burton (1968) has developed the concept of the vulnerable child, based on Stott's idea of congenital impairment. Here the attitudes and behaviour associated with suicide seem to be those also linked with being taken into care, accident proneness and juvenile delinquency. After self-injury, one should scan the child's developmental history for this pattern of vulnerability. This provides a useful guide to the event's likely significance. If a pattern of maladjustment and proneness to accident is found, then we can consider referring the case for further psychiatric investigation.

It is difficult, however, to predict with any degree of certainty that a particular individual will harm himself. Every attempt to delineate a precise pre-suicidal syndrome has broken down in practice. Part of our dilemma derives from the fact that self-harm is often a sudden impulsive reaction to stress, when some additional event, sometimes trivial, breaches the individual's threshold. This may be a quarrel with parents or the breakdown of a close relationship. Many adolescents who attempt suicide have problems which alienate them from parents, and this is often accompanied by a compensatory romantic relationship which contains unrealistic elements which foredoom it to failure. The resulting breakdown is likely to lead to a temporary disintegration of the individual, who then makes a suicide attempt. Bergstrand and Otto (1962) in a study of 1,727 cases found that twenty per cent of the boys and eighty per cent of the girls had attempted suicide apparently because of difficulties in an intimate relationship.

Adolescents who attempt suicide tend to be withdrawn and self-punitive, unable to direct hatred outwards. Loneliness often assumes intolerable proportions for them, especially if there is doubt about their sexual identity. The inability to tolerate frustration is often strong, and self-pity characterizes many of them. The Edinburgh study suggested that many who attempt suicide are self-critical and self-punitive, and simultaneously critical and suspicious of others. Pressures in the school which reduce self-respect are also pressures which push the vulnerable pupil towards self-injury.

A pupil at risk might have a long-standing history of problems in childhood, which escalated during the early stages of puberty. If there is evidence that the pupil has had to struggle to establish his autonomy from a possessive mother, this gives us additional cause for concern. Indications of progressively worsening relations with teachers and peers add to this picture. Adam *et al*. (1973) suggest that the loss of a parent early in life is also a significant indicator. Sabbath (1969) talks of the suicidal adolescent as the expendable child, rejected by his parents. This pattern, of course, does not necessarily lead to suicidal attempts—the child could resort to violence—but he or she is certainly at risk.

Suicide and maladjustment seem to be bed partners. Impulsive character disorders are present, as Finch and Poznanski (1971) point out. After attempting suicide, adolescents of this type will often deny that they intended to harm themselves severely.

Some are depressive, but their depression remains unrecognised because it is hidden by truancy, disobedience, and the type of self-destructive behaviour which accompanies adolescent offences such as "driving and taking away". We must learn to recognise defences against despair and depression and try to discover the person's inner feelings. Other adolescents are paranoid, and will accept our help only to prove us wrong. They punish those who offend them by their acts of self-harm, for they manage to prove that this was caused by others' gross insensitivity.

One factor associated with self-injury in girls is premenstrual tension. Certainly girls seem more at risk, especially when an emotional tie has been cut or a prized relationship disrupted. Yet suicidal attempts seem to be increasing amongst boys, and may be more serious. Bergstrand and Otto report that although boys formed only about one-fifth of the total number of cases they studied, twice as many as girls actually committed suicide. An attempt by a boy is a very serious signal for help.

Communication must be built up positively with pupils who show tendencies towards self-harm. Disturbed behaviour is inevitably associated with confusing and destructive patterns of communication within the family. Conflicts arise from the very style of family communication, because what Manocchio and Petitt (1975) have described as the 'blame frame' emphasises the discrediting of the individual's motives, the blocking of attempts to escape from the position, and the attribution of negative intent. So the adolescent's motives and behaviour are continuously misinterpreted. Denial of the adolescent's right to be himself is predominant with such parents: he is their child and nothing more.

What then can we do? We can at least ensure that we do not replicate the destructive home communication patterns which erode self-respect. We can examine carefully the nature of the signals which reach pupils in many classrooms. These give the pupil a picture of how we view him, but sometimes they carry messages which we have neither intended nor recognized. Sarcasm can be often more destructive than physical punishment.

Our task is to help such pupils function more adequately in school and reduce their sense of isolation. We can help them with their social skills and take steps to link them with a group of stable peers, in which the skills of dealing constructively with day-to-day problems are methodically built up. Pupils from residential or foster homes may need more support after the attempt at self-harm than those from apparently more secure homes, although they are not necessarily at greater risk.

We must know our limits, and often psychiatric and psychological expertise is necessary. Every threat should be taken seriously, but this, of course, does not imply hasty and dramatic action. The adolescent needs the support of a calm and steady person. We learn not to react to threat and blackmail when handling such adolescents in school and yet to preserve and demonstrate our concern. We need to provide a firm and positive structure within which they can begin to experience success in living.

The problem often lies in the family relationships rather than in the adolescent alone, and it is not our task to attempt to modify this. At the most we can interpret it to the adolescent and help him behave more positively because he understands the roles thrust upon him. Finally, we can check what happens to the pupil during holidays and, if we are concerned, we can either use any existing educational opportunities, such as school camps, to relieve him of the burden, or in confidence inform the social services or school psychological service of our anxieties. Throughout we should provide good experiences within the school setting which build up the pupil's self-respect.

Anorexia nervosa

Many adolescents are sensitive about their bodies and the acceptability of their bodies to others, and I would like to give the reader some insight into *anorexia nervosa*, the extremely dangerous condition of compulsive self-starvation. Often the girl who suffers from this condition deteriorates and has to be hospitalized, with a poor prognosis. Indeed it is an open question whether an anorexic is ever free from her obsession about eating, so certain warnings must be given immediately. The emphasis will be on the female anorexic. Although Dally (1969) argues that ammenorrhea or the cessation of menstruation is an essential component of the illness, a parallel condition does occur in the male, but girl anorexics vastly outnumber males.

By dealing with this topic here, the writer is not suggesting that the teacher is competent to deal with the illness. But the pastoral team must be sufficiently alert to initiate referral for further medical and psychological investigation and not let a girl drift into the severe form of anorexia. They should know how to provide support and tolerate the irrational behaviour which accompanies recovery in some girls. And it may eradicate some of the crass ignorance of the problem found in staffrooms.

Girls are more likely to be concerned about their weight, physical appearance and, most crucially, personal relationships than boys. This may account for their greater susceptibility to the disease. Early studies of anorexia nervosa ignored psychological factors related to interpersonal bonds and indentity, although the work of Bruch (1974) and Palazzoli (1974) has done much to correct this. Girls seem to turn aggression against themselves rather than express it actively towards others. Hence covert ways of dealing with anger often appear. A girl is acutely worried if her physical appearance is at odds with the norms of her age group, but she can turn those negative attitudes into self-hatred. Some elements of this can be found in the anorexic, though they do not explain the illness.

Intuitively we know that obesity and anorexia nervosa are mirror images of one another, a perception further strengthened when we identify common underlying factors. At the physiological level, both types fail to interpret accurately the sensations of hunger or satiation; indeed Schachter (1959) suggests that the signals the obese person labels as those of hunger are actually very different from those of the normal person. Both rely on signals from outside themselves and deny the validity of inner ones.

Food manifestly plays an undue part in the anorexic's life, for she centres much of her emotional life around it. Both the anorexic and the obese are deeply concerned with food. Food and power are synonomous for the anorexic, but the power attributed to food is that of harm. Sufferers therefore induce vomiting and misuse laxatives to get rid of the dangerous substance.

Most mothers are guilty of using food to placate or reward their troublesome offspring, but in the family of the anorexic, food is a dominant element in bargaining between its members. Many mothers with an adolescent daughter who is anorexic stress that she was a good girl. They omit to make clear their curious definition of goodness. A good child is one who accepts the food thrust upon her by the mother, whilst the bad one rejects it. Meal-times become a source of stress in the family where a dominant and possessive mother creates a situation which weakens the girls's autonomy in this vital area. The prototype is the situation where the young girl claims that she has eaten enough, but the mother vehemently denies this, insisting that she "*must* feel hungry". Constant exposure to such experiences leads to the confusion described by Schachter.

It is likely, however, that this is merely a specific instance of a more general state of affairs. More generally, the family has become a system of interaction in which the child's independence and psychological wholeness are eroded by the mother's emotional blackmail and coercion. This is matched by the growth of devious tactics on the daughter's part. Both Bruch and Palazzoli argue that distorted feeding experiences in conjunction with continuous denials of the reality of the girl's inner life, make her feel almost totally controlled by external forces. In such a family, goodness is defined in passive terms, and the mother's definition of the girl's need for food override her own physical reactions. Vulnerability to anorexia is therefore created with the added stress of puberty. It is no accident that the onset is typically between the ages of thirteen and sixteen.

The argument could be interpreted psychoanalytically, but its developmental progression has a straightforward logic. The girl has not managed to separate from her mother—a bondage clearly expressed in areas associated with food. Again, some of these mothers have an obsessional interest in the state of their daughter's bowels. Inevitably when the girl reaches the identity task of adolescence, together with the emotional turbulence due to physiological changes, she lacks the wherewithal to cope. It is not that such girls reject the feminine role, but that sexuality is a challenge for which they are unprepared.

It is not true to say that the anorexic girl does not want to grow up. Most experts now see the anorexic girl as indulging in a determined attempt to achieve autonomy. It is both intense and maladaptive, and therefore foredoomed to failure. When invasion of personal boundaries and denial of independence have centred around eating, the struggle for autonomy will be expressed in the same terms. Anorexia also involves a disturbance of the body image of almost delusional proportions. Only in this way can the anorexic who is a handful of bones and skin maintain her position. But the anorexic is not to be trusted. She lies convincingly about her food intake, and she may well lie when she claims to see herself as normal, if not elegant. Deviousness is part of her survival kit; but while some girls are indulging in an insidious form of emotional blackmail when they claim that one square meal will make them fat and ugly, others are honestly stating their perceptions of themselves. Emaciation and the skin troubles which follow prolonged starvation do not worry such girls, and it is difficult to decide whether the reaction is one of rebellion or of genuine unawareness.

Anorexia brings amenorrhea and other malfunctioning, which can separate the girl from her peers. Autonomy therefore becomes isolation. The anorexic girl is often hyperactive, denying fatigue. At the same time she may experience a paralysing sense of depersonalization, feeling herself merely a passive respondent to others' actions, incapable of freely initiating action.

The price for over-intense and ambivalent attachment between mother and daughter is high, and evidence often emerges of hidden conflicts within the family. There seems to be an exaggerated fear of sex in some anorexic girls. Not only has the mother eroded her daughter's autonomy, but she has ensured that the conflict centres around the body image. Mothers tend to be older than the run of parents for the age group, although they also initiate competitive relationships with their daughters. Hence the dress of both the anorexic and the obese reflects the self-distaste which suggests that they see their bodies as unworthy of adornment. Such attitudes simultaneously convey an acceptance of the mother's views about the daughter's unattractiveness and a statement that at least she is different from the domineering mother. Both the obese and the anorexic often talk about their bodies as if they did not own them. This is a serious symptom which the teacher should not ignore. It is better to run the risk of an occasional unnecessary referral than allow a crisis to develop which demands prolonged treatment.

What can be done at school about anorexia? We may need to relax demands whose imposition replicates the home situation and probably increases the severity of the condition. We can get a dialogue going with the girl, but this can be dangerous because the anorexic girl is liable to blackmail emotionally those who try to assist her. The manipulated become the manipulators!

The mother needs help, but surely this is not our function. Where a girl is really anorexic, skilled family therapy is essential. Relief from undue stress, protection from the limelight and situations in which she is publicly evaluated, may be all that we can do to help the girl.

This is just as true for the much rarer male anorexic where the onset is earlier, usually between the age of ten and thirteen. Does this mean that the male condition has not the same connection with puberty? The boy may react more sharply to the competitive demands and the sudden expansion of social relationships when transferred to the secondary school. Preoccupation with body size and shape is marked in the male, and case histories seem to indicate the same inner doubts about competence as girls have.

In both sexes, the condition is often associated with a major change in the family environment through bereavement, birth or in the wider social setting. A move to a new school, leaving an area in which they have lived for a number of years, or the disappearance through death or divorce of the father who has acted as a buffer against the emotional forays of the mother, can be apparent precipitating factors. Occasionally, anorexia becomes manifest when the pupil moves from a school where he had achieved high status to one where he is submerged or the competition is more intense. At times, I have found some slight link between the condition and a high drive towards success unbacked by aptitude.

Gooch (1976) makes some interesting suggestions for breaking into the vicious circle in which many adolescents with weight problems are trapped, although they are far from anorexic. They make sporadic attempts to cope with their weight problems, but fail to maintain the effort. The relapse causes guilt, and the attempt begins again, ending as before. The cycle then becomes part of their life pattern. Gooch advocates a version of the strategy used by Weight Watchers, a club designed to help members lose weight. Members would be committed publicly to do this. Regular checks on weight, setting of targets, dietary advice and suggestions for muscle-toning exercises would be part of it; so would help with dress and the improvement of appearance. Individual counselling would be available.

Peer supports make the likelihood of success greater than when the effort is conducted in isolation. The school nurse, physical education department and counsellor would have much to contribute, but there should be medical consultation before any child in indifferent health is admitted. Gooch remarks that such a club would have to impose penalties for failure to carry out the self-imposed tasks, if the guilt which is part of the failure pattern is to be avoided. Of course, the anorexic will not be attracted to the club. Emotional conflicts and the pressing need for autonomy prevent their seeing it as a viable or attractive way of gaining their ends.

The reader may well feel disappointed that so little that is positive has been said, but my aim has been to give some idea of what it feels like to be an anorexic, in order that we can avoid mawkishness or insensitivity.

Sexual deviance

Lesbianism and male homosexuality may seem unusual topics for a book on pastoral care. These problems, however, are age-old and we should responsibly examine them as carefully as possible, avoiding both prejudice which may stem from our own immaturity and fear, and brash forms of permissiveness.

The new climate of apparent frankness, coupled with the odd offerings of the mass media, have brought these topics into adolescent thinking in ways unknown to many of us. Jokingly I remarked to an eleven-year-old girl that she would probably be thinking about acquiring a boy friend shortly. Her response was terse and unexpected. "No, but you needn't think that I'm a lesbian." She did not come from a particularly sophisticated background, yet her reply was both spontaneous and natural. Such an anecdote illustrates that we are now working with pupils who approach topics which would have been taboo to many of us at their age. But this openness does not mean that we can take for granted that pupils have any deep understanding of the complications and difficulties of sexual deviancy.

The moral element poses grave difficulties for some teachers when they have to deal with an incident which seems to involve sexual deviancy. Confusion of what we find distasteful with what is immoral is a form of philosophical immaturity. Echoes of the old cries of decadence and corruption are not far away in many discussions of what to do when a pupil shows signs of homosexuality or undue interest in forms of sexuality which we regard as unusual. Patronage and pity are of little use; nor should we deny that deviance is a problem for its possessor. This discussion will try to understand the genuine distress that a real or imagined sexual difference causes the young person, and to look at the situation with honesty.

We must not forget that the sexual drive is remarkably plastic, for it can be easily conditioned and directed towards not only the opposite sex, but the same sex, leather or rubber garments, whips, handbags and even perambulators. This recognizes hard facts to which many psychiatrists and psychotherapists would testify. The demand on busy teachers, that we should cope honestly with sexual problems when we have not entirely discarded our own adolescent prejudices and emotional conflicts, is intimidating. Many of us still have inbuilt reactions of guilt which originally belonged to adolescence. When we find ourselves reacting to someone who seems sexually different, with revulsion or contempt, it may tell us more about ourselves than about their problem, and we should cast a suspicious eye at ourselves. We react most negatively to that which we see in others but which is also present in us, although we attempt to deny its existence.

Before taking the discussion further, I must make my position clear, I am not advocating the introduction of unstructured discussions on the topic into programmes of guidance. Observation has taught me that this can increase the prejudice of the rough and tough sections of the school rather than modify it. Although my aim is to provide a climate of greater understanding for those who are sexually different in our schools, I am not arguing for permissiveness or the flaunting of deviance. Decent inhibitions are essential for the smooth functioning of society, and mutual adjustments have to be made. Reality exists, and one must accept that the sexual deviant will not meet tolerance in some schools and settings.

251

I am, however, trying to build on the teacher's goodwill and concern, so that we learn to give true respect to those who differ from us. We must avoid the "nothing but" approach which treats the problem as if it were the totality of the pupil's being. People are far more than their sexuality. Above all, we must help them learn the value of commitment, trust and love. Good experience or exposure to real concern may be more profoundly therapeutic than anything else. But let us remember that although therapy means healing; it does not necessarily imply sickness. The hurt which has to be healed comes from the sexual deviant's guilt and anxiety, rather than from anything inherent in his sexual orientation.

Learning to understand and help

I will being this section by quoting from the profoundly compassionate Quaker document (1963) which gets at the heart of the problem: "as society changes and modes of conduct with it, we must always be searching below the surface of human behaviour to discover what is in fact happening to people, what they are seeking to express, what motives and intentions they are satisfying, what fruits, good or bad, they are harvesting". We have to admit that we do not know why one person is heterosexual, another homosexual and yet another bisexual. When such ambiguity reigns it behoves us to proceed cautiously, avoiding condemnation or rash endorsement of the pupil's claimed sexual identity. The fact that homosexual tendencies do not always lead to a homosexual way of life should make us refrain from precipitate action that could cause a false crystallization of identity from which it will not be easy to retreat.

Homosexuality has, in the past, been regarded as a disease, and this still seems to operate. Freud saw male homosexuality as the product of over-attachment to the mother which led to a neurotic fear of heterosexual relationships. Hence homosexuality was basically a neurotic fear of sexual relationships with females deeply instilled during early childhood. Many people now reject this hypothesis, although there is some evidence that the family backgrounds of some homosexuals, female and male, contain some unusual features. Clinicians have drawn attention to the frequency with which a background containing a dominant mother and a weak, passive father figures in their cases. Bene (1965), who attempts to clarify the function of the parents in the creation of male homosexuality, is one of a number of workers who report such findings.

However, association does not necessarily mean a direct causal link, and this pattern may apply only to sexual deviants who also experience neurotic conflict and maladjustment. Whilst we have no British equivalent to the survey of Kinsey *et al.* (1953), it seems that many homosexuals are well adjusted and that the condition is more frequent than many of us imagine. This means that we may have to return to theories concerned with the impact of labelling and the derivative sense of stigma to explain the unhappiness and conflict of some sexual deviants. Plummer (1975) argues that behaviour is the emergent product of social interaction. The feeling of difference, perhaps of inferiority and badness, comes from the reactions of others, although self-labelling has most impact. Once this occurs, the chances are that the individual will move into overt expression of his sexual identity, unless he or she remains trapped in a state of guilt or conflict.

This is a reminder that condemnation and moralizing can have the opposite effect to that which was intended. Punishment and disapproval may effectively create or confirm deviant identities. The greater the hostility encountered by the individual, the stronger the tendency to self-label. In an age when the traditional boundaries between the sexes are diminishing, there are also strong compulsions towards sexuality. If doubts exist in the adolescent and then he receives signals which seem to categorize him adversely, his vulnerability leads to grave anxiety.

Developmental psychologists have noted that there is a period in earlier adolescence when the individual strongly identifies with heroes and models of the same sex. To interpret this as homosexuality perhaps tells one more about the person who labels, than of the adolescent. The deprived, possibly not very bright girl, who develops the equivalent of the old-fashioned "crush" on a sixth-form pupil or the P.E. mistress, is only expressing something about the sex-role model to which she aspires. Only very rarely is it more. A little gentle humour, encouragement with her school work, and helping her to make the best of her appearance are more appropriate than the over-reaction which I have seen in some schools.

If we realize that bisexuality may be more common than homosexuality, we shall begin to temper our harsh conception of the dichotomy between so-called normal sex and so-called deviance. After all, we all carry the hormones of the opposite sex within ourselves, and should consider why some old ladies tend to develop moustaches, and old men become rounded. Such facts as these can help us develop real acceptance rather than woolly permissiveness.

How can we be of service to the pupil who finds himself or herself in a dilemma of sexual identity? First, one must realize that legally there is an irrational difference between the sexes. Two consenting male adults can now legally commit a homosexual act in private, provided that both are over twenty-one. But homosexual acts between women are subject to no such restrictions, and indeed have never been illegal. This difference in the law is a source of great difficulty for the male pupil who feels that he is homosexual. His anxiety, alarm and resentment require wise and calm counsel.

The greatest fear is that of their parents' finding out. Most males are deeply worried about the parents' reactions, and although they often are afraid of paternal violence, they are more afraid of their mother's rejection. The fear of parental discovery and of the reaction that may have to be faced, means that if exposure does occur, the youth will need strong support whilst his father and mother work through their reactions. The homosexuality of a son or daughter may be more of a problem for the parents than it is for the boy or girl. I am currently working with a boy whose father reacted violently to the discovery and although he felt true affection for the boy, he saw him as almost evil. It was his own panic and fear that were the real problem. The mother, on the other hand, was so determinedly liberal in her approach, that she went around trumpeting the news to friends and acquaintances in a highly dramatic way. We may validly ask whose problem is the most severe.

The reaction of the head of the school and the staff is sometimes another problem. Many heads and senior staff behave in a way which earns my admiration, accepting that the welfare of the pupil comes before all other considerations. I have met cases, however, when the pupil was arbitrarily suspended from school, even though nothing was done on school premises. As with similar reactions to drug-taking, the justification is the fear that others will be "corrupted". A moment's thought would suggest that this is unlikely, and that the deviant pupil is the one at risk.

Many of these boys and girls need counselling which does not see them as problems, but which honestly faces the fact that their declared sexual orientation will create problems for them. The males often find they have to maintain two groups of friends, one of which knows about their sexual proclivity and the other which does not.

They then worry in case the two groups should interact. This leads to a daunting awareness that they may be moving towards a life of double standards and pretence, although the act of declaring themselves is often more so. Concealment can aggravate the sense of having an identity imposed upon them, which is a common feature of later adolescence.

Both sexes may need special help in talking through their feelings about finding a satisfying relationship. They may need to look at the distasteful aspects of the sub-culture to which they are drawn. They need to be aware of the frustrations, shallowness of relationships and the possibility of exploitation, but romanticism and blind self-justification may hide these aspects from them. Although I do not accept the concept of fixation at an early stage of development, there is often a need to deal with immaturities. Many such pupils maintain a blind belief in their creativity, without any evidence of talent. They constantly search for an outlet for what they believe they possess, ignoring their real ability. Perhaps this indicates nothing more than that they have accepted cultural stereotypes. In one area in South Wales, boys remiss enough to indicate an interest in music, art or, even worse, drama, run the risk of being dubbed a "billo" or homosexual. The belief in the artistic ability of the sexual deviant may be the same phenomenon viewed in a looking glass.

One key factor is the age at which subjects report their awareness of attraction to the same sex. In Kalmund's (1975) study of male homosexuality, some of his subjects said that they were attracted to the same sex at as early as ten years old, although they vary widely. Saghir and Robins (1969) in their investigation of females found that emotional and sexual attachments to the same sex began before the age of fourteen. Thus there is evidence that the sexual identity of some adolescents has been establishing itself over a number of years and that a change of orientation is unlikely.

It seems sensible, however, to behave as if identity was still open. Such organizations such as the Campaign for Homosexual Equality have a very useful role in society, helping us adjust to new vistas, but they can be unhelpful to the lonely adolescent who may begin to feel that he will only be accepted within the homosexual group. Doors which should remain open may then prematurely close, and questions which the individual should raise about his inner self are submerged, probably because a temporary relief from anxiety and isolation is experienced.

Finally, let me make my position clear. I would neither encourage nor inhibit, but I would help someone think the situation through in an atmosphere of trust and peace. If he or she is clear and convinced, then I see little need for counselling, unless the pupil is worried about the future and the sexual identity itself is problematical. If, however, they feel that they are "freaks", if fear or confusion is present, if they become obsessed with the problem or label themselves as abnormal, then we must help them. If we feel this beyond us, we must see that they are directed to agencies of known integrity.

In the end, we are still left with questions that each of us must answer for ourselves. Should we try to help the adolescent who says that he is sexually deviant adjust to his orientation, or should we try to change it? If we concentrate on the so-called problem, are we making matters worse; but if we stress his general adjustment, are we indulging in evasion? Certainly we must develop respect for the integrity of the other, but such questions can only be answered according to our conscience, remembering that what we sometimes call conscience is more concerned with the negative than the positive, with prohibitions rather than positive injunctions. The old story of the therapist and the patient may raise healthy doubts in us. The patient enters and says to the therapist, "I'm God". After surveying him coldly, the therapist rejoins, "Very well, I'll let you be God". Whose then is the omnipotence? Is it possible that in the matter of sexual deviancy we may possess a hidden omnipotence which makes a mock of our finest pretensions?

REFERENCES

Adam, K., Lohrenz, O., Hard Harper, D. (1973) Suicidal Ideation and Parental Loss, *Canadian Psychiatric Association Journal*, Vol. 18, pp. 95–100.

Bagley, C. (1975) Suicidal Behaviour and Suicidal Ideation in Adolescents: a Problem for Counsellors in Education, *British Journal of Guidance and Counselling*, Vol. 3, No. 2, July.

Barrett, A. (1976) *Some causes of stress among fifth form pupils.* Unpublished D.S.C. Dissertation: University College of Swansea.

Bene, E. (1965) On the Genesis of Male Homosexuality: An Attempt at Clarifying the Role of the Parents, *British Journal of Psychiatry*, 3.

Bergstrand, C. and Otto, U. (1962) Suicidal Attempts in Adolescence and Childhood, *Acta Paediatrica Scandinavia*, Vol. 51, January, pp. 17&26.

Bruch, H. (1974) *Eating Disorders*, London: Routledge & Kegan Paul.

Burton, L. (1968) *Vulnerable Children*, London: Routledge & Kegan Paul.

Dally, P. (1969) *Anorexia Nervosa*, London: Heinemann.

Durkheim, E. (1952) *Suicide*, London: Routledge & Kegan Paul.

Finch, S. and Poznanski, E. (1971) *Adolescent Suicide*, Springfield, Illinois: Thomas.

Gooch, C. (1976) *The Body-Image of the Adolescent Girl*, Unpublished D.S.C. Dissertation: University College of Swansea.

Jacobnizer, H. (1965) Attempted Suicides in Adolescence, *Journal of the American Medical Association*, Vol. 191, No. 1 January.

Kalmund, P. (1975) *Identification and Adjustment of the Male Adolescent Homosexual*, Unpublished D.A.D. Dissertation: University College of Swansea.

Kessell, N. and McCulloch, W. (1966) Repeated Acts of Self-Poisoning and Self-Injury, *Proceedings of Royal Society of Medicine*, Vol. 59, 89.

Kessel, N., McCulloch, W. and Simpson, E. (1963) Psychiatric Service in a Centre for the Treatment of Poisoning, *British Medical Journal*, Vol. 2, p. 985.

Kinsey, A., Pomeroy, W., Martin, C. and Gebhart, P. (1953) *Sexual Behaviour in the Human Female*, Philadelphia: Saunders.

McCulloch, J. and Phillip, A. (1972) *Suicidal Behaviour*, Oxford: Pergamon.

Manocchio, T. and Petitt, W. (1975) *Families Under Stress*, London: Routledge & Kegan Paul.

Otto, U. (1965) Suicidal Attempts Made by Children and Adolescents Because of School Problems. *Acta Paediatrica Scandinavia*, Vol. 54, July. pp. 348–356.

Palazzoli, M. (1974) *Self-Starvation*, London: Chaucer.

Plummer, K. (1975) *Sexual Stigma: An Interactionist Account*, London: Routledge & Kegan Paul.

Quaker Document. A Group of Friends (1963) *Towards a Quaker View of Sex*, London: Friends Home Service Committee.

Rutter, M., Graham, P., Chadwick, D. and Yule, W. (1976) Adolescent Turmoil: Fact or Fiction, *Journal of Child Psychology and Psychiatry*, Vol. 17, No. 1, January.

Sabbath, J. (1969) The Suicidal Adolescent—The Expendable Child. *Journal of the American Academy of Child Psychiatry*, Vol. 8, pp. 272–289.

Saghir, M. and Robins, E. (1969) Sexual Behaviour of the Female. *Archives of General Psychology*, Vol. 20.

Schachter, S. (1959) *The Psychology of Affiliation: Experimental Studies of the Sources of Gregariousness*, Stanford: Stanford University Press.

Waldenstrom, J., Larson, T. and Ljungstedt, N. (Eds.) (1972) *Suicide and Attempted Suicide*, Stockholm: Nordiska Bokhandelns Forlag.

Winterbottom, N. (1958) The relation of heed for achievement to learning experiences in independence and mastery. In Atkinson, J. (Ed) *Motives in Fantasy, Action and Society*, Princeton, N.J.: Van Nostrand.

CHAPTER NINE: KEY POINTS

LINKS WITH OUTSIDE INFLUENCES

PLANNED USE OF:

1. SCHOOL PSYCHOLOGICAL SERVICES

2. SOCIAL SERVICES

3. PTA OR OTHER REGULAR SYSTEM OF CONTACT WITH PARENTS

+

MOBILISATION OF RESOURCES WITHIN THE SCHOOL

ACTION TO DEVELOP:

1. IN-SERVICE TRAINING

2. MANAGEMENT OF THE PASTORAL SYSTEM

3. PLANNED INNOVATIONS

4. REGULAR EVALUATION

=

NECESSARY CONDITIONS FOR CREATING AN EFFECTIVE SYSTEM OF PASTORAL CARE

SOME WIDER ISSUES: IN-SERVICE TRAINING, INNOVATION, EVALUATION, AND LINKS WITH THE OUTSIDE WORLD

Summary

THE GENERAL ARGUMENT

This chapter surveys the processes and factors which form the sub-structure upon which the good management and success of the pastoral system rests. It looks at the conditions which have to be created if innovations are to be introduced successfully. The need for evaluation to be accepted as an essential part of the pastoral endeavour is mooted; and the perceptual processes which are often neglected in our deliberations, despite their salience in determining the outcome of our effort, are highlighted.

IN-SERVICE TRAINING

The school must assume responsibility for extending the skills of form tutors by arranging training courses specifically designed to foster the professional development of this particular group of teachers working within the context of a particular school. Such

261

courses are the responsibility of the heads of year or house in conjunction with the deputy head of pastoral care and other members of staff with relevant skills. Whilst a job specification is a prerequisite for accountability and for efficient performance by the form tutor, by definition it only states what has to be done. A skills analysis which states how the objectives can be achieved is essential. This then acts as a basis for the training courses.

HOME AND SCHOOL LINKS

There must be clearly stated objectives for improving links between school and home. A start may be made by using the critical incidents as points of contact. It is crucial to evaluate current procedures to detect any aspects which make them counter-productive or negate the avowed aims of such contacts. Parental interest and understanding are probably best stimulated by activities which give parents first-hand experience of teachers' methods, rather than by lectures. Placing the parents in helping roles may be the most effective means of ensuring their co-operation. The ways in which the P.T.A. can become an active source of support for the school are touched upon.

THE EDUCATIONAL PSYCHOLOGIST

The training and role of the educational psychologist are rapidly extending, and so their advisory and training functions are more relevant to the secondary school than they were a few years ago. Hence it is sensible to involve the psychologist in training courses for the pastoral team. In particular, the school will find his knowledge of behaviour modification, the detection and reduction of stress, and the nature of learning disability, of particular relevance. Regular case conferences will not only ensure more effective guidance for the pupils concerned, but will help the teacher acquire the skills of assessment of problems.

THE SOCIAL SERVICES

Schools can have unrealistic expectations of the social services, and teacher and social worker can be suspicious of each other. Barriers to co-operation with the social worker exist in some schools. These could be removed by mutual dialogue to promote the establishment of procedures for communication and action. The knowledge and skill of the teacher can often reinforce those of the social worker if professional boundaries are not allowed to inhibit communication. It is obvious that the social worker should have the opportunity of direct contact with the form tutor.

Wider issues

The pastoral team can learn much from the history of curricular innovations at secondary level, where the need to plan systematically for the dissemination and implementation of new methods has been gradually accepted. We should carefully examine how the pastoral team is trained to meet the needs of a particular school. Teachers' centres do extremely valuable work, yet if no structured arrangements exist within the school to spread the knowledge gained to those who have not attended the courses, little impact is made on the school as a whole.

Richardson (1973) gives some useful insights into the inertia and determination to maintain the *status quo* which can inhibit in-service training. In any case it must be introduced gradually. I believe in a form of in-service training which uses the resources of the whole school, and in my own courses, heavy emphasis is given to the provision of skills and experiences that will allow the students to undertake the in-service training of their colleagues.

The responsibility of the senior management and the specially trained person is reinforced by that of the year or house head. He has to develop materials, institute training programmes for those for whom he is responsible and face the difficulties which accompany the concept of accountability, if he or she is to justify their allowances. The same arguments apply to the senior managers, the head of lower and middle school or the deputy head who is in charge of the pastoral system.

In-service training is merely one component of good management which involves decisions about the purpose and nature of pastoral activities and the mobilization of the human and material resources to accomplish them. It is concerned with the professional performance of members of the pastoral team within a specific school, and contains an unique blend of organizational and personal features. The senior management must recognize that form tutors need co-ordination of effort, the necessary materials to carry out the task, and a sound structure of management of the pastoral team. They must also realize that form tutors and subject teachers must not hold negative attitudes towards pastoral care. Structured programmes of training should be organized by the deputy head responsible for the pastoral system. Such courses may be concerned with measures to combat truancy or disruptive behaviour or to meet the pastoral needs of certain sectors of the school population. Senior management should also institute training groups to provide the year and house heads with technical and managerial skills. This might be done by advanced training courses provided by institutes of higher education and university departments of education.

Training and change with the school

The person responsible for the development of pastoral methods must avoid confrontation and be credible, especially in a school where existing relationships are marked by excessive formality and rigidity. As important, is the confidence inspired by those whom the innovator involves in the project. It seems to me that senior members of the pastoral team often fail to anticipate the difficulties of innovation and how their ideas will work out in real life. The first step towards implementing change is a diagnostic one. Many modifications of pastoral method are basically an attempt to alleviate some problem, yet too little time and effort are devoted to defining the problem clearly and analysing the underlying causes. A problem of the drop-out of non-traditional sixth-form students during their first year could be met with attempts to make the curriculum more relevant; yet investigation might show that promised changes in teacher-pupil relationships had not occurred and that demands for unsupervised study, for which these pupils lacked the skills, actually caused the dissatisfaction. During the diagnostic period we must question our original definition of the problem. We may then find that a problem about the wearing of school uniform has something to do with how the ideal pupil is envisaged, rather than rejection of the teacher's authority.

Pastoral care always begins by assessing the individual's strengths and then building on them, rather than emphasizing his or her

264

weaknesses. This is just as true for our assessment of the system. We identify the areas in which the team is coping and build outwards from these, provided that we take certain precautions. Gross *et al.* (1971) show the limitations of the usual explanations of failure in innovation. These commonly stress the inability of individuals attempting to introduce new ideas to overcome teachers' initial resistance to the changes. But it neglects the possibility that individuals originally favourable to the change are discouraged by barriers and frustrations stemming from the educational organization and the structure of the school. New methods will be only partially implemented because such hazards are ignored; and also, as usual, teachers change them because they perceive them differently from the person who introduced them. Two essential points arise from this. First, the headmaster and his deputies should acquire the skills to detect such barriers and hazards, and then take steps to remove them. Second, there must be discussion of the reasons for an innovation with the staff before its introduction.

Parlett and Hamilton (1972) suggest that evaluation should be conceived as a gradual process of illumination, unravelling the nature of the processes and problems. Problems may emerge which were not present at first, and we may fail to detect them. This approach pays due respect to the emotional climate of the school and key beliefs about the educability of some groups of pupils, and also to the type of innovation which merits the expenditure of time and effort. Hence, it is argued that it is only the insider who can meaningfully analyse the latent features of a particular school that will determine the success or failure of a particular project.

Without clear objectives none of the above is workable, but this does not mean that our objectives are immutable. Davies (1976) argues that, without some statement of our goal, we cannot assess how nearly our final results match the intended ones.

Davies presents findings which suggest that it is the pupil of middle ability who benefits most from teaching methods with clear objectives. By definition these pupils are the majority. Equally, may not this finding be true of the majority of teachers? Many of them are aware that their pastoral duties form only one element of their teaching task, and so they need help to use constructively the limited time available to them. A framework given by clear objectives which they have helped to formulate keeps them on target, yet allows the form tutor to experiment profitably in areas where he feels able.

Having provided a framework, the next step is to look at the changes in job specifications which spring from the objectives and associated methods. In many cases management finds it useful to analyse these changes in terms of the work load on year heads, their assistants and the form tutors. For this a year or house head should be able to produce diagrams or statements which indicate how the tasks are phased over the year.

The allocation of resources, including personnel, forms part of this planning. Year and house heads must learn to analyse the workload on certain members of staff, but they must also recognize that certain year groups may need extra personnel for special tasks. Outmoded conceptions of the form tutors' task can lead us to think that all we have to do is provide one tutor for each class and a head of year, and all will be well. Efficiency demands that we have teachers, apart from form-tutor and head of year, who are responsible for the development of materials and the implementation of certain parts of the guidance programme. Truants, the aggressive and the very withdrawn can also benefit from smaller pastoral-care groupings planned specifically for their needs.

Some schools have realized the need to control information and to find methods of presenting it which do not encourage distortion. Two devices help. First, the number of yearly reports is reduced giving more time for them to be written in a form meaningful to the reader. Second, reports should concern the actual behaviour of the pupil rather than personal interpretations of it, and should make clear practical suggestions for improvement. They can also be written at different times of the year for different classes, so that they are not hurried.

The managers in the pastoral team should train themselves to consider that latent factors may be more significant than the manifest aspects of a problem or a situation. Tensions, malfunctioning and anxiety can lead to defensive attitudes in which displacement of blame obscures the difficulty. Caseworkers express this clearly when they say that the presenting problem is not necessarily the true problem. The pastoral team and those responsible for innovation and management within it must always maintain open minds.

In counselling we have learned to build on the individual's strengths rather than dwell upon his weaknesses. Similarly, if we wish to induce development in the pastoral system, we must identify areas of strength and success and build outwards from these. The positive approach leads us to ask about rewards for participants in the new activity. These will take many forms. Those which motivate the teacher are concerned with raising the level of the pupil's performance, an increased sense of professional competence and improved interaction with pupils.

If rewards are unduly delayed, great commitment is required to continue working. The principle of working from areas of strength allows planners so to introduce new methods as to secure reasonably quick returns, for it is the equivalent of the principle of graduation of difficulty in behaviour modification. If this strategy is profitable for the pupil who wishes to change, it is equally useful for those who wish to innovate within an existing system. Alternatively, one can begin innovation in an area where the problem is acute and where most members of staff feel that something has to be done urgently.

Successful innovation allows those who will implement it some measure of choice. Therefore the year head should offer the form tutors a range of ideas from which they can select. It is imperative to begin gradually, formulating the new method as a feasibility study. Both innovator and form tutors can then approach the experiment objectively, feeling neither threatened by its success or depressed by its failure. If it is presented in a workmanlike way, with clearly stated boundaries of time and effort, and explicit and strictly limited objectives, then it is possible to build on success, if this occurs, or discard the innovation without feeling too disappointed. Modification will be usually necessary, and the form tutors should be involved in these modifications.

A pastoral-care system, must, therefore, be ready to introduce and foster new methods. Its planning must be carefully assessed, so that tutors feel involved, and pupils' needs are met realistically. Let us remember that our planning is always related to a particular situation rather than to an ideal state of affairs, for what can be done in one school in one way, would be inappropriate in another.

A successful pastoral system must allow for constant reappraisement so that emerging problems can be identified, many of which could not be anticipated until the tutors work on the project. This may lead to the discovery that the emergent target is more appropriate than that originally set. The year or house head must always specify the prerequisities for success. If these include new skills on the part of the form tutor in the use of games and simulations, we must provide training within the school. Consensus about the objectives only gradually develops, but we must beware of confusion which allows destructive elements and conflict to predominate.

From the first teaching practice the teacher's major concern is with order and control; yet we can fail to pay sufficient attention to this in planning new developments. If new methods violate pupil's expectations about the teacher's role, then we ask for trouble, because pupils can be more resistant to change than their teachers. Tutors have their own ideas about their role, and if new methods risk destroying order and lead to problems of control, then one cannot blame the tutor for rejecting them. Again, in-service training to build up the skills of classroom management is needed in the school anxious to innovate within the pastoral area.

The good innovator and manager is one who pays as much attention to social relationships, perceptions and processes as to the basic task and techniques. To ignore either broad element is foolish, for to emphasize the task alone is to open oneself to the danger of taking a superficial approach to the intellectual and personal growth that the pastoral system should foster. This simple approach can be backed by reference to other work such as that of Davies (1971), Daunt (1975), Hughes (1970), Richardson (1973) and Marland (1971). These works provide a basis for working out the routines and procedures which form the basis of the orderly structure essential for pastoral care.

If those of us responsible for the growth and efficiency of the pastoral system blind themselves to the fact that many young teachers see our attempts at helping children as a not too subtle form of paternalism, directed both at pupils and at them, we will not understand the resistance that we meet. Paternalism is a highly emotive word, although one could ask what is society without the father? Failure to comprehend the latent aspects of resistance, leads the senior people to clumsy measures which the protester takes as confirmation that he was correct in his original assessment. Heads of year or house do not always see that resistance may reflect a defensive attitude, based often on concern that demands are being made which the form tutor lacks the skill to meet. To avoid this painful exposure, they summarily dismiss the demands. Training would prevent this situation from assuming serious proportions; and it is a central task in the management of the pastoral system to anticipate relevant criticism although this does not mean stifling it.

The management of the pastoral system, apart from the setting of objectives and the development of appropriate methods and activities, should be, therefore, equally concerned with the modification of patterns of interaction between individuals and between groups. Richardson (1973) points out that the task of management includes the recognition of groups which impede performance, and the pastoral team must develop constructive strategies for their modification and dissolution. We have already seen how some processes such as the allocation of reputations and the continuance of unnecessary points of conflict worsen the situation. A pastoral team which does not account for the way the subterranean life of the classroom and the methods of organization influence performance, will not make a creative contribution to pupils' quality of life. One gets the impression that many guidance teams are future-orientated, which is essential, but forget that pupils live their lives now. What happens this week shapes what we and our pupils will do next year.

Links with parents and other professionals

Management of the pastoral system includes the monitoring of links with other agencies and with parents. Such contacts have always tended to be a source of anxiety, conflict and adverse publicity. Today many more teachers are involved than in the past. They have to interact with professionals and parents who can be highly critical of the school's objectives, methods and output. It is not surprising that the management of such links is becoming an increasingly important element in our comprehensive schools, so that no ill-considered action is taken which may be further misinterpreted by the outside audience.

Links with parents are critical for maintaining effort and raising pupils' standard of performance, especially in the first three or possibly four years of the secondary stage. It must be accepted, however, that parents are becoming increasingly critical of educational practices, though some still expect the school to produce results for their children without any effort or co-operation from them. As a profession, we must build good relationships which will help the neighbourhood form its image of the school. Without this, parents are only too ready to allocate a school a poor reputation. We must, therefore, be prepared to invest time in helping parents understand new methods and explaining our objectives.

Difficulties undoubtedly exist in parent-teacher relationships. For one thing, as Lindley (1976) demonstrates, pupils after the fourth year have reservations about, if not an active dislike of, parent-teacher contacts. Unless there is trouble, they see these links as a threat to their autonomy.

Mutual suspicion between parents and teachers often exists, whilst such visits to school as do take place may lead to an increased sense of grievance and acrimony. However, Plowden (1967) argued that teachers and parents should be partners in more than name; Newsom (1963) that schools cannot undertake the educative task alone: parents cannot abdicate responsibility for guiding their children.

Parental contact with the secondary school brings sharply into focus the possibility of the clash of values between parents and teachers. Enquiry One (1968) shows that parents and their children stress different aspects of the teacher's role and the school's functions from those that teachers stress. Other sources of misunderstanding spring from attitudes built up from the moment of entry to infant school, which colour pupils' responses to the learning situation. By the time the pupil from a disorganized home reaches the secondary school this may have hardened into a life-style for school hours which incorporates avoidance of demands, minimal effort and disruptive behaviour. Only a concerted pastoral effort, linked with the curricular and including real contact with parents, has a chance of modifying this pattern of behaviour. Some children from deprived backgrounds have learned little at home that they can transfer to the schoolroom. They have to acquire the skills of planning, prudential thinking, and setting ever more difficult targets.

Links with parents from poor backgrounds are essential. They are even more so with parents from good backgrounds, who are concerned about their children's achievement but have limited views of the nature of education, lacking understanding of how modern methods equip pupils for life in a rapidly changing world. Their emphasis on progress produces "mark-hungry" children.

We know that many other factors besides intelligence play a part in achievement in school: indeed a significant part of the variation between individuals is accounted for by factors other than intelligence. We who work in the pastoral system, become very aware that a pupil chooses to work or not to work, whether this choice is worked out consciously or reflects the influence of others. Faced with curricular activities apparently suitable for him, he can eagerly approach them, actively avoid them or indulge in minimal performance. Parental attitudes may play a large part in shaping his reactions.

Banks and Finlayson (1973) found, in the groups of able pupils whom they studied, that the mode of discipline at home was strongly related to success or lack of it. Material punishments, such as being sent to bed early, loss of pocket money or food, and physical punishment were assocatied with lack of success. These parental attitudes fail to provide the pupil with the necessary supports when he or she meets difficulties. There is no straightforward relationship between paternal approval and filial achievement, but those pupils who were subject to psychological rather than physical discipline seemed to cope better.

The pastoral team will need to discuss these subtle aspects of success and failure with parents. Group discussions can build up bonds between school and home in a way which less intimate groupings are unlikely to manage. However, form tutors must be trained to take such groups and use constructively the informal situations that develop from them. It is also advisable for the tutors to stay with their groups for longer than a year, so that they have greater opportunity to build up helpful links with parents.

Parent-teacher associations seem well established these days, but a school's management must ask if best use is being made of their association. Parents would often appreciate real contact with teachers, but have been rebuffed when they attempted to begin a dialogue, and so feel that there is no point in striving after the unobtainable. Also, if parents are unaware of the benefits of teacher-contact, they are hardly likely to feel a need for it. Provision of the facilities and education of the potential recipients create the need.

It is foolish to allow the picture of the school to come to parents solely through the eyes of their children. The pastoral team must consider the points at which parents should be involved and at which they will wish to be consulted. Two such points have already been mentioned: entry to the secondary school and choice of subjects. It is also likely that parents will respond well to contact during the year preceding O level and C.S.E. Attitudes to homework seem closely associated with success in school, and parents can either erode or strengthen the child's desire to do homework. Yet rarely are parents given real help with this problem.

A working party, consisting of teachers and parents, should be set up to consider carefully ways and means of linking home and school. Parents should be involved in concrete activities. These can be joint teacher-and-parent projects, although pupils can beneficially be included. Cave (1970) provides a useful account of such joint projects in Cambridgeshire; and the writer has first-hand experience of the worth of parent-teacher co-operation, including participation in outside visits, contribution to careers, education, work experience and the organization of fifth year activities.

If education is to progress, we must educate parents about the real nature of modern methods by providing first hand experience. Pupils can explain what they do, and parents are put into a learning situation. It is only by so doing that some parents can be persuaded to drop their stubborn prejudice against new ideas.

A well-planned parent organization can become a ginger group, modifying perception of the school in the neighbourhood and pulling in other parents. The full use of parents as resources in a joint endeavour necessitates providing them with meaningful tasks which orientate them to the neighbourhood and to other groups of parents, apart from directing their attention to events within the school. This can be achieved only gradually. It is hoped that active parental contact rather than passive acceptance of views will help to solve some of our current difficulties.

We are inclined to use inadequately both the educational psychologist and the school psychological service. The good pastoral system should detect in good time pupils in danger of developing an unsatisfactory way. The educational psychologist can diagnose and assess the needs of the more severe cases who do not respond to the usual measures of reward, punishment, encouragement and containment.

The function of the psychologist in relation to the pastoral team is largely advisory, and he can be of great help, especially if he has experience of teaching in the comprehensive school. Unfortunately, Chazan and Hamblin (1977), in a study of the relationships between educational psychologists and school counsellors, found that despite goodwill on both sides, the actual contact was less than desirable. The psychologist often did not reach the form tutor or those members of the staff who really knew the child.

The psychologist can act as a consultant to help senior members of the team resolved conflict. Most psychologists possess a sensitive understanding of the type of conflict which arises when time and skilled help are in short supply. Marshall (1973) shows how the educational psychologist can contribute to the training and support of counsellors within the school; and this is equally important for the year or house head. The latter have responsibilities which expose them to many contradictory demands, but if they are supported by the psychologist through after-school meetings or individual discussions, their task may be reduced to manageable proportions. The tutors, however, are not cut off from contact with the psychologist because the school has, or should have, programmes of in-service training in which the educational psychologist can play a useful part. He can also advise on the application of behaviour modification to the special conditions of the secondary school. As regards the basic problem of control and achievement, under the psychologist's guidance, we can explore punishment in depth, and realise that the form of discipline must be adapted to the particular individual. At meetings which discuss these key issues, the presence of the educational psychologist makes it easier to approach areas of tension and disagreement. Part of the in-service training might well consist of short courses which look in depth at such topics as anxiety, stress, sexual development, learning difficulties and attitudes.

Perhaps the greatest contribution that the psychologist can make to the pastoral team is to extend and sharpen their skills of assessment. Courses on the tentative diagnosis of pupils and the significance of early signs of stress would be useful. The psychologist should then show how his recommendations can be implemented, and see that arrangements are made for follow-up discussions.

The experienced psychologist learns to beware the inflated expectations of many teachers. Nobody can put right what has been going wrong for years without prolonged treatment. Yet some teachers still act as if they believed in a recipe, known only to the psychologist, to modify long-standing behaviour. They then react adversely when nothing happens. The type of contact advocated here prevents misperceptions of the psychologists' role as irrelevant. On the one hand, ideas that psychology is loosely permissive can be eradicated; on the other, so can any belief that the psychologist has immediate answers. A healthy working relationship can then be established.

Another source of outside help is the social services, which often seems to be under-utilized by the school. At the moment both school and social services seem to expect the other to initiate action. It is scarcely surprising, then, if communication becomes sporadic and inefficient. But, it is imperative that all members of the pastoral team should know the procedures in their area for dealing with cases of suspected violence towards children. Such procedures reflect, however, the atmosphere of emergency which the pastoral team seeks to avoid by preventative measures and early detection.

It is therefore essential that the senior management of the pastoral system should build good relationships between the school and the social services. However, if the results of Jones (1975) are typical, it seems that social workers are allergic to what they call the "hierarchy and policy-makers of the school". She also found that on the whole social workers prefer to work with teachers at what they term "field-level", whom they regard as more sympathetic towards the social-work approach. This reinforces the emphasis that we have given to the role of the form tutor. Such arrangements need to be structured, and there should be considerable liaison between senior social workers and senior members of the pastoral team in planning constructive action.

Barriers to real co-operation exist on both sides. Teachers feel that social workers are difficult to contact and, when reached, evasive about their responsibilities. Teachers are liable to be seen equally negatively by social workers. Many of them seem oblivious of changes in school and modern methods of teaching. I sometimes feel that they must have had very bad experiences at school from which they have never freed themselves.

Both teachers and social workers would benefit from regular meetings where each discusses the viewpoint of the other profession and develops mutual respect. In some schools the social services and interested members of the staff meet on a monthly basis to discuss topics of interest. This is a device for extending understanding and developing the links essential for effective action. In some schools, the social services and senior members of the pastoral team, together with the psychologist and form tutors, hold regular case-conferences on pupils. This has meant for some children a continuity of approach that was previously lacking.

Another outcome of such contacts may be an improved standard of reports on pupils who are going to appear in court. Teachers often write reports that are irrelevant and unhelpful to social workers and magistrates. Discussion about the purpose, content and format of such reports is one way of breaking the barriers to communication. Social workers are not entirely without fault in this, for they tend to undervalue information provided by the school. They disregard the possibility that the form tutor or head of year or house, who has known the child for several years, is at least as likely as the social workers to make valid judgements of the child. Jones (1975) found

274

that social workers limited their communication with schools because they felt that teachers were unable to comprehend the meaning of confidentiality. Only by regular contact will trust develop.

One fear for social workers is the labelling that can occur when teachers learn that a girl is either promiscuous or delinquent or both. In the majority of cases, teachers are already aware of the situation and coping with it constructively. Certain teachers are unable to accept the girl's presence and deal with her professionally, but their behaviour is far from typical. Schools usually manage to see that these teachers have minimal contact with pupils in pastoral care.

The "Teachers into industry" scheme yielded good results in careers education. One wonders if social workers might spend more time in school during their training, and if teachers, even those not on a specialist course, might have closer contact with the social services. Intermediate treatment schemes which involve youth clubs and other forms of group activity might well be the basis for constructive dialogue between teacher and social worker.

Conclusion

The argument in this book has been simple. It is that, with the backing of a planned and systematic effort, teachers have the power to create an environment within which standards of excellence are actively pursued, and healthy social and emotional development is encouraged. This has little to do with the formality of informality of teaching methods but is a product of the relationships between teacher and taught, of the development of effective communications and of the setting of clear directions. None of these can exist for long without constant evaluation of our underlying intentions and values. The pastoral team will play a major part in this, focussing on the feelings and perceptions which either impede or facilitate learning. From such analyses, will develop imaginative methods of teaching which build on what the pupil has, extending his skills and abilities, rather than reinforcing his current mode of functioning, or, as in some fifth-year courses, merely entertaining him.

To achieve this, we have to understand the hidden processes and latent meanings in the school's interactional patterns. Otherwise the introduction of innovations and the implementation of plans for development, however carefully devised, may either founder or become unrecognisable. Without this understanding, which only comes into being gradually through informed experience within a particular school, it is unlikely that evaluation, which is a primary educational and professional responsibility of the school's upper management, will be productive. To overcome resistance to evaluation it is necessary for the pastoral team, who incorporate the socialization functions of the secondary school to acquire habits of thinking which automatically focus on good communication. Let us be clear that socialization means taking up responsible social roles which may or may not embody change, and does not mean unthinking compliance!

It is therefore to communication that I turn in this brief final section, although I will not repeat what has been already written by Creber (1972), McQuail (1975), Pool *et al.* (1973) and Wilkinson (1975). A minimal definition of communication is given by McQuail (1975) as the "sending from one person to another of meaningful messages". This reaches the heart of the matter in the secondary school, where many of the messages sent and received are either meaningless or of only peripheral significance for those supposed to receive them, with the inevitable result that they are ignored.

Even if this is not the case, the messages often mean something very different to the recipient than the sender intended. We must take into account that messages sent to individuals in practice assume meaning only in the context of the receiver's group affiliations. That the meaning of a communication is determined by the membership groups which offer social and emotional rewards to the individual, is as true of the staff in a large school as it is of the pupils.

The two key elements in the acceptance and rejection of messages are coding and context. It is a commonplace that good communication is, at least partially, dependent upon coding which attempts to adjust the presentation of the content to the individual's standpoint, taking into account his or her position in the social structure of the organization. This skill which is at the heart of good communications is singularly lacking in some teachers. Most of their classroom messages seem to take little account of the pupils' viewpoints. Hence we can unwittingly humiliate and antagonize, and then blithely blame the negative response on pupils personality and background.

It is imperative that the pastoral team approach problems of communication in a flexible way which allows them to ask questions such as, "What shapes our punishments?" and "When are our punishments actually rewards?" It is salutary to look at such possibilities and detect how they act as barriers to change. Without seeking to understand such factors, we will not be able to anticipate the responses which our attempts at pastoral work elicit from colleagues.

Feedback is part of clear communication. Clarity here means that what is received, is what the sender intended. Yet we often fail to check that this happens. We have a remarkable capacity for ignoring, at the beginning of a sequence of interaction, feedback which would indicate that our messages have been misunderstood or have aroused bad feeling. A spiral of misunderstanding then begins, which often accelerates in other ways, finally resulting in alienation, which will need much energy and patience to correct. If we are sincere in our wish to tackle ritual performances, psychological truancy and growing alienation in our schools, we must acquire sensitivity to our pupils' reactions. One-way communication will only mean that our pupils reject us as credible sources of information and strengthen their feeling that our actions are the outcome of indifference and dislike. We also need to examine the growth of disenchantment amongst our junior colleagues, if the secondary school is to become what, in rather unfashionable terms, I would call a healthy organism.

It is hard to realize that our complaints about the inadequate language of our pupils may hide the sterility of our proposed remedies. The observer in the classroom might well assume that many of us merely require a superficial conformity in which outward forms are more significant than inner meanings. School procedures can unthinkingly reinforce attitudes and behaviour learned at home which militate against learning. When our concern with order takes these sterile forms, the pupil from the poor home background has little chance of gaining the skills of study and planning ahead which will allow him to overcome the handicaps of his environment.

Poor communication impinges upon teachers even more strongly than upon pupils. King (1973) shows that many schools now tend to rely on formal and standardized communication. This may lead to inflexibility and poor coding of messages, barriers to co-operation and experimentation. The form tutor who has to rely unduly on paper directives and shortened discussions feels no commitment because he receives little encouragement from the very people who bitterly complain about its absence. The middle management of the pastoral team often behave as if it is up to the form tutor to bring commitment and enthusiasm to the task, and if he fails to do this, then all is lost. We are lucky when this enthusiasm is present, but we should see that commitment is an emergent product of the tutor's growing appreciation of the importance of his task, reinforced by success.

A good pastoral team therefore invests time and energy in invesigating blocks to communication as they realize their existence. Such realization results from clear objectives: indeed this book has stressed that without this clarity of direction, there is little point in pastoral care. Clear objectives are not identical with rigid ones, and indeed one suspects that only when we specify our objectives are they amenable to rational modification.

The underlying argument of this book is that the inarticulate pastoral system is an underfunctioning one, more likely to separate the pastoral from the curricular than integrate them. The team which cannot state what it is attempting and then evaluate that attempt, is one which will maintain the *status quo* in which certain groups of pupils are given negative reputations and identities, rather than actively strive to raise the level of performance of every pupil by building on strengths. An inarticulate pastoral team is an impediment to progress of which the school would do well to rid itself. Throughout this book it has been my earnest endeavour to give the pastoral team a tongue with which to speak—a tongue which is not merely mouthing empty phrases, but one which is backed by a sense of purpose and direction and the discipline of stern love.

REFERENCES

Banks, O. and Finlayson, D. (1973) *Success and Failure in the Secondary School*, London: Methuen.

Cave, R. (1970) *Partnership for Change*, London: Ward Lock.

Chazan, M. and Hamblin, D. (1976) *Educational Psychologists and School Counsellors: Role Relationships*, Leicester: Occasional Publications, British Psychological Society, 11 Autumn.

Chazan, M., Moore, T., Williams, P. and Wright, J. (1974) *The Practice of Educational Psychology*, London: Longman.

Creber, J. (1972) *Lost for Words: Language and Educational Failure*, Harmondsworth: Penguin.

Daunt, P. (1975) *Comprehensive Values*, London: Heinemann.

Davies, I. (1971) *The Management of Learning*, London: McGraw-Hill.

Davies, I. (1976) *Objectives in Curriculum Design*, London: McGraw-Hill.

Enquiry One (1968) *Young School Leavers*, London: H.M.S.O.

Gross, N., Giacquinta, J. and Bernstein, M. (1971) *Implementing Organizational Innovations*, London: Harper and Row.

Hughes, M. (1970) *Secondary School Administration*, Oxford: Permagon.

Jones, S. (1975) *A Study of Communication and Co-operation Between the Social Services and the Secondary School*, Unpublished D.S.C. Dissertation: University College of Swansea.

Lindley, L. (1976) *An Investigation of the Perceptions of the Links Between Home and School Held by Teachers, Parents and Pupils in a Comprehensive School*, Unpublished D.S.C. Dissertation: University College of Swansea.

Marland, M. (1971) *Head of Department*, London: Heinemann.

Marshall, M. (1973) Counselling and the Schools Psychological Service, *Journal of the Association of Educational Psychologists*, Vol. 3, 5, pp. 43–45.

McQuail, D. (1975) *Communication*, London: Longman.

Newsom Report (1963) *Half Our Future*, Report of Central Advisory Council for Education. London: H.M.S.O.

Parlett, M. and Hamilton, D. [1972] *Evaluation as illumination: A new approach to the study of evaluatory programmes, Occasional Paper 9*. Edinburgh: Centre for Research in the Educational Sciences.

Plowden Report (1967) *Children and their Primary Schools*, London: H.M.S.O.

Pool, I., Schramm, W., Frey, F., Maccoby, N. and Parker, E. (1973) (Eds.) *Handbook of Communication*, Chicago: Rand McNally.

Richardson, E. (1973) *The Teacher, the School and the Task of Management*, London: Heinemann.

Summerfield Report (1968) *Psychologists in Education Services*, London: H.M.S.O.

Wilkinson, A. (1975) *Language and Education*, London: Oxford University Press.

NAME INDEX

INDEX